Herbert A. (Herbert Alonzo) Howe

A Study of the Sky

Herbert A. (Herbert Alonzo) Howe

A Study of the Sky

ISBN/EAN: 9783337041779

Printed in Europe, USA, Canada, Australia, Japan

Cover: Foto ©ninafisch / pixelio.de

More available books at **www.hansebooks.com**

THE CHAUTAUQUA LITERARY AND SCIENTIFIC CIRCLE.

Founded in 1878.

This volume is a part of the course of home reading the essential features of which are:

1. **A Definite Course** *covering four years, and including History, Literature, Art, Science, etc. (A reader may enroll for only one year.) No examinations.*
2. **Specified Volumes** *approved by the counselors. Many of the books are specially prepared for the purpose.*
3. **Allotment of Time.** *The reading is apportioned by the week and month.*
4. **A Monthly Magazine,** THE CHAUTAUQUAN, *with additional readings, notes, and general literature.*
5. **A Membership Book,** *containing suggestions on reading, review outlines, and other aid.*
6. **Individual Readers,** *no matter how isolated, may have all the privileges.*
7. **Local Circles** *may be formed by three or more members for mutual aid and encouragement.*
8. **The Time Required** *is on an average forty minutes a day for nine months.*
9. **Certificates** *are granted at the end of four years to all who complete the course.*
10. **Advanced Courses,** *for continued reading in special lines —History, Literature, etc.*
11. **Pedagogical Course** *for secular teachers.*
12. **Young People's Reading Course,** *to stimulate the reading of good literature by the young.*

For all information concerning the C. L. S. C. address
The Chautauqua Office,
Buffalo, N. Y.

THE REQUIRED LITERATURE FOR 1896-7.

THE GROWTH OF THE FRENCH NATION (illustrated). George B. Adams, Professor of History, Yale University $1.00
FRENCH TRAITS. W. C. Brownell, of Scribners', New York 1.00
A STUDY OF THE SKY (illustrated). Herbert A. Howe, Professor of Astronomy, University of Denver 1.00
A SURVEY OF GREEK CIVILIZATION (illustrated). J. P. Mahaffy, Professor of Ancient History, University of Dublin, Ireland 1.00
A HISTORY OF GREEK ART (illustrated). F. B. Tarbell, Professor of Archæology, University of Chicago 1.00
THE CHAUTAUQUAN (12 numbers, illustrated) . 2.00

THE MOON PARTIALLY ECLIPSED.

Chautauqua Reading Circle Literature

A STUDY OF THE SKY

BY

HERBERT A. HOWE, A.M., Sc.D.,

Director of the Chamberlin Observatory, University of Denver; author of "Elements of Descriptive Astronomy."

MEADVILLE PENNA
FLOOD AND VINCENT
The Chautauqua-Century Press

| NEW YORK : | CINCINNATI : | CHICAGO : |
| 150 Fifth Avenue. | 222 W. Fourth St. | 57 Washington St. |

1896

Copyright, 1896
By FLOOD & VINCENT

The Chautauqua-Century Press, *Meadville, Pa.*, *U. S. A.*
Electrotyped, Printed, and Bound by Flood & Vincent.

TO HUNDREDS OF MY PUPILS,

WHOSE STEADFAST DEVOTION

TO THEIR DAILY TASKS

IS A DELIGHTFUL MEMORY,

THIS BOOK IS

AFFECTIONATELY DEDICATED

The required books of the C. L. S. C. are recommended by a Council of six. It must, however, be understood that recommendation does not involve an approval by the Council, or by any member of it, of every principle or doctrine contained in the book recommended.

PREFACE.

ASTRONOMY is at once the most ancient and the noblest of the physical sciences. For thousands of years successive generations of men have gazed with admiration and delight at the brilliant orbs which glitter in the diadem of night. The shining constellations, the roving planets, the ever-changing moon, the splendid Galaxy, a celestial river bedded by suns and banked by the ether, all these display their beauties before the ravished eye.

> "The sky
> Spreads like an ocean hung on high,
> Bespangled with those isles of light
> So wildly, spiritually bright.
> Who ever gazed upon them shining,
> And turned to earth without repining,
> Nor wished for wings to flee away,
> And mix with their eternal ray?"

To the study of these inspiring objects our book is devoted. Their story is told with plainness and simplicity. The standpoint adopted is that of the astronomer, who observes, records what he sees, studies his observations, digs out the truths which they contain, and weaves them into laws and theories which embrace the visible universe, reaching from unknown depths of past ages up to unmeasured heights of futurity.

The historical development of the science is sketched. An explanation of the apparent daily motion of the heavens is given. The chief constellations are set forth in detail, that the learner may have ample guidance in his endeavors to become acquainted with them. The reader is introduced to the astronomer, inspects an observatory, and becomes acquainted with the most important instruments and their uses. Thus he is prepared to listen appreciatively to an unvarnished tale, in which are set forth the principal things which are known or reasonably surmised concerning the worlds around us.

The effectiveness of the presentation of the subject is much enhanced by the illustrations, for many of the finest of which the thanks of both reader and author are due to the directors of the Lick and Harvard College Observatories, and to the editors of *Popular Astronomy*, *Knowledge*, and *The Astrophysical Journal*.

Notice of any error will be gratefully received by the author, whose address is Chamberlin Observatory, University Park, Colorado.

CONTENTS.

CHAPTER		PAGE
I.	Introduction and Historical Sketch	15
II.	The Heavens and their Apparent Daily Revolution	36
III.	The Constellations in General	48
IV.	The Constellations for January and February	56
V.	The Constellations for March and April	79
VI.	The Constellations for May and June	95
VII.	The Astronomer	111
VIII.	A Great Telescope	128
IX.	The Astronomer's Workshop, and Some of His Tools	143
X.	Time	167
XI.	The Sun	179
XII.	The Moon and Eclipses	205
XIII.	Mercury and Venus	231
XIV.	Mars and the Asteroids	236
XV.	Jupiter, Saturn, Uranus, and Neptune	253
XVI.	Comets and Meteors	271
XVII.	The Fixed Stars	301
XVIII.	The Nebulæ	321

DIAGRAMS AND ILLUSTRATIONS.

The Moon Partially Eclipsed . . . . *Frontispiece.*

FIGURE		PAGE
1.	The Moon	19
2.	Cycle and Epicycle	25
3.	Tycho	28
4.	Kepler	30
5.	Galileo	31
6.	Sir Isaac Newton	33
7.	Laplace	34
8.	A Section of the Milky Way	37
9.	The Great Dipper	40
10.	Measurement of an Angle	41
11.	The Two Dippers	45
12.	Ursa Major	59
13.	Ursa Minor	61
14.	Cassiopeia	63
15.	Pegasus	65
16.	Aquarius	66
17.	Pisces	68
18.	Andromeda	70
19.	Aries	71
20.	Cetus	71
21.	Taurus	73
22.	Orion	75
23.	Auriga	77
24.	Gemini	80
25.	Perseus	82
26.	Cancer	83
27.	Canis Major	84
28.	Canis Minor	85
29.	Lepus	85
30.	Leo	86
31.	Boötes	88
32.	Virgo	90

Diagrams and Illustrations.

FIGURE		PAGE
33.	Corvus	91
34.	Corona Borealis	92
35.	Hydra	93
36.	Lyra	95
37.	Hercules	97
38.	Cygnus	98
39.	Draco	100
40.	Sagitta	101
41.	Scorpio	102
42.	Libra	103
43.	Delphinus	104
44.	Aquila	105
45.	Serpens and Ophiuchus	106
46.	Sagittarius	108
47.	Cepheus	109
48.	Capricornus	110
49.	Charles A. Young	112
50.	Edward S. Holden	114
51.	Simon Newcomb	115
52.	Benjamin A. Gould	116
53.	Edward C. Pickering	117
54.	William H. Pickering	119
55.	Edward E. Barnard	120
56.	James E. Keeler	121
57.	First Position of the Spider-webs	123
58.	Second Position of the Spider-webs	123
59.	A Micrometer	124
60.	Third Position of the Spider-webs	124
61.	Seth C. Chandler	125
62.	Sherburne W. Burnham	126
63.	The Yerkes Telescope at the Columbian Exposition	129
64.	Alvan G. Clark	130
65.	Lump of Optical Glass	132
66.	The Lump Cut Down	133
67.	The Lump Molded	133
68.	The Lump after Further Cutting	134
69.	The Lump Cut Down Still More	134
70.	Machine for Polishing Lenses	135
71.	Alvan Clark's Workshop	136
72.	John A. Brashear	137

Diagrams and Illustrations.

FIGURE		PAGE
73.	The Two Lenses of an Object-Glass	138
74.	An Equatorial Telescope	139
75.	The Chamberlin Telescope of the University of Denver	141
76.	The Yerkes Observatory	144
77.	The Chamberlin Observatory	145
78.	Main Floor of the Chamberlin Observatory	147
79.	A Meridian Circle	150
80.	The Spider-webs	152
81.	The Spire on the Cross Wires	153
82.	The Lick Observatory	155
83.	A Chronograph	157
84.	A Portion of a Chronograph Sheet	158
85.	The Lick Micrometer	159
86.	Measurement of a Planet's Diameter	160
87.	Bisection by Spider-webs	161
88.	Essentials of a Spectroscope	162
89.	A Spectroscope	165
90.	A Watch Balance	177
91.	Sun-spots	183
92.	Changes in a Solar Spot	184
93.	A Portion of the Photosphere	187
94.	*Faculæ*	190
95.	Prominences	191
96.	A Quiescent Prominence	192
97.	The Corona of July, 1878	194
98.	The Corona of January, 1889	195
99.	The Corona of April, 1893	196
100.	Lunar Formations	207
101.	Lunar Plains, called Seas	210
102.	Copernicus	213
103.	The Apennines	216
104.	The Mare Crisium	219
105.	A Rugged Region near Tycho	223
106.	Moon's Shadow on the Earth, as seen from the Moon	227
107.	Conjunction and Elongation	232
108.	Markings on Venus	235
109.	Mars	236
110.	Projections on the Polar Cap	238
111.	The Lake of the Sun	239

xii *Diagrams and Illustrations.*

FIGURE		PAGE
112.	Canals	241
113.	Projections on the Edge of the Disc	242
114.	Canals connected with Lacus Solis	243
115.	The Polar Cap in July and August, 1892	244
116.	Canals in August, 1892	245
117.	The Cap Diminishing, August 24–9, 1892	246
118.	Asteroid Trail on a Photograph of the Pleiades	249
119.	Jupiter	254
120.	The Great Red Spot	256
121.	Saturn	261
122.	Sir William Herschel	266
123.	Discovery of a Comet by Photography	272
124.	Paths of Comets	273
125.	Jets and Envelopes	276
126.	Photographs of Swift's Bright Comet of 1892	279
127.	Holmes's Comet	282
128.	Photograph of Rordame's Comet, showing Masses of Matter driven off into the Tail	285
129.	Comet c, 1893 (Brooks)	287
130.	A Besprinkling	290
131.	Photograph showing a Meteor's Path among the Stars	293
132.	A Meteorite seen July 27, 1894	298
133.	Outlines of Dark Structures in the Galaxy	302
134.	A Part of the Milky Way in Cygnus	304
135.	Motion of the Components of a Double Star	308
136.	A Rich Portion of the Milky Way	312
137.	The Great Globular Cluster in Hercules	315
138.	Cloudy Region in the Milky Way	318
139.	A Spiral Nebula	322
140.	The Nebula of Orion Photographed. Exposure, fifteen minutes	324
141.	The Nebula of Orion Photographed. Exposure, two hours	324
142.	The Nebula of Orion Photographed. Exposure, nine hours	325
143.	A Drawing of the Central Part of the Great Nebula in Orion	329
144.	The Ring Nebula in Lyra	334

A STUDY OF THE SKY.

CHAPTER I.

INTRODUCTION AND HISTORICAL SKETCH.

"The heavens declare the glory of God :
And the firmament sheweth his handywork."

THE starry spheres which roll and shine, uncounted millions, in the infinite depths of space call us away from the common things of earth, and bid us plume our spirits for the loftiest flights. Not in the garish glory of the day, when men's eyes are well-nigh blinded by the affluence of light which the sun pours forth, and their minds are caged in the narrow round of daily toil, are the wonders of the sky revealed. But when the clangor and roar of the world's traffic have died away, and the last glint of the retiring sun has vanished from the mountain top ; when the soft shades of the evening twilight gradually melt into the darkness of the night, and the blessed shadow of the earth steals over the abodes of men, bringing rest and refreshment of mind, then come forth the troops of radiant orbs, filling the sky with their splendid array, and giving to the mind of the beholder a portion of their own eternal calm. *The starry spheres.* *The blessed shadow.*

"The starry skies, they rest my soul,
Its chains of care unbind,
And with the dew of cooling thoughts
Refresh my sultry mind.

"And like a bird amidst the boughs
I rest, and sing and rest,
Among those bright dissevered worlds,
As safe as in a nest."

A Study of the Sky.

Mysteries are unraveled.

With this calmness of mind comes reflection, followed by a keen thirst for knowledge. The enigma of the universe is thrust upon the beholder, and he accepts the challenge to solve it. Year after year, century after century, has the dauntless mind of man climbed the arduous steep which leads to a knowledge of the stars. Each defeat has stimulated it to greater exertions and more glorious victories. Barrier after barrier has been surmounted or broken down. Difficulty after difficulty has vanished before persistent effort.

Powerful instruments.

Ingenious and powerful instruments have been devised, which reveal wonders otherwise unimagined, and the end is not yet. Each new telescopic giant is expected to win fresh laurels in old fields of endeavor, or to make discoveries which shall link its name forever with the stars. When the great thirty-six-inch glass, the fame of which has spread throughout the world, was set up on Mt. Hamilton, a poet's fancy was stirred, and he addressed the ensuing lines to the lens.*

> " Perchance that thou
> With cloudless vision slowly sweeping up
> The mighty Nave that cleaves the Galaxy—
> God's visible Tabernacle in the skies,
> Star-built from shining undercroft to dome,
> Past pillared pomp of worlds, and columns wrought
> With fair entangle of amethyst and pearl,
> Thro' jacinth portals hung with mist of stars,
> And fiery fringe of suns—mayst come at last
> Even to the chancel of the Universe ;
> And so thro' glories veiled and far, behold
> The Choral Stars that sang so loud and sweet
> On the first morning when creation sprang
> In dewy beauty from Jehovah's hand.
> Mayhap that thou, with swiftness unconceived,
> Wilt overtake the light and see the things

---

* " Handbook of the Lick Observatory," page 76.

Introduction and Historical Sketch. 17

That have been, and that shall be nevermore ;
Follow the dying star in her swift flight
Athwart Eternity ; track the lost world,
That drifting past our ken, still gleameth fair
Upon the confines of some far-off realm ;
Perchance the Star which first spake peace to men
Will dawn through thee upon the waiting earth ;
And O far-seeing Eye, perchance mayst thou
Reveal the City Beautiful which lies
Four-square in midst of heaven, whose shining walls
Are of fair jasper builded and pure gold ;
Whose battlements are crystal and whose ways
Are sapphire paven, and whose gates are pearl."

No astronomer has any expectation of such good fortune as the poet has outlined. But the spacious firmament, to the study of which he gives his nightly vigils and his daily toils, is the handiwork of the Most High, and continually reveals to the earnest student the majesty and glory of the omnipotent, the ever-living God. *The majesty of God is revealed.*

Many and toilsome have been the steps by which the astronomers of centuries past and present have mounted the long ladder whose base rests on the earth, and whose summit is now to be found among the star-clouds of the Milky Way. *The ladder of progress.*

The first astronomer was Adam : his observatory was one of the flower-decked mounds of the Garden of Eden. His two telescopes were fresh from a celestial workshop. What must have been his feelings as the glowing orb of day, which had warmed his body and cheered his spirit, sank in the west and the evening twilight deepened ! Was he to be imprisoned in a dungeon of darkness, and the beautiful creation about him to fade into nothingness? *Adam as an astronomer.*

Behold ! a new light appears in the sky ; the silvery moon, which has been appointed to rule the night, stands out in all her beauty, and casts dim shadows of

The moon and stars appear.

the foliage on the darkening turf. But hers is not the only light. Here and there, scattered over the broad expanse of the sky, appear the brighter stars, set like jewels as a crown upon earth's brow. They have various colors and degrees of brightness : a multitude of lesser lights gradually come forth, forming strange configurations. Now, for the first time, the solitary observer notices that the moon is following the sun to a grave in the west, and that the stars too are joining in the general movement. Will all at last be lost to his vision, and darkness rule supreme? He faces eastward and sees new groups of stars rising to take the places of those which are passing away. The moon sinks in the west ; earnestly he watches the glow on the horizon at the point where she disappeared, until it fades away.

The Milky Way.

Upward again he throws his inquiring glance, and beholds the most wonderful sight of all. Athwart the star-sphere a broad river of light pursues its tortuous way. In places it glows as if pent-up fires were about to burst forth ; in other places are black rifts, which seem to intensify the darkness of the night. Upon all nature has fallen a solemn hush, broken only by the faint notes of a far-away nightingale. A strange drowsiness creeps over our great ancestor and fills him with dread : in vain he

Adam sleeps and wakens.

fights against it : overcome he sinks down and is lost in slumber. What visions may have come to him we know not. The hours roll on, and the stars keep silent vigil over the slumberer : at last the aurora of approaching day glows along the eastern horizon. He awakens and feels the pleasurable glow of fresh life and vigor. The stars fade from view, and the first glint of the glad sunshine greets his vision. The sun arises in its full glory, and animate nature is awakened. The man wonders and adores. Surely he will be a lover of nature for life.

Introduction and Historical Sketch. 19

The majestic revolution of the heavens, the waxing and waning of the moon, the movements of the brilliant planets, an occasional outburst of a comet, all these will

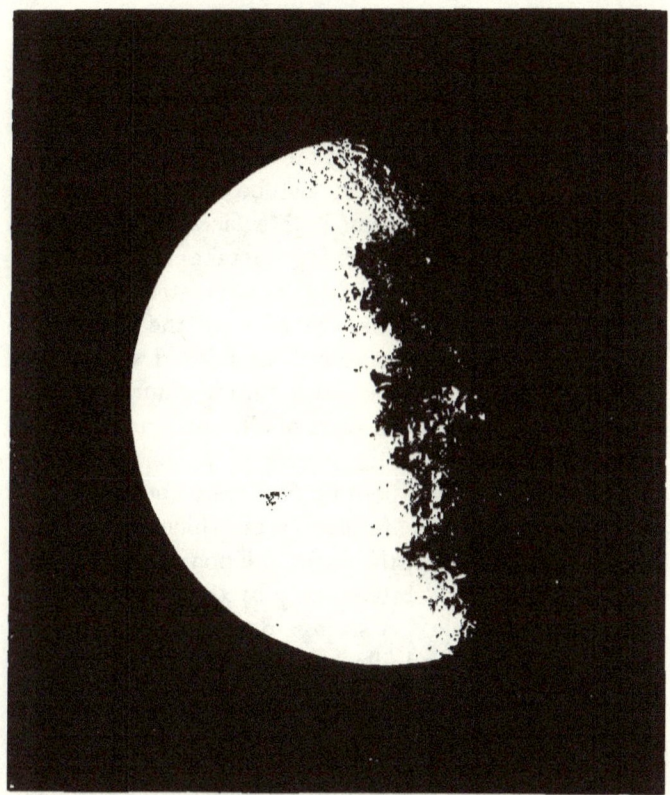

FIG. 1.—THE MOON.

continually delight him, and will ever lead to fresh adoration of his Creator.

How rudely are our bright expectations of Adam's astronomical joys shattered! For a rationalistic instructor in the domain of theology, the wily serpent, took

The first application of scientific method.

Adam and his companion in hand. Under his tuition they introduced the genuine scientific method of investigation, the method of experiment and observation, into fields theological. Inestimable as may be the value of this method, it brought ruin and desolation to the first experimenters.

Brought sharply to his senses by being driven from his beautiful dwelling place, forced to earn his subsistence by the sweat of his brow, burdened with increasing cares and sorrows, Adam's spirit was much broken, and, like Bunyan's man with a muck-rake, he acquired the habit of looking downward instead of upward.

A step forward. We must take a long step forward to find the first glimmerings, more or less historic, of the lamp of astronomical knowledge. We thus emerge from the realm of fancy in which we have disported ourselves for a time into the dim borderland, in which history and myth are interwoven, and we shall press on speedily into the full light of historic fact.

The "Rigveda." Among the first of astronomical allusions are those contained in the writings of the early Aryans, by whom the hymns of the "Rigveda" were written. These writings, however, serve only to reveal to us primitive notions about the earth and the firmament, and do not contain astronomical observations. The earth is represented as a flat surface, on whose broad expanse rests the blue and ever-changing vault of heaven. Below this star-spangled vault is the home of the life-giving light.

Josephus. Josephus states that one reason why the lives of the antediluvian patriarchs were prolonged was that they might perfect the sciences of geometry and astronomy, which they had discovered. He also informs us that these primitive scientists had learned from Adam that the world was to perish by water and by fire ; fearing therefore that the results of their centuries of labor would be lost, they built two columns, one of brick and the other of stone, which bore inscriptions intended to preserve the knowledge which their toil had wrested from the sky. In case the deluge destroyed the brick column, the stone one at least would come through unharmed. Josephus would have us believe that the stone monument was still to be seen in his day.

Herodotus, the father of history, makes the astonishing statement that the Egyptians had made astronomical observations for 11,340 years, and had seen the earth's equator perpendicular to the plane of its orbit. But the present refinement of astronomical theory forbids a belief that the equator and ecliptic have been perpendicular within the memory of man, and lends no countenance to the theory that they ever were. *Herodotus.*

A high antiquity is claimed for the beginning of astronomy among the Chinese. Forty-five centuries ago the emperor Hoang-Ti is reputed to have built an observatory, and to have appointed an astronomical board, upon the members of which devolved the duties of regulating the times of the religious festivals. The ancient chronicles also relate that once upon a time the astronomical board, which consisted of two learned gentlemen bearing the rather hilarious names of Hi and Ho, forgot the dignity of its high position, and indulged in riotous living. Meanwhile the moon stole a march on the board, and eclipsed the sun. China was thus exposed to the wrath of the gods, because the eclipse had not been foreseen and the proper religious rites observed. The emperor at once accepted the resignation of the board, by the sword of the executioner. The Chinese astronomical records of the past twenty-six centuries are thought to be fairly reliable; they contain *Early Chinese astronomy.*

accounts of the appearances of remarkable comets, as well as data concerning eclipses.

<small>Babylonian astronomy.</small>

We must look to the plains of Babylonia for the most valuable early observations. The mild climate and open sky of Central Asia favored the development of the science of the stars. We are not surprised, then, to find that the Chaldeans were acute and patient observers through many generations, and accumulated a very respectable store of observational knowledge. Their greatest achievement lay in the line of observations of eclipses of the sun and moon. By careful study of the times at which eclipses had happened, they discovered that those phenomena repeated themselves in cycles of about eighteen years. Thus they were enabled to foretell eclipses with considerable accuracy. But of the real causes of those interesting phenomena they were ignorant.

<small>Grecian philosophers.</small>

To the ancient Greeks modern astronomy owes a great debt. So sublime and mysterious are the heavenly bodies, and so intricate their motions, that the speculative minds of the early Grecian philosophers were irresistibly attracted to a study of them. Though many of their theories were groundless, and many of their statements obscure and mingled with metaphysics in a most curious fashion, yet gems of truth are to be found here and there, which well repay the labor spent in searching them out.

Though Plato suggested that the world was a cube, which seemed to him the most perfect of solids, Eudoxus, Archimedes, and Aristotle made it a sphere. Nicetas is said to have ascribed the apparent daily revolution of the celestial sphere to the revolution of the earth upon its axis.

<small>Pythagoras.</small>

To Pythagoras is attributed the beautiful but utterly

erroneous doctrine of the crystalline spheres. In the outermost of these were set the fixed stars, which had, long before his time, been grouped in constellations, and associated with mythological characters. Each planet too had its sphere. To him also is ascribed the theory that the sun is the center about which the earth and the other planets move; this would nowadays be called a "class-room theory," because it was not promulgated except in a private way among his students. Philolaus, a follower of Pythagoras and a contemporary of Socrates, taught the doctrine openly.

But the overwhelming influence of Aristotle soon erased it from the Greek mind. He placed the earth immovable in the center of the universe, and did not allow it to rotate upon its axis. The celestial bodies were permitted to revolve around the earth in decorous fashion. So powerful was the influence of this intellectual giant upon the minds of thinking men for centuries afterward, that the earth was not finally and forever displaced from the erroneous position which he assigned to it till the days of Copernicus. *Aristotle.*

To the second century before Christ belongs Hipparchus, justly called the father of astronomy, who rescued Greek astronomy in large measure from the bog of speculation into which earlier philosophers had plunged it, and made it a science of observation as well as of theory. He was a genius of the highest order, being at once an accurate observer of the celestial bodies, a profound mathematician, and a brilliant theorist. He devised the system of locating places on the earth by means of their latitude and longitude. In order to facilitate his computations he invented that branch of mathematics now called trigonometry. The first catalogue of the fixed stars is due to his labors. The apparent motions of the *Hipparchus.*

sun and moon he explained by an ingenious theory, which he tested by observation and computation. In determining the length of the year he made an error of only four minutes.

Ptolemy. After Hipparchus the most distinguished astronomer of antiquity was Ptolemy, who lived at Alexandria in the second century of our era, and wrote the "Almagest," which has come down to us entire, and in which is preserved nearly all our knowledge of Greek astronomy. As the Ptolemaic system was the orthodox astronomy of the next fourteen centuries, we notice a few of its chief principles.

The shape of the earth. The earth, said Ptolemy, must be round. For if one go southward new stars appear above the southern horizon, and stars in the north seem nearer the horizon than before. Besides this, the heavenly bodies do not rise at the same moment for two observers, one of whom is east of the other. Furthermore, when a sailor approaches the coast, the bases of the headlands are at first hidden from view by reason of the curvature of the sea.

The earth's place. The earth must also be in the center of the celestial sphere, for if it were nearer to the eastern portion of the heavens than to the western the stars in the east would seem to move with greater rapidity than those in the west. Since the stars sweep across the sky each day at a perfectly regular rate, the earth must be equally distant from all of them, and thus in the center of the universe.

What is the shape of the curve in which every heavenly body moves? Ptolemy replies that it is a circle, the most perfect of all curves. Now an objector might say that this would do for the fixed stars, the sun, and the moon, which move with exceeding regularity, but how could it explain the apparent motion of Saturn, or of Jupiter, both of which move irregularly? Here Ptolemy had recourse to the device of the epicycle, introduced by Hipparchus. The word *epicycle* is derived from two Greek words, meaning "upon" and "a circle." The epicycle was a circle the center of which moved along the circumference of another circle. The idea is easily grasped by reference to Fig. 2. E represents the earth; Jupiter, located at J, moves uniformly around the circumference of the small circle, while P, the center of that circle, moves along the circumference of the large circle.

Cycles and epicycles.

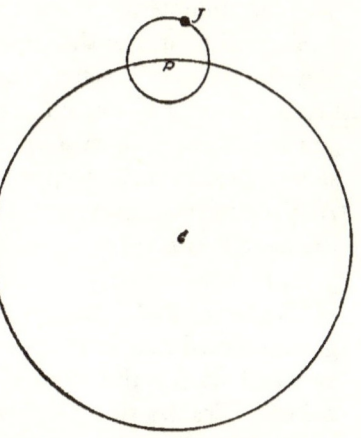

FIG. 2.—CYCLE AND EPICYCLE.

Ptolemy found, by comparing his observations with those of Hipparchus, that he could not explain the motions of the sun, moon, and planets with sufficient accuracy by so simple a device. But by adding additional epicycles, and by placing the earth at a short distance from the center of the large circle in the diagram, he could explain the irregularities which perplexed him.

After Ptolemy's death the study of astronomy gradually declined, and suffered a decided set-back in the burning of the great library at Alexandria, in the middle of the seventh century. To the Arabians, who now made Bagdad the literary center of the civilized world, we must look for the next advances. They were assiduous observers, and thus furnished a groundwork of fact

Arabian astronomy.

upon which later generations might build theories, and by which those theories might be tested.

The awakening of Western Europe. At last the intellectual aspirations of the peoples of Western Europe were awakened, after a slumber of centuries. The lamp of learning, which was burning in the Moorish universities of Spain, shed its beneficent rays among more northern nations. The Arabic version of Ptolemy's "Almagest" was translated into the Latin language in the thirteenth century, under the patronage of Frederick II., emperor of the Holy Roman Empire. In the same century Alphonso X., king of Leon and Castile, who was surnamed "The Wise" and also "The Astronomer," published the celebrated Alphonsine tables, which were prepared with immense labor by the best mathematicians of the Moorish universities. Observations were at this time so much more accurate and numerous than in the days of Ptolemy that many epicycles had to be added to the original system, in order to make theory correspond with observation. The entire heavens were said to be

"Scribbled o'er
With cycle upon epicycle, orb on orb."

Alphonso's remark. So complicated had the celestial machinery become that Alphonso is said to have told a notable gathering of bishops that if the Almighty had done him the honor to consult him concerning the mechanism of the universe, he could have offered some good advice. This irreverent remark may have been inspired by the depleted condition of the royal purse after the publication of the tables.

Copernicus. Three centuries had yet to roll away before deliverance from the thraldom of Ptolemy came. On February 12, 1473, Nicholas Copernicus was born at Thorn in

Prussia. During thirty-six of the seventy years that were allotted to him he studied the motions of the planets. Throughout a large part of his life he held high ecclesiastical rank as canon of Warmia, and had leisure for his favorite investigations. The variations in the brightness of Mars in different parts of its orbit were so great as to lead him to think that the earth could not be the center about which Mars revolved. The results of his meditations are set forth in the following translation of his own words :

And I too, on account of these testimonies, began to meditate upon the movement of the earth, and though that theory seemed absurd, I thought that as others before my day had devised a system of circles to account for the motion of the stars, I also might endeavor, by supposing that the earth moved, to find a more satisfactory scheme of the movements of the heavenly bodies than that which now contents us. After long research I have become convinced that if we assume the revolution of the earth to be the cause of the wanderings of the other planets, observation and calculation will be in better agreement. And I doubt not that mathematicians will be of my opinion, if they will take pains to examine carefully and thoroughly the demonstrations to be given in this book. *The new theory.*

Copernicus broke with the Ptolemaic theory at two points. He placed the sun in the center of the planetary system, and explained the diurnal rotation of the heavens by the revolution of the earth on its axis. For a long time he hesitated about publishing the new doctrines, knowing that they would at once make him a target for the ridicule and abuse of the unthinking and of the narrow-minded. *The new vs. the old.*

The insistence of his warmest friends, particularly of the bishop of Culm, finally led to the publication of his great work, which was entitled "De Revolutionibus Orbium Cœlestium." It may well be called the Magna *His work is published.*

Its importance. Charta of astronomical science. Copernicus did not live to see the reception which was accorded it; the first copy, fresh from the press, was placed in his hand only a few hours before his death. In one important particular Copernicus failed to break with Ptolemy; he still retained the system of epicycles, but the innovations which he introduced simplified it greatly.

FIG. 3.—TYCHO.

The new system was soon to be put to a much more searching test than Ptolemy's had been subjected to. In 1546, three years after the death of Copernicus, there came into the family of a Danish nobleman a son, who afterward became the famous Tycho Brahé. In those days it was little

Tycho Brahé. short of a misdemeanor for a member of an aristocratic family to engage in scientific researches; to hunt animals and to kill men according to the canons of war were the proper pursuits. The young noble was therefore destined for the army.

An eclipse. When but fourteen years of age Tycho's curiosity was aroused by the occurrence of an eclipse. From that time forth his mind was with the stars. Sent to Leipzig to study law, he could not be induced to devote himself to it; his money was spent for astronomical books and instruments, and his time was largely engrossed with observations of the stars. In 1563 he observed a conjunction of Jupiter and Saturn, which he thought to be the cause of the Great Plague. As the Copernican tables did not give the time of the conjunction accurately he resolved to make new ones. He constructed instruments of large size, and began to observe with fresh vigor. The king heard of his doings, and offered him a site for an observatory, £20,000 for the building, and a life pension of £400. The observatory, which was called Uranienburg (the Castle of the Heavens), was erected on the island of Huen, near Copenhagen. It was stocked with the largest and finest instruments which the mechanics of that day could build. For twenty years he worked with the utmost ardor, accumulating a vast store of observations of far greater accuracy than any which had been made previously. Of the subsequent death of his patron, his own impoverishment and virtual banishment, we may not give the details. On October 24, 1601, he died, after a painful illness, during which he frequently called out, "Ne frustra vixisse videar" (May I not seem to have lived in vain!). *Uranienburg.*

    Two years before Tycho's death, Johann Kepler became his pupil. Tycho was one of the greatest of observers, but his pupil was preëminent as a theorist. Taking up Tycho's observations of Mars he endeavored to discover the laws of the planet's movement. Hypothesis after hypothesis was tried and rejected; at one moment he was at the summit of hope; at another he was in the depths of disheartenment. Struggling with indomitable perseverance against sickness, poverty, and misfortune, harassed by domestic troubles, and hampered at every turn, he pressed on through weary years to final victory. *Kepler.*

Three laws came to light through his labors:

Kepler's laws.

Law I. Each planet moves in an ellipse, at one focus of which is the sun.

Law II. The line joining a planet to the sun sweeps over equal areas in equal times.

Law III. The squares of the times of revolution of any two planets are to each other as the cubes of their mean distances from the sun.

FIG. 4.—KEPLER.

His exultation.

Upon the discovery of the third law his exultation knew no bounds, as the following exclamation shows:

Nothing holds me: I will indulge in my sacred fury: I will triumph over mankind by the honest confession that I have stolen the golden vases of the Egyptians to build up a tabernacle for my God far away from the confines of Egypt. If you forgive me, I rejoice: if you are angry, I can bear it: the die is cast, the book is written, to be read either now or by posterity, I care not which: it may well wait a century for a reader, as God has waited six thousand years for an observer.

Galileo.

While Kepler was making his immortal studies in theoretical astronomy, the science of observation took a tremendous stride. Galileo, then a professor in the University of Padua, heard that a Dutch spectacle-maker had found a combination of glasses through which the weathercock on the church spire looked larger. Being familiar with the laws of optics he began to ponder over the matter. All night long he sat in a brown study ; by morning the solution came, and he soon had an old organ pipe with a glass at each end, which was the forerunner of the great telescopes of our day. The Senate doubled his salary, and he went at telescope-making in earnest ; having completed one which magnified thirty times he began to explore the heavens.

The moon displayed to him the rocky ramparts and battlemented crags of her mountains. The Milky Way was resolved into countless stars ; Discoveries.

"Infinity's illimitable fields,
Where bloom the worlds like flowers about God's feet."

Jupiter was found to be attended by four moons, the entire system being a miniature of the solar system. The motions of these bodies powerfully confirmed the theories of Copernicus. The surface of the sun was seen to be marred by spots. Venus became a waxing and waning crescent.

The Aristotelians were confounded again and again. But they had their revenge upon this pestilent fellow, who was turning the world of natural philosophy upside down. The hand of the Inquisition was laid upon him. But The Inquisition.

FIG. 5.—GALILEO.

why relate the painful tale of the rigorous examinations, and the recantation finally forced upon the feeble old man? In the year 1642 the shattered body of the philosopher was laid to rest, but in unconsecrated ground, for the iron heel of the Inquisition must even grind his bones! Many of his manuscripts were destroyed, and his friends were not permitted to raise a monument in his honor.

Truth triumphant.

But the truth, which had thus been ruthlessly trampled under foot, beneath the blue skies of fair Italy, rose in adamantine strength amid the sturdy oaks of old England. On Christmas Day of the year in which Galileo died there was born a boy who was to supplement the work not only of Galileo, but also of Copernicus, Tycho, and Kepler, and to be recognized as the master mind among the world's philosophers.

Isaac Newton.

Isaac Newton was not a very promising lad, until the day when a bigger boy conferred a signal blessing on the world by kicking him. Young Isaac retorted by thrashing his assailant, and then proceeded to show the rest of the boys at school that he could beat them in their studies. So keen became his interest in books that he was sent to Trinity College, Cambridge, where his remarkable aptitude for mathematics displayed itself. We cannot recount all the marvelous researches to which Newton's genius lent itself. The discovery which concerns us at present is that of the law of gravitation.

Copernicus had proved that the planets revolved about the sun as a center. Tycho had observed with all assiduity, and Kepler, by discussing these observations, had discovered the three laws which bear his name. Galileo had not only enlarged astronomical knowledge by the use of the telescope, but had promulgated the laws of motion of bodies on the surface of

the earth. These laws were admirably restated by
Newton, and are now called Newton's laws. But the   Newton's laws.
crowning glory of his achievements is the proof that the

FIG. 6.—SIR ISAAC NEWTON.

same force which pulls the apple to the earth controls
the motion of the moon, and binds the planets to the   The law of gravitation.
sun. This force is not constant in intensity, but varies
inversely as the square of the distance. Kepler's laws
have been proven to be necessary consequences of the

Its wide application.

law of gravitation. The entire mechanism of the planetary movements, not their elliptical paths alone, but also their small departures from true ellipses, caused by their

FIG. 7.—LAPLACE.

attractions for one another, are all explained by this simple law.

If Newton's law be correct, will not the mutual attractions of the planets so derange their orbits that at last there will be wreck and ruin, where now are order and beauty? During the last century Lagrange and Laplace, the most illustrious of French mathematicians, proved that though the orbit of each planet alters somewhat, changing in both shape and position, the disturbances are confined within narrow limits, and the system of planetary worlds is therefore stable. Lagrange and Laplace.

We now bring our rough historical outline to an end, having come up to the close of the eighteenth century, when the construction of large telescopes by Sir William Herschel and others gave a special impetus to observational astronomy, and led to the unfolding of the science along new lines. William Herschel.

CHAPTER II.

THE HEAVENS AND THEIR APPARENT DAILY REVOLUTION.

"The sad and solemn night
Has yet her multitude of cheerful fires;
The glorious host of light
Walk the dark hemisphere till she retires:
All through her silent watches, gliding slow,
Her constellations come, and climb the heavens, and go."

The arm-chair.

PERMIT the author to talk to you, the reader, for a moment. Perchance you are seated in an arm-chair, with your feet on the fender, and this book in your hands. You have vanquished Chapter I. and are ready for fresh victories. The next foe to be overcome is the arm-chair. For you will never take a deep interest in astronomy if you confine yourself to an arm-chair and a book. A young man rarely becomes enamored of a young lady into whose face he has never gazed. You must look into the eyes of the goddess Urania; they spangle the heavens, and will well repay your most ardent gazing. Surely you know the Great Dipper, which performs the endless round of motion about the north pole of the sky. But are you acquainted with Vega the beautiful, Arcturus the magnificent, Capella the icy, and Sirius the glowing? Why do we call Vega beautiful? When you have observed its hue, you will know. Why is Arcturus magnificent? If you shall be led to think that it is thousands of times as large as our sun, you will not begrudge it the adjective. In the dead

Bright stars.

of winter look up through the frosty air at Capella, as it stands at the apex of the starry vault, shining with a clear white light. You will be ready to admit that it is a fit jewel for the crown of the ice-king. As soon as your own eyes have marked the fact that Sirius is, in point of brightness, a seven-fold Vega, its splendid scintillations will glow in your memory.

Have you seen that storehouse of uncreated worlds, the great nebula in Andromeda? Have you at any time turned your opera-glass upon the famous double cluster in Perseus, or upon the Pleiades? How many stars can you see within the bowl of the Great Dipper? Is your eye sufficiently keen to split the double-star Epsilon Lyræ, which lies but three moon-breadths from Vega? Has a telescope ever split again each of these stars for you, so that you realized that they formed a system of four revolving suns? Have you seen Venus at mid-day, or can you recognize her in the evening, as

Nebulæ and clusters.

FIG. 8.—A SECTION OF THE MILKY WAY.

Venus and the moon

she glows with silvery sheen in the west, and weaves her way in and out among the stars, from night to night? Can Venus be seen at midnight? Is the full moon visible at noon? Do the horns of the crescent moon point toward the sun? Does the moon always set directly in the west? In what direction does the moon move among the stars, eastward or westward?

The Milky Way. On some night when the sky was perfectly clear, and the moon was not in sight, have you made a study of the wonderful river of light which foams across the sky? Have you seen the dark rocks against which it dashes, the foaming eddies here and there, and the profusion of starry spray with which it besprinkles the adjoining constellations?

Urania. Must you give a negative answer to most of these questions? Then let the arm-chair control you no longer. Yield to the charms of Urania: woo her, and make her your friend. How shall this wooing proceed? This chapter and the next four shall be your guide in this matter. In them will be developed an orderly method of procedure, which will lead, by easy stages, to the attainment of the desired end.

First we mention briefly the classes of objects with which our study will be concerned.

The fixed stars. The fixed stars, or more simply the stars, are those brilliant points of light which stud the heavens, remaining in the same relative position from year to year, and from century to century, as nearly as the unaided eye can judge. Had an ancient Assyrian made a rude representation of the Great Dipper on one of his tablets of clay, we should at this day instantly recognize the configuration as one with which we are familiar. The fixed stars are suns, at such amazing distances from us that their motions seem exceedingly small.

The Heavens and their Apparent Revolution. 39

The nebulæ are cloud-like masses of matter of vast extent, which are as far away as the stars. The great nebula in Andromeda can be seen easily with the naked eye, and the nebula in the sword-handle of Orion can be glimpsed. The vast majority of these objects, however, are visible only with powerful telescopes. Quite a number are invisible even in the largest instruments, but have imprinted themselves on photographic plates exposed for hours in the foci of special star-cameras. *The nebulæ.*

The planets look like the fixed stars, when viewed with the naked eye, except that they do not twinkle. Jupiter and Venus are usually brighter than the brightest fixed stars. Mars, Mercury, Saturn, Uranus, and Neptune are less brilliant, Neptune never being visible to the unaided eye. The ancients, who were unacquainted with Uranus and Neptune, discovered that the other planets changed their apparent positions among the stars. From this circumstance arose the designation "planet," which signifies "wanderer." These bodies are all comparatively near us, the most distant being less than three thousand million miles away. The minor planets, also called asteroids, are small bodies coursing about the sun in paths which lie between those of Mars and Jupiter. *The planets.*

Comets derive their name, which means "hairy ones," from their tails or trains, which often attain to great magnificence. Some of them are to be regarded as members of the solar system, since they revolve about the sun in closed curves. Others are simply visitors, which display their beauty for a time, and then whisk off to regions unknown. *Comets.*

Meteors are those rash little bodies which plunge headlong into the earth, and thus end their careers in an outburst of evanescent glory. *Meteors.*

40 *A Study of the Sky.*

Sun, moon, and earth. The sun, moon, and earth need no particular mention, the earth being one of the sun's family of planets, and the moon being her attendant; the moon belongs to the class of bodies known as satellites, which revolve about the planets.

We are now in a position to understand any mention

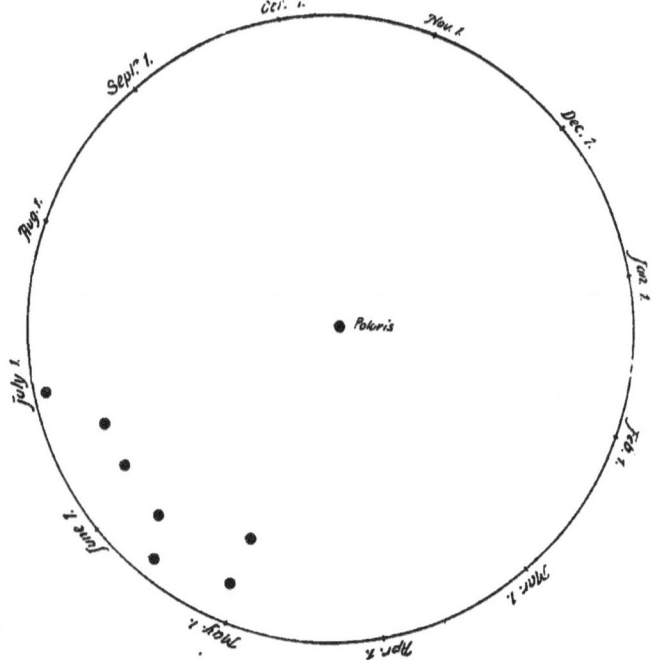

FIG. 9.—THE GREAT DIPPER.

which may be made of these celestial objects, prior to the detailed discussion of them which will come later.

The Great Dipper. Our present business is to get acquainted with the fixed stars. The Great Dipper is the first configuration to be learned (Fig. 9). Around the margin of the diagram are given dates, which will aid in finding it. To locate it on February 1 at 8 p. m., the book is to be held out in front of the reader, with the center of the diagram on a level with his eyes, and the point marked February 1 at the uppermost part of the circle. The diagram then shows that the Dipper is at the right of Polaris, the pole-star. Two of the stars in the bowl are called the Pointers, because they point toward Polaris. The distance between the Pointers is about five degrees, and should be fixed in mind as a sort of yardstick with which to estimate distances between other stars. The distance from Polaris to the nearest Pointer is about five times our yardstick.

The yardstick.

In order to get an accurate notion of measurement by degrees, imagine that the stars are fastened upon the inner surface of a huge celestial sphere, the distance from the earth to the surface of the sphere being so great as to be beyond adequate comprehension (Fig. 10). Let E be the position of the observer on the earth, while S and S' are two stars said to be 30° apart. Through these stars a circle whose center is at E is drawn on the surface of the celestial sphere. From E two lines, ES and ES', are drawn, making the angle SES'. This angle is measured by the number of degrees in the arc SS', there being 360° in an entire circle. If the arc SS' is one twelfth of the entire circumference, the angle SES' is an angle of 30°.

Angular measurement.

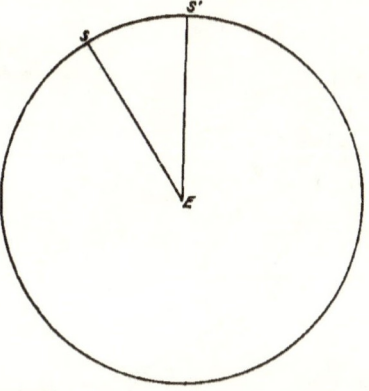

FIG. 10.—MEASUREMENT OF AN ANGLE.

Now the diameter of the earth, which is less than

8,000 miles, is very minute in comparison with the distance from the earth to any fixed star, for the latter distance is expressed by many millions of millions of miles. In consequence of this, the angular distance between any two stars always appears the same, wherever the observer may be on our planet.

<small>Boston and San Francisco.</small>

If an astronomer in Boston were to measure the angular distance between Polaris and one of the Pointers, with the most perfect instrument ever devised for such work, and another astronomer in San Francisco were to make a similar measurement, the two results would agree if the observations were free from error. This remark applies only to the fixed stars, and is not true of the moon or the planets, which are much nearer to us.

<small>Center of the sphere.</small>

For all our naked-eye observations we may therefore assume that the eye of the observer is located in the center of the celestial sphere, and that all of the fixed stars are fastened to the sphere, turning with it as it turns. We are thus taken back to the crystal spheres, studded with golden nails, with which the ancient Greeks dealt. We may imagine the moon, the planets, and comets to be likewise located on the inner surface of the sphere, but to be endowed with powers of locomotion, so that they can move about among the golden nails.

<small>Rotation of the sphere.</small>

Remembering then that we are in the center of the celestial sphere, we ask the question, "How does the star-sphere appear to turn?" In answering this we have recourse to the cause of the apparent turning, which is the spinning of the earth upon its axis with such evenness of motion that we experience no jar or shock.

<small>A sleeping car.</small>

Every reader has had similar experiences with motions on the earth's surface. A sleeping-car passenger awakes suddenly in the middle of the night, and concludes by the comparative silence and the absence of noticeable jarring that his train is stopping at some station. Looking out of the window he sees a freight train apparently slowly backing on the next track. The truth is that the freight train is at rest, while his own train is just starting up.

A passenger steamer leaves Chicago at night; having gotten fairly out of the harbor, it turns in order to head in a certain direction. While it is turning the lights of the city and the stars in the sky appear to the passengers to be revolving in the opposite direction to that in which they themselves are turning. *A steamer.*

Conceive the axis of the earth to be prolonged till it strikes the celestial sphere. The north end of the axis strikes near Polaris, at a point called the north celestial pole. The south end strikes at the opposite point of the celestial sphere, called the south celestial pole. A straight line joining these two points is the axis of the celestial sphere, about which it appears to rotate. If there were a bright star at each pole, and we could see both of them at the same time, we should have little difficulty in getting an accurate idea of just how the heavens rotate. *The poles.*

A line drawn from the eye of the observer parallel to the earth's axis, and prolonged to the celestial sphere, would strike so near the centers of the stars, which we have imagined to be at the celestial poles, that no astronomer could measure the deviation. We are therefore entirely justified in laying down the following principle to guide our thinking in this matter of the apparent daily rotation of the star-sphere: *The axis of rotation.*

The star-sphere appears to turn once a day about an axis drawn from the observer's eye to the north celestial pole, which is in the vicinity of Polaris.

The north pole. We may now locate the north celestial pole more accurately than by saying that it is in the vicinity of Polaris. The star which is situated at the bend of the handle of the Great Dipper is called Mizar. Let the eye travel slowly from Polaris directly toward Mizar; when it has gone a distance equal to one fourth of the distance between the Pointers, it has reached the north celestial pole.

Observations and records. But the explanation which has just been given does not suffice for our needs. The motion of rotation can be well grasped only by repeated observations of the heavens. Since we now purpose to get acquainted with the heavens, gaining knowledge which will be a source of delight throughout life, we must not only observe, but also record some of our observations, that they may be the better fixed in mind. A common blank book will answer our needs.

The first drawing. A picture of the Great Dipper is first to be drawn. We get it and Polaris well in mind by looking at them a minute or two. Polaris is considerably brighter than any other star within fifteen degrees of it, and is almost directly north of us, about half way from the horizon to the zenith. It is also at the end of the handle of the Little Dipper, which is shown in the figure. The distance from Polaris to the furthest corner of the bowl of the Little Dipper is nearly twenty degrees, and the curved handle is about twelve degrees in length.

Polaris and the Pointers. We first locate Polaris on a page of the blank book, and then draw a faint line directly down from it, to represent a vertical line; we also draw a horizontal line similarly. These are only to assist in getting the Dipper correctly located. The Pointers are next drawn, care being taken that the distance from Polaris to the nearest Pointer shall be five times the distance between the Pointers. Then come the other two stars of the bowl in their proper relative positions, and lastly the handle. After this the Little Dipper may be drawn.

The picture now resembles Fig. 11, except that the vertical and horizontal lines may not lie in the same positions with reference to the stars as in the diagram, and that the dotted lines have not been drawn. The date of observation and the time (within five minutes) when the drawing was finished are recorded. If the drawing was made early in the evening, another similar one should be made just before retiring for the night. A comparison of the two will show that the Dippers have shifted their positions with reference to the vertical and horizontal lines. After watching the Dippers for two or three nights the answers to the following queries may be written down in the note-book:

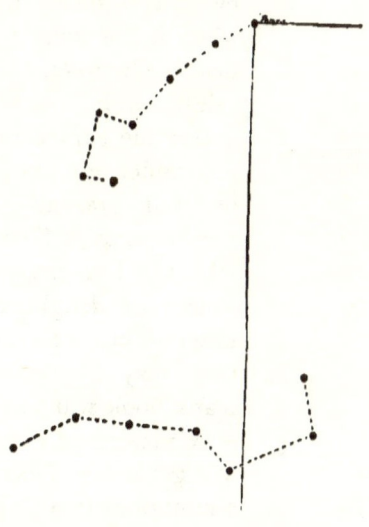

FIG. 11.—THE TWO DIPPERS.

Is Polaris as bright as either of the Pointers? Is any star in the bowl of the Little Dipper brighter than the faintest in the bowl of the Great Dipper? How many stars can be seen within the bowl of the Great Dipper? There is a faint star, called Alcor, which is within a degree of Mizar; what is its color? The distance from Alcor to Mizar is what fraction of a degree? What is the color of each of the Pointers (white, yellowish, reddish, bluish)? Is the Great Dipper higher up late in the evening than early? At some time during the night

Queries.

46   *A Study of the Sky.*

<small>How the Dipper moves.</small>

would the bowl of the Great Dipper be near the zenith? If so, would the handle be east or west of the bowl at that time? At about what time on the day of observation was the bowl underneath Polaris? Where was the bowl of the Little Dipper with reference to Polaris, when the large bowl was underneath? If a watch were held between your eye and Polaris in such a position that you looked squarely at its face, would the extremity of the minute hand travel around the face in the same direction in which the Dippers go around the pole-star, or in the opposite direction? Twelve hours after the time of your first observation where would the Great Dipper be with reference to Polaris? Does Mizar keep at the same distance from Polaris? Does the bowl of the Great Dipper ever disappear below your horizon? Does this bowl move downward, when at the left of the pole-star as you face it? If it were below Polaris would it appear to be moving toward your right as you face it? Is there any time during the twenty-four hours which are consumed by a revolution of the star-sphere when Alcor appears to be exactly in line between Mizar and Polaris?

<small>Motion of other stars.</small>

Did you ever see the moon close to either Dipper? If you turn your back on the pole-star and face southward will a star off in the south appear to be traveling toward your right? If you face westward and look up at a star near the zenith, will that star be moving westward down the vault of the sky? Will its distance from Polaris apparently alter as the hours of the night roll on? Will the star slide straight down the sky, as if endeavoring to reach the horizon by the shortest path, or will it veer off toward the north? A star has just risen close by the east point of the horizon; as it climbs the sky will it go straight toward the zenith, or will it veer off toward the south? Are there any stars except Polaris and those

The Heavens and their Apparent Revolution. 47

in the Dippers which never disappear below your horizon?

If the reader is not sure about the answer to any of these queries, he should watch the heavens until doubt gives way to certainty.

The expression "celestial sphere," which we have used so freely, has a technical meaning among astronomers. They define it as a sphere whose radius is infinite, so that the remotest stars lie far within it. The apparent position of any object on this sphere is the point where a line drawn from the observer's eye through the object, and extended to an infinite distance, pierces the sphere.

The definition of the celestial sphere.

Our first and most difficult lesson in astronomy is at an end.

CHAPTER III.

THE CONSTELLATIONS IN GENERAL.

" Look how the floor of heaven
Is thick inlaid with patines of bright gold;
There's not the smallest orb which thou behold'st,
But in his motion like an angel sings;
Still quiring to the young-eyed cherubins."
—*Shakespeare*.

The menagerie.

MEN of the earliest ages were quick to perceive that there were certain striking groups of stars, some of which rudely resembled men and animals. To these they gave names, according to their fancy. Even the most savage nations have not failed to name certain groups. A celestial globe of the present day is covered with a veritable menagerie of monsters, the names of which are largely taken from Greek mythology. We cannot trace the origin of these names satisfactorily; some of them occur in the most ancient writings. Many of the groupings are highly artificial, and were apparently devised to immortalize the heroes and heroines of mythological tales.

Andromeda.

The story of Andromeda is a case in point. She was a daughter of Cepheus, a king of the Ethiopians. Her mother, Cassiopeia, imprudently boasted that the beauty of Andromeda excelled that of the Nereids, who were lovely divinities inhabiting the depths of the Mediterranean. Incensed at this, the Nereids betook themselves to Poseidon, the chief divinity of that sea, and prevailed upon him to visit Libya by an inundation,

The Constellations in General. 49

and further to send a sea-monster to ravage the unhappy land. An oracle promised deliverance if Andromeda were given up to the rapacious maw of the leviathan. The clamor of his people obliged Cepheus to yield, and Andromeda was chained to a rock.

It so happened that a brave youth, Perseus by name, had just accomplished the daring feat of slaying Medusa, one of the Gorgons. Her snaky head, which turned the beholder to stone, was borne aloft by Perseus in triumph. From her blood sprang Pegasus, the winged horse. As Perseus journeyed homeward through the air, with his horrid trophy, he spied Andromeda. Everybody will admit that the only proper thing for this prehistoric knight to do was to kill Cetus, the sea-monster, break the chains of Andromeda, and marry her. He proved equal to all these demands, though her color did not match his. *Perseus.*

Among the stars we now find Andromeda, Cassiopeia, Cepheus, Cetus, Perseus with Medusa's head still in his hand, and Pegasus.

The Great Dipper, to which we paid so much attention in the last chapter, is a portion of the constellation of the Great Bear. One of the Greek legends is that Jupiter, who had a penchant for falling in love with fair women, wooed the nymph Callisto, and metamorphosed her into a bear, lest Juno should enliven his domestic affairs unduly. But Juno was not deceived by this ruse, and persuaded Diana to slay the bear. Jupiter then gave Juno a standing lesson about meddling with his royal prerogatives by placing Callisto among the stars, under the name of Arctos, the Greek word for bear. *The Great Bear.*

The Iroquois Indians, when America was discovered, are said to have called this star-group Okouari, which signifies bear. *The Iroquois.*

The Greeks also applied the designation "The Chariot" to the Great Dipper. The bowl may be considered as the body of the chariot, and the handle as the pole. This conceit survives in England, where the appellation "King Charles' Wain" is used, and in France, where it is often called "David's Chariot."

Ptolemy, who did so much in systematizing the astronomy of his day, has transmitted to us forty-eight constellations, which are now called the "ancient constellations," and are accepted and retained largely on account of their historic interest. Their names are thoroughly woven into astronomical literature, both popular and scientific.

Some attempts have been made to dispossess the ancient heroes of their happy hunting grounds. Early in the eighth century the Venerable Bede advocated a plan for Christianizing the heavens. Henceforth the apostles were to have conspicuous places in the sky. Peter was to take the place of the Ram, as was fitting, and the other disciples were to be distributed around the zodiac after him.

In the seventeenth century Professor Weigel, of the University of Jena, proposed that a series of heraldic constellations be formed, the zodiac being composed of the arms of the twelve foremost families in Europe. But this attempt to displace the old scheme, as well as all others, failed.

The zodiac, or zone of animals, is a belt sixteen degrees wide, which extends around the sky like the stripe on a croquet ball. From antiquity onward much attention has been paid to the constellations in it. Imagine that a line from the center of the sun to the earth's center is prolonged through the earth, and extended till it meets the celestial sphere.

The Constellations in General. 51

While the earth travels round the sun in its annual journey, the extremity of this line traces a circle on the celestial sphere. The name of the circle is "the ecliptic." To an eye situated at the sun's center the earth would appear to travel around the ecliptic. To an eye placed at the earth's center the sun would similarly appear to course along the ecliptic, taking a year to make the complete circuit, passing through the zodiacal constellations in succession. The ecliptic lies in the middle of the zodiac, which extends eight degrees each side of it. As we watch the sun, moon, and planets, they always appear to lie in the zodiac.

The ecliptic.

The ancients gave to certain small and conspicuous groups special names, such as the Pleiades and the Hyades. Individual stars of pronounced brightness were also named. We glance for a moment at some interesting facts concerning the Pleiades.

Other names.

The Pleiades were often used in connection with the calendar by ancient peoples, and are still employed thus by some savage tribes. This group of stars is situated near the ecliptic. The sun, therefore, in his annual journey, gets so near them at one time of the year that they cannot be seen for several days. Six months after this time, when the sun has gone half way round the heavens, it is opposite the Pleiades, so that they rise when it sets, and *vice versâ*. From Hesiod we learn that the Greeks in his day accounted the winter season as commencing when the Pleiades were seen low down in the east soon after sunset, and the summer season when they set soon after the sun.

The Pleiades.

The Society Islanders are said to have divided the year into two parts, according to the position of the Pleiades. That half of the year during which they could be seen early in the evening was called "the

The Society Islanders.

Pleiades above." The other half was "the Pleiades below."

The Druids.
The rising of the Pleiades at sunset occurs about November 1. On that night was one of the most noteworthy festivals of the Druids, in which they celebrated the destruction and rejuvenation of the world. The sacred fire, which had burned continuously in the temple during the past year, was extinguished, and then the spirits of those who had died during the year embarked in ghostly array in the boats which were to take them to the seat of judgment, where the god of the dead apportioned to each his lot. In the church calendar of to-day November 1 is known as All Saints' Day. The preceding evening is Hallowe'en. The following day is All Souls' Day, and is celebrated in the Roman Catholic Church by supplications for the souls of the pious dead.

The Peruvians.
A festival commemorative of the dead is held at this time of year in many parts of the world. The Peruvians visit the tombs of their relatives, to bring food and drink for the departed, and to lament with plaintive songs and weeping. In India the month of November is called the month of the Pleiades, and a Hindu festival of the dead is celebrated about the middle of the month. The Persians once named the month after the angel of death.

Australian savages.
Australian savages are said still to hold a "corroboree" at this season, in honor of the Pleiades, which, say they, "are very good to the black fellows." These occasions are also festivals of the dead; the savages paint white stripes upon their bodies in such fashion that they appear like skeletons, as they execute weird nocturnal dances about their fires.

From Prescott's "History of the Conquest of Mexico" we learn that the Mexicans celebrated a great

cycle of fifty-two years, the celebration occurring on
a November night. There was a tradition that the *The Mexicans.*
world was once destroyed at this time. When the
shades of evening fell, and the Pleiades rose, the cere-
monies began. As this group of stars approached the
zenith a human sacrifice was offered, to avert a repetition of the dreadful calamity. When once the Pleiades
had passed the highest point of their course, and were
seen to be descending in the west, the gloom and
dismay of the people gave place to rejoicing.

The names now used for most of the stars of the first
magnitude come from Greek or Latin sources, and
are significant. Thus Arcturus comes from the Greek, *Proper names of stars.*
and means "the bear-driver." Antares, the red star in
the heart of the Scorpion, shows by its name that it
is the rival of Ares (the Greek name for Mars, the ruddy
planet). The word Sirius is probably derived from the
Greek σείριος, and therefore signifies "the scorching
one." Quite a number of names were given by the
Arabians. Aldebaran signifies "the follower"; it is
supposed to have received this designation because it
rises shortly after the Pleiades. Altair, "the flying
eagle," is the brightest star in the constellation of
Aquila, the Eagle. Betelgeuse is a modification of the
Arabic *Ibt-al-jauza*, which means "the giant's shoulder"; the star is located in the shoulder of Orion, the
mighty hunter.

Stars which had no proper names were, up to the beginning of the seventeenth century, usually designated
by referring to their positions in the constellations.
Thus we read of the star in the right knee of Boötes, or
in the club of Hercules. This inadequate plan is
happily no longer in vogue.

In 1603 Bayer published a star atlas in which he made

use of the letters of the Greek and Roman alphabets. According to this system the brightest star in the constellation Lyra is called Alpha Lyræ.* The next star in that constellation, in point of brightness, is Beta Lyræ. When the letters of the Greek alphabet have been exhausted, and there remain stars yet unlettered, the Roman alphabet is taken up.

The modern system of naming.

If all the letters of the Roman alphabet have been used and there yet remain naked-eye stars which are unnamed, numbers assigned by the astronomer Flamsteed are employed. At present every star visible to the unassisted eye can be referred to by letter or number. The system of numbers is entirely independent of the letters, every star in a given constellation having a number, even though it may have been previously called by a letter. The numbers were not given in order of brightness. When the daily revolution of the stars brought the constellation Taurus to the meridian of Greenwich, the first naked-eye star which crossed the meridian was called by Flamsteed 1 Tauri; the next star was 2 Tauri, etc.

Flamsteed's numbers.

The hundreds of thousands of faint stars whose positions have been determined by modern astronomers receive their names from their current numbers in star catalogues. For instance the 1634th star in Lalande's catalogue is known as Lalande 1634. The stars in all modern catalogues are arranged in the order in which they cross the meridian of any place, without reference to the constellations within whose boundaries they lie.

Catalogues.

What does a modern catalogue tell about each star which it contains? This question cannot well be answered until we learn the meanings of two simple ex-

---

* *Lyræ* is the genitive case, or, as we would say in English, the possessive case of the Latin word *lyra*.

The Constellations in General. 55

pressions, "right ascension" and "declination." These terms are analogous to those used in geography in locating places on the earth. As there is a terrestrial equator, so there is a celestial equator, as heretofore explained. As the latitude of a city is its distance, expressed in degrees, from the terrestrial equator, so the declination of a star is its distance from the celestial equator. There is a prime meridian on the earth, *e. g.*, the meridian of Greenwich, from which longitude is reckoned eastward or westward; there is also a certain celestial meridian which passes through the celestial poles, and cuts the celestial equator at a particular point called the "vernal equinox," the location of which we shall explain more particularly hereafter. As the city of Denver has a longitude of seven hours, so some star has a right ascension of seven hours. While longitude on the earth is reckoned either eastward or westward from the principal meridian, the right ascension of a star is reckoned eastward only.

Right ascension and declination.

In a star catalogue we expect to find three things stated about each star, its right ascension, its declination, and its brightness. An explanation of the method of estimating brightness will be given in the next chapter.

The letters of the Greek alphabet are given below, for the benefit of those who may not know them. They will slip easily into the memory, in the process of learning the constellations which are given in the next three chapters.

The Greek alphabet.

α	Alpha.	ι	Iota (iŏ′tä).	ρ	Rho.
β	Beta (bā′tä).	κ	Kappa.	σ	Sigma.
γ	Gamma.	λ	Lambda.	τ	Tau (tou).
δ	Delta.	μ	Mu (mū).	υ	Upsilon′.
ε	Epsilon′.	ν	Nu (nū).	φ	Phi (phē).
ζ	Zeta (zā′tä).	ξ	Xi (ksē).	χ	Chi (kē).
η	Eta (ā′tä).	ο	Omicron′.	ψ	Psi (psē).
θ	Theta (thā′tä).	π	Pi (pē).	ω	Omĕ′ga.

CHAPTER IV.

THE CONSTELLATIONS FOR JANUARY AND FEBRUARY.

" Ye quenchless stars ! so eloquently bright,
Untroubled sentries of the shadowy night,
While half the world is lapp'd in downy dreams,
And round the lattice creep your midnight beams,
How sweet to gaze upon your placid eyes,
In lambent beauty looking from the skies ! "
—*Montgomery.*

A review. WE are now ready to confront the sky for the purpose of getting a hailing acquaintance with the most interesting of the star-groups. For we have already learned something of their origin, of the methods of naming the stars in each constellation, and the way of locating them by right ascension and declination. We have also obtained ideas concerning the apparent daily motion of the star-sphere, and can therefore foresee, to a certain extent, the effect of this motion on the position of a constellation during the successive hours of the night.

Every reader will not find time to learn all the constellations described in this and the next two chapters. *Three constellations a month.* But every one should form the acquaintance of at least three constellations a month. Therefore the three most conspicuous constellations of those given for each month are named in **black letter**. One may read the remainder of the book before the constellation work is finished. The work is so arranged that it may be done, a little at a time, during the first six months of the year. During the vacation months of summer the pleasant evenings

The Constellations for January and February. 57

will tempt the observer to review those constellations which are then visible, and thus to fasten them in the memory.

Only those stars which form the characteristic configuration of each constellation are given in the illustration of it. Many other adjoining stars, which are generally fainter, are within the arbitrary boundaries of the constellation, as laid down on standard maps of the heavens. To these extra stars we pay no attention; an attempt to learn them would be a waste of energy, as not even professional astronomers are familiar with them. It is not advisable to learn the Greek letter for every star. If any particular star interests the reader especially, it is well to remember its name. For example, Epsilon Lyræ is a famous quadruple star, which consists of two adjoining pairs of revolving suns, and is used as a test of acuteness of vision. It is best to learn the names of those bright stars which, like Sirius, Arcturus, and Vega, are among the most splendid objects in the sky. Such names are printed in the diagrams.

The characteristic configuration.

The faintest star which can be seen by an average eye is said to be of the sixth magnitude. A star which is two and one half times as bright as this, and can be seen easily, is of the fifth magnitude. A fourth magnitude star is two and one half times as bright as one of the fifth. Thus the scale of magnitudes is ascended till we reach the first magnitude. Fewer than twenty of the fixed stars are bright enough to be rated as of the first magnitude, and some of them are much brighter than others. A standard first magnitude star is one hundred times as bright as one of the sixth magnitude. The magnitudes of the stars are indicated by the symbols given on the next page :

Stellar magnitudes.

First magnitude, •
Second magnitude, ─●─
Third magnitude, ━●━
Fourth magnitude, ─╂─
Fifth magnitude, •

Estimation of distance. Two stars which appear in a diagram of the same magnitude may seem to the observer quite different. Both stars, for instance, may be given of the third magnitude, though one is only a little fainter than magnitude three and one half, while the other is nearly as bright as magnitude two and one half. For small distances the observer may use as a measuring rod the distance between the Pointers, which is close to 5°. For longer distances it will be convenient to remember that the distance from the extremity of the handle of the Great Dipper to the Pointer at the top of the Dipper bowl is 26°.

Hints. In learning a constellation one should first familiarize himself with the illustration given in the book, studying it till he can make a rude sketch, showing the relative positions of the stars. Having this mental picture, he can face the sky with a good degree of assurance, and will generally have little difficulty in picking out the stars desired. The constellations will not usually appear the same side up as in the book. But if the observer imagines a line drawn on the sky from the north pole, or practically from Polaris, directly toward the desired constellation and through its center, this line will run from the center of the upper edge of the diagram to the center of the lower edge.

Observation exercises. After the description of each constellation are given a few queries, the answers to which may be written in the observer's note-book. If two or more persons observe

The Constellations for January and February. 59

together, the work will prove quite fascinating. But in answering the queries one should never allow his judgment to be swayed by that of a companion. The eyes of one person are not like those of another, and each should put down what his own eyes reveal.

Independence.

Ursa Major.

The Great Dipper, with which we have already become familiar, is a portion of Ursa Major, the Great Bear.

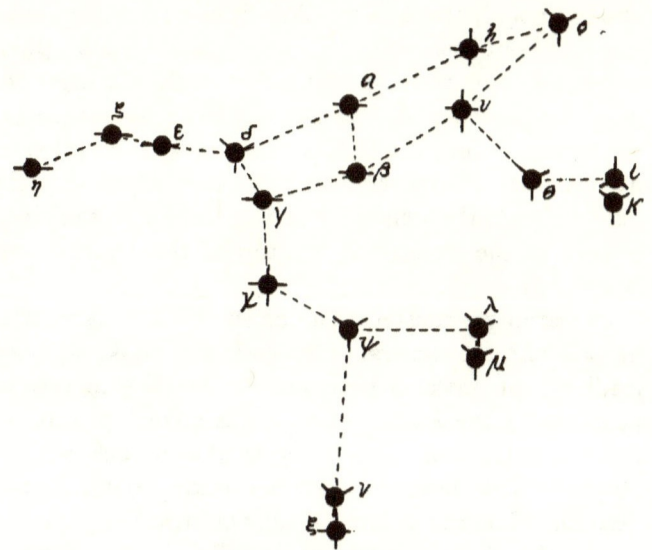

FIG. 12.—URSA MAJOR.

About 9 p. m. during any evening in January this constellation is found at the right of Polaris. The Bear appears at that time to be balancing himself upon the tip of his tail. The star *o* (Fig. 12) marks the tip of the creature's nose. The animal is short one fore leg, but map-makers are accustomed to supply the missing member, despite the absence of available stars. Each of the three existing feet is marked by a couple of stars ; the

Description.

components of each pair are less than two degrees apart. ι and κ mark the front foot ; λ and μ mark the forward hind foot. The remaining hind foot is located by ν and ξ. These three pairs of stars lie almost in a line, the central pair being about twenty degrees from each of the others.

The handle of the Dipper is the tail of the Bear, and is of appropriate length for a cow. This anomaly, we are told by an old writer, is due to the fact that Jupiter lifted the bear by its tail, when he raised it to the sky.

The Bear's tail.

The stars in the Dipper have received proper names, which are sometimes used even by astronomers, who, except in the case of the stars of the first magnitude, usually prefer the Greek letter nomenclature. α Ursæ Majoris is Dubhe ; β is Merak ; γ is Phecda ; δ is Megrez ; ε is Alioth ; ζ is Mizar ; η is Benetnasch or Alkaid.

The Dipper.

Mizar is one of the finest of double stars, as seen with a small telescope, and was the first of such objects which the telescope revealed ; it was discovered in 1650, soon after the invention of that instrument. These two magnificent suns, one of the second, the other of the fourth magnitude, are slowly revolving about their common center of gravity. The time of a complete revolution is roughly estimated at 20,000 years. In 1889 Prof. E. C. Pickering* discovered by means of observations with the spectroscope that the brighter of the two components of Mizar is itself a double. The two stars composing it are thought to make one revolution about one another in one hundred and four days, the diameter of their orbit being about 140 million miles. The mass of the system is forty times that of the sun. Near Mizar is the faint star Alcor, which the average eye should see without difficulty.

Mizar.

---
* Director of the Harvard College Observatory.

According to mythology, Ursa Major is the nymph Callisto, who was so pleasing in Jupiter's eyes that Juno became jealous. One version of the legend is that Jupiter changed Callisto to a bear, to avoid Juno's jealousy; another version is that Juno took revenge upon her rival by changing her into a bear. Being unwilling to lose his favorite in this way, Jupiter transported her to the stars. *Mythology.*

What is the magnitude of Alcor, and its distance (fraction of a degree) from Mizar? Which is the brightest star in the Dipper? How many stars are visible within the bowl of the Dipper? Twelve hours after the time of sketching the constellation, what is its position? *Queries.*

Ursa Minor.

At 7 p. m., on any evening early in January, the Little Bear is suspended by his tail, the end of which is fastened at Polaris (Fig. 13). It has been suggested that the inordinate length of his tail is an illustration of the Darwinian law of adaptation to environment, the tail having been stretched in the process of swinging the Bear around once in every twenty-four hours, for hundreds of years. *Description.*

This star-group is commonly called the Little Dipper; the handle of the utensil is a neat curve containing four stars, including

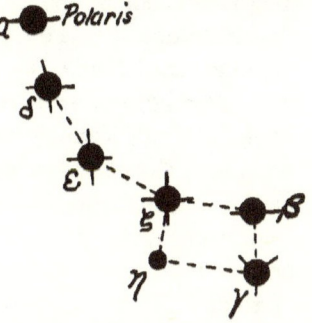

FIG. 13.—URSA MINOR.

the one by which it is joined to the bowl. The two brightest stars in the bowl are called the "Guardians of the Pole." The constellation guided the Phenicians in *The Little Dipper.*

their voyages on the Mediterranean, just as the pole-star now affords to a seaman a method of checking the indications of his compass, should he fear that it is awry.

Polaris.

Polaris is one of the nearest of our neighbors among the fixed stars. Yet a railway train, speeding continuously at the rate of sixty miles an hour, would require 600 millions of years to reach it. So enormous a distance is very difficult to measure, and is subject to considerable uncertainty arising from the unavoidable errors inherent in even the most careful measurements of experienced astronomers.

The north celestial pole.

The north pole of the heavens lies on a line from Polaris to Mizar, being a little more than a degree from the former. Polaris has not always been the pole-star. Because of the attractions of the sun and moon upon the equatorial protuberance of the earth, the direction in which the axis of the earth points is continually changing. The result is that the north celestial pole moves in a circle on the surface of the sphere. One revolution is made in 25,800 years. The circle passes near Vega, in the constellation of the Lyre, its center appearing to lie about half way from Polaris to Vega, not quite on a line joining them. Twelve thousand years hence Vega will be the pole-star, unless some unforeseen catastrophe gives an unexpected shift to the earth's axis.

A double star.

Polaris is a double star, having a companion of magnitude 9.5, which can be detected with a telescope of two or three inches' aperture. By the "aperture" of a telescope is meant the diameter of the object-glass, which is the lens at the large end of the telescope.

Cassiopeia.

Description.

The pole-star is midway between the Great Dipper and a striking group of five stars, three of which are of the second magnitude, the other two being of the third.

The group resembles a dilapidated W, and consists of the stars β, α, γ, δ, ε, shown in Fig. 14. By adding κ the figure is brought to a rude likeness to a broken-backed chair, γ and κ forming the seat of the chair, while δ and ε outline its back.

<small>A dilapidated W.</small>

Cassiopeia is often called "The Lady in the Chair," and one is thus led to suppose that she is seated in the chair. But the map-makers have ordered otherwise, and the queen disdains to sit on anything more substantial than the ether.

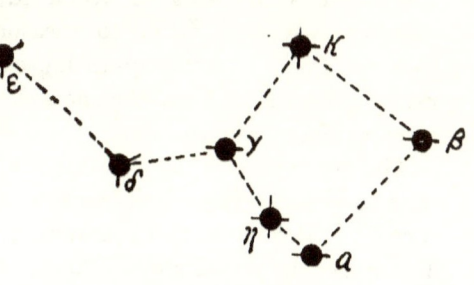

FIG. 14.—CASSIOPEIA.

β, α, γ, and κ form her body; δ lies in her knee, and ε marks her foot. Her hands are upraised, as if in prayer to the gods to spare her beautiful daughter Andromeda, the story of whose danger and rescue has already been told.

<small>"The Lady in the Chair."</small>

Less than two degrees from κ, on the opposite side of it from γ, appeared in November, 1572, a new star, which was bright enough to be seen in full sunshine. Tycho perceived it while out for an evening stroll, and thenceforth observed its changes assiduously. In December its fires paled perceptibly, and after a lapse of sixteen months it became invisible to the naked eye. When it first appeared it inspired great terror among the ignorant, and was thought to presage the end of the world.

<small>Tycho's star.</small>

An opera-glass reveals many beautiful regions in Cassiopeia, where the stars besprinkle the sky like diamond dust. A line drawn from κ to β, and prolonged half as

<small>Clusters.</small>

far again, terminates at a cluster of small stars discovered by Caroline Herschel, the sister and assistant of Sir William Herschel. A degree from δ another fine field of stars is located. Any one who has a small telescope may spend considerable time pleasurably, exploring the Milky Way in and adjacent to Cassiopeia.

Double star. Between α and γ lies η, a star of the fourth magnitude, which is comparatively near us, its light taking not much over twenty years to come to us. It has a colored companion too close to it to be detected without a telescope. The hue vies with that of the chameleon, having been called by various astronomers green, purple, blue, red, and lilac. Such a diversity is best explained by changes in the star itself, though such changes seem improbable.

Queries. Is η in a direct line between α and γ? How many stars are at the end of a line drawn from β through the middle point between α and η, and prolonged nearly an equal distance? If β is now at the left of the pole, and as high above the horizon as Polaris, will it be lower two hours hence, or higher?

Pegasus.

Description. Pegasus, the winged horse, is a very large constellation, the conspicuous portion of which is a large square, whose sides average 15° in length (Fig. 15). Three of the four stars in the square are of the second magnitude. One corner of the square lies at the extremity of a line drawn from Polaris to β Cassiopeiæ, and prolonged an equal distance beyond β. The star at this corner is common to the two figures of Pegasus and Andromeda, and is universally called α Andromedæ. The same line prolonged 14° further meets γ, which is at another corner of the square. The square lies west of the zenith, about half way down to the horizon, at 7 p. m. in the middle of January, its uppermost side being the one just described. The square is the body of the horse, which has no hind quarters. At the opposite corner of the square from α Andromedæ lies α Pegasi. A line from the first of these stars to the second, prolonged an equal distance, passes through ζ in the neck, and terminates at θ, which is at the top of the head. ε is in the nose. The two fore legs start at β, and are marked by dotted lines in the diagram.

The square.

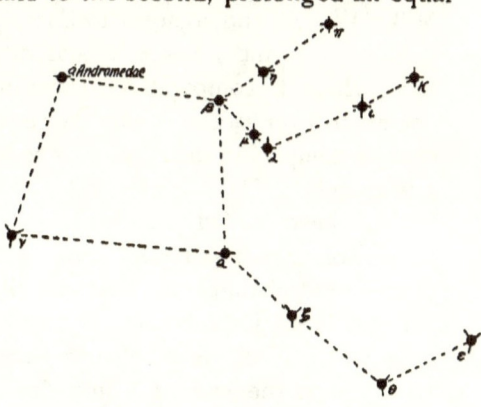

FIG. 15.—PEGASUS.

A line from θ to ε, prolonged a little more than half its length, reaches a globular cluster, which can be seen with a good opera-glass, and is one of the finest condensed clusters in the sky. Star crowds upon star, and the center of the cluster is a blaze of glory, which seems to defy separation into individual stars. We have here a system of thousands of suns, each of which undoubtedly moves under the attraction of all the others. The cluster is at least one hundred millions of millions of miles away.

A star cluster.

When Perseus had killed the Gorgon Medusa, Pegasus, the winged horse, sprung from her blood. Rising to the abodes of the immortals he became Jupiter's charger for a time. When Bellerophon wished to slay the Chimæra, it was necessary for him to bestride Pegasus. Minerva gave him a golden bridle, with which he caught the horse as he was drinking at the well Pirene.

Mythology.

The Chimæra vanquished, Bellerophon attempted to ascend to heaven on the back of his winged steed. But Jupiter sent a gad-fly, which stung the animal and caused him to throw his rider. Pegasus then flew on to the stars.

Queries. How many stars can you count on a moonless night, within the boundaries of the square? Is π double to the naked eye? Does the square set at the west point of the horizon, or north of that point? Which is the shortest side of the square?

Aquarius.

Aquarius is low in the west in January, in the evening, and should be looked for as soon as the sky has become fairly dark.* A line from β Pegasi to ζ Pegasi, when

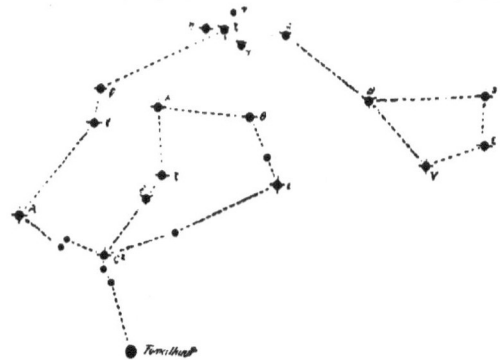

FIG. 16.—AQUARIUS.

Description. prolonged two thirds of its length, reaches an equilateral triangle, composed of three stars of the third, fourth, and fifth magnitudes respectively, in the center of which lies a third magnitude star. The sides of the triangle are 3° long; the four stars resemble a Y (Fig. 16). This is

---
*Should the reader fail to get hold of this constellation because it is low in the west, further study of it may be postponed until early summer, when it is seen in the east, late in the evening.

The Constellations for January and February. 67

the water-jar of Aquarius; from it flows a stream, which winds its way southward and eastward into the mouth of the Southern Fish, where lies the first magnitude star Fomalhaut (Fo-ma-lo). The stars π, η, γ, and ζ form the Y or water-jar. The stream flowing down to Fomalhaut follows the dotted line in the diagram through φ, ψ, etc. The line is marked by several groups of faint stars, near ψ, a, etc. β Pegasi lies nearly midway between Polaris and Fomalhaut. At the right of the Y lies a rude short-handled dipper, which the observer will fail to find unless he looks very early in the evening, and as near the first of the month as practicable. Most of the stars which stand guard between the dipper and the stream, that the fish be not defrauded of the water, belong to the constellation. Lines joining the brighter ones of them form a configuration not unlike the outline of South America; c^2 is at Cape Horn, the continent touching the stream at this point. τ in the center of the Y lies close to the celestial equator, and therefore sets very near the west point of the horizon. Fomalhaut.

There is a remarkable nebula situated 1° from ν toward ϵ, which, in a large telescope, exhibits a resemblance to the planet Saturn. It appears to be a world or system of worlds in formation. Should it, in the ages to come, become a gigantic Saturn-like form, having a central globe, surrounded by a thin flat ring composed of a myriad of smaller worlds, how magnificent and awe-inspiring a spectacle! Saturn-like nebula.

Aquarius is thought by some to represent the youth Ganymede, the most beautiful of mortals, whom Jupiter snatched to Mount Olympus to be his cup-bearer. With a fine appreciation of the distress of the bereaved parents he endeavored to assuage their grief by a present of a team of fine horses! Mythology.

68   *A Study of the Sky.*

Queries.
How many faint stars can be seen close to ψ? Are there five groups of faint stars (from two to four stars in a group) lying in the stream, between φ and Fomalhaut? When the water-jar is nearly setting in the west, what two stars in it lie most nearly in a horizontal line?

Pisces.

Description.
Like Aquarius, this constellation is largely composed of faint stars, the brightest one being of only the third magnitude. But the group lies in a dull region of the

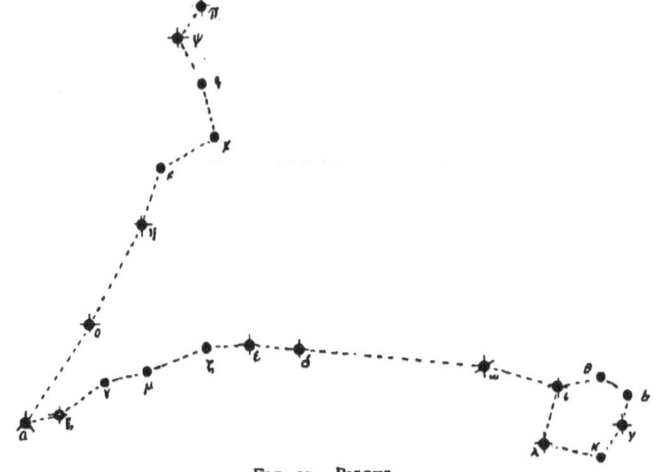

FIG. 17.—PISCES.

sky, so that the ribbon joining the two fishes can be readily traced (Fig. 17). The southernmost fish is composed of a circlet of seven stars, 5° or 6° in diameter.

The circlet.
Three of these stars, γ, ι, and λ, are of the fourth magnitude; the distance from ι to λ is 4°. γ is 6° from each of the other stars. The center of the circlet lies 12° south of the southern side of the square of Pegasus; ι is equidistant from α Pegasi and γ Pegasi. From ι in the circlet a row of stars runs eastward to α, a distance of

35°, and is a portion of the ribbon joining the two fish. α is called El Rischa, the Knot, and lies 10° west of the western side of a well-marked, five-sided polygon, the average length of one side of which is 5°. The polygon, as we shall learn hereafter, is the head of Cetus, the sea-monster. At the Knot the ribbon turns at a sharp angle, and runs northwesterly a distance of 30°, terminating in a coarse group of faint stars, which may be found by prolonging a line from β Pegasi to α Andromedæ eastward 15°, a little more than its own length.

The vernal equinox, which is the point in the sky at which the sun's center appears to lie, when it crosses the celestial equator in March, and ushers in the spring, lies in a barren spot of sky just east of the circlet of stars forming one fish. A line from γ to λ, extended as far again, ends at the equinox. The vernal equinox.

FEBRUARY CONSTELLATIONS.

Andromeda.

This constellation is found early in the evening in the northwest. α has already been mentioned as one corner of the square of Pegasus; it is located by drawing a line from Polaris to β Cassiopeiæ, and prolonging it an equal distance. A line from Polaris to the middle point between ϵ Cassiopeiæ and ι of the same constellation, prolonged an equal distance, ends at γ (Fig. 18). The bright stars β and δ lie nearly in line between α and γ; these four form one side of the maiden's form, α being in the head and γ in one foot. β is in her waist and δ at one shoulder. Her outstretched arms run from π to λ, and from δ to η. Description.

A line from β across her waist to μ, when prolonged an equal distance, ends at the great nebula, which is plain to the naked eye. Here is a storehouse of un- The great nebula.

70   *A Study of the Sky.*

created worlds, which is vast beyond all human comprehension. The entire solar system, if flung into this mighty abyss of chaotic matter, would be as a few grains of sand in a wagon-load.

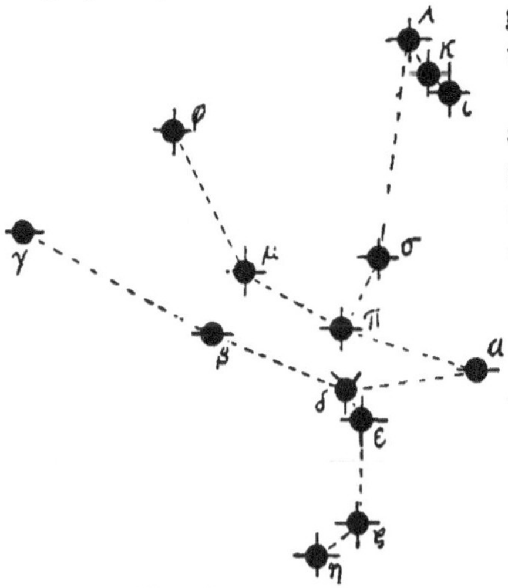

A double star.

γ is a fine double star, as seen with a small telescope, the components being of widely different hues, the smaller one being of the fifth magnitude; a large telescope splits the small star in two, showing that it is composed of two revolving suns. The mythological story of Andromeda has been told at length already, and is therefore omitted here.

FIG. 18.—ANDROMEDA.

Queries.   What is the color of γ? Which is the brighter, β or γ? Is the great nebula round or oval to the naked eye?

Aries.

Description.

Aries lies in the northwest early in the evening in February. A line from Polaris to γ Andromedæ, when prolonged nearly 20°, terminates at a, the brightest star in the small triangle composed of a, β, and γ (Fig. 19). The distance from a to γ is only 5°. The entire triangle is located in the head of the Ram. East of this triangle, between it and the Pleiades, are scattered a number of faint stars, which are sprinkled quite at random over the Ram's body.

The Constellations for January and February. 71

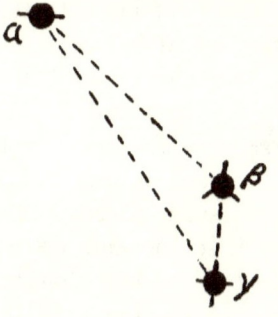

FIG. 19.—ARIES.

According to Grecian mythology a ram with a golden fleece, the gift of Mercury, flew with two children, Helle and Phrixus, over a sea. Helle was so unfortunate as to drop off into the sea, which was accordingly named the Hellespont (the sea of Helle). The famous Argonautic expedition was for the recovery of the golden fleece.

Mythology.

Cetus.

Cetus should be studied early in February, and as soon as it is dark, for the constellation is then in the southwest, and sets early. The monster resembles a walrus; his head alone is above the celestial equator.

The body of the leviathan is marked by a kite-shaped figure formed of the stars β, η, θ, ζ, and τ (Fig. 20). β lies on a line from Polaris through ζ Andromedæ (which is in one of the lady's arms), and is nearly 45° beyond the latter. The kite is 20° long from β to ζ. The tip of the tail of Cetus lies at ι, 11° northwest of β. The position of the pentagon forming the head (a, γ, etc.) is shown in the diagram, ζ being equi-distant from β and γ,

FIG. 20.—CETUS.

Description.

but not directly in line with them. υ marks the extremity of a flipper. A line from α to γ, when extended 10° further westward, nearly strikes α Piscium.

Mira. A little more than half way from ζ to γ lies ο. This star has received the proper name Mira, the Wonderful, because of the remarkable changes of its brightness. It is visible to the naked eye only three months in a year; on one occasion in the eighteenth century it became as bright as a first magnitude star. τ is one of the most rapidly moving stars known. It is traveling across the kite toward η, which it will reach in 19,000 years, if it keeps on at a uniform rate.

Mythology. Cetus is the sea-monster, frequently called "the Whale," that was to devour Andromeda, by order of Neptune. But Perseus intercepted and killed him.

Queries. Which is the brighter, α or β? Does the naked eye show that υ consists of more than one star? Less than half a degree from ζ lies a star of the fifth magnitude ; does it lie within the kite?

Taurus.

Description. Taurus, the Bull, is noteworthy because it contains the Pleiades, the Hyades, and the first magnitude star Aldebaran. It resembles Pegasus, in that only its head and fore shoulders have reached the sky. Nevertheless it makes a brave show of charging at Orion, the mighty hunter, of whom we have still to learn.

Pleiades and Hyades. The Pleiades are readily recognized. They are 25° east of α Arietis. Ten degrees east of the Pleiades, and less than that distance south is a V-shaped figure, which constitutes the face of the Bull, and contains Aldebaran. The horns are between 15° and 20° long, their tips being β and ζ (Fig. 21). The V-shaped group is called the Hyades. Both the Pleiades and the Hyades should be examined with an opera-glass, as they contain many stars, which are thus brought out well. Six of the Pleiades should reveal themselves to the unaided eye. On a good night, when the moon is below the horizon, a dozen stars may be seen by an acute eye. Alcyone, the brightest of the Pleiades, was once surmised to be the center of the universe, but the theory had no sufficient foundation and was soon abandoned. Photography has shown that shreds of Alcyone.

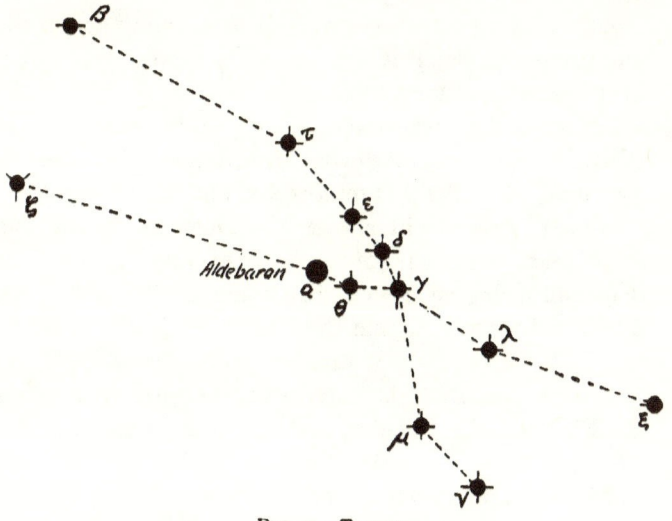

FIG. 21.—TAURUS.

nebulosity cling to many of the Pleiades, as if they were the remnants of an original nebula from which the cluster has been evolved.

In the eye of the Bull glows a, which is usually called by its Arabic name Aldebaran. Its distance from us, according to some of the latest measures, is about 100 millions of millions of miles. Aldebaran.

Taurus, in common with the majority of the constellations of the zodiac, is one of the ancient Egyptian star- Mythology.

groups, and was associated with the bull Apis. The Greeks described it as a mild and milk-white bull, into which Jupiter changed himself when he wished to seek the favor of beautiful Europa. The Pleiades were seven in number, being the daughters of Atlas, and sisters of the Hyades; one fell in love with a mortal, and hid herself from shame. When Atlas had joined the other Titans in an attack upon Jupiter, and had been conquered, he was condemned to uphold the sky. His sad fate led the Pleiades to make way with themselves. Both Atlas and Pleione, the father and mother, were placed in the sky in the same group with their devoted children.

Queries. What is the color of Aldebaran? What star in the V is double to the naked eye? Is any one of the Pleiades double, as seen with an opera-glass?

Orion.

Description. One who can look upon this magnificent constellation without a thrill of delight has no eye for the beauties of the heavens. At 8 p. m. in the middle of February it is on the meridian in the south, half way from the horizon to the zenith. It resembles the figure of the mighty hunter, who stands facing us (Fig. 22); with his right hand he brandishes a club, with which he is about to smite charging Taurus full in the face. The top of the club is marked by two stars of the fifth magnitude, $2\frac{1}{2}°$ apart, which point nearly at ζ Tauri, which is 5° west of them, at the top of one of the Bull's horns. The belt of the giant is marked by the three second magnitude stars δ, ϵ, and ζ. The length of the belt, which is often called the Ell and Yard, is 3°; it points westward toward the Pleiades, and eastward toward Sirius, the brightest of the fixed stars. On either side of the belt, at distances of about 10°, lie Betelgeuse in the right shoulder,

The Constellations for January and February. 75

and Rigel in the left foot. These are respectively α and β. In the left shoulder is γ, also called Bellatrix, and in the right knee is κ. The head is marked by a small isosceles right triangle. Over the left arm is thrown the skin of a lion. From the belt dangles a sword, which consists of the third magnitude star ι, and two faint stars immediately above it; a good eye sees in the sword four faint stars, in a row. The first star above ι is θ, which is involved in the great nebula of Orion. It has a hazy appearance to the naked eye.

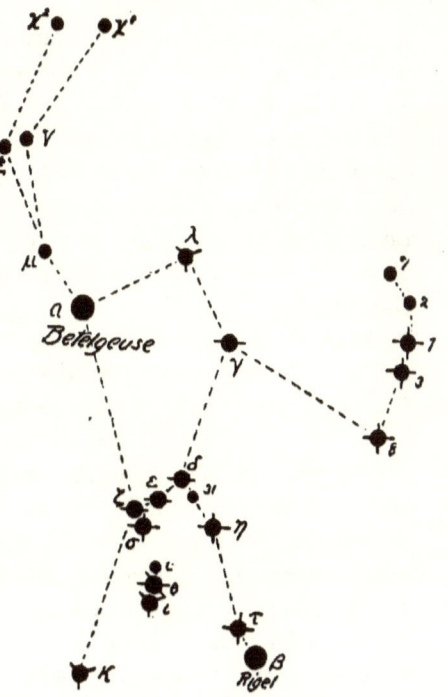

The sword.

FIG. 22.—ORION.

The celestial equator passes nearly through δ, the uppermost star in the belt.

Betelgeuse and Rigel must be bodies of amazing magnitude, for they are so far away that astronomers have not been able to measure their distances; yet they are among the brightest of the stars. It is safe to say that their distances exceed 200 million million miles.

Betelgeuse and Rigel.

The great nebula, which is situated in the sword, is the most marvelous object of its kind in the entire

The great nebula.

sky. Even an opera-glass reveals a little of the central portion of it; in a large telescope its magnificence baffles description. In viewing it with a large telescope it is well to point the telescope just west of the nebula, and allow it to drift through the field of view. θ, which is involved in the nebula, is a sextuple star; the four brightest stars in it have received the name of the Trapezium.

The Milky Way runs hard by Orion, and has apparently besprinkled it with a shower of starry spray. The entire constellation, seen through an opera-glass, is well spangled with faint stars.

Mythology.

Orion was a handsome giant and great hunter; he led an unhappy life, on account of his beauty and accomplishments. He lost his eyesight in consequence of his first love affair; after he recovered it by looking full at the rising sun, Aurora, the goddess of the dawn, fell in love with him and carried him off. According to another account no less a personage than Diana, whose heart was supposed to be Cupid proof, became enamored of him. Her indignant brother Apollo took occasion one fine day to tease her about her skill in archery, and asserted that she could not hit a certain shining mark, which bobbed on a distant wave. She hit it, and lo! it was Orion's head.

Queries.

What is the color of Betelgeuse? What is the color of Rigel? Does the middle star in the belt lie above or below a line connecting the other two? Are there two stars, or three, in a line a degree south of the belt, and parallel to it, the line being as long as the belt?

Auriga.

Description.

A little less than half way from Bellatrix (γ Orionis) to Polaris is Capella, a first magnitude star, which is the leading luminary of Auriga. It is at one corner of an irregular five-sided figure, the other corners being at β, β Tauri, θ, and ι (Fig. 23). The distance from Capella to β Tauri is 20°. The remainder of the constellation consists chiefly of inconspicuous stars, lying on the north and east sides of the five-sided polygon. Auriga signifies "the charioteer." A line from θ to β, prolonged northward an equal distance, meets the fourth magnitude star δ, which is in the man's head. His feet are at ι and β Tauri. Near Capella is a little triangle of fourth magnitude stars; two sides of it are 3° long, and the third side only 1°. One vertex of the triangle is in a line from Capella to ι. The triangle represents a kid, which the charioteer carries in his arms.

"The charioteer."

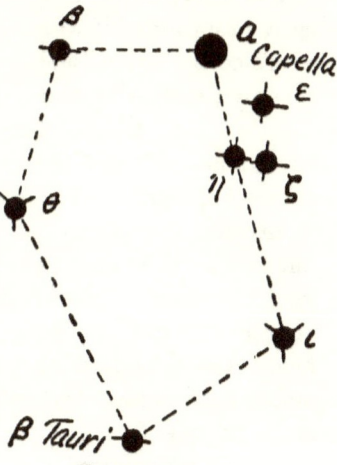

FIG. 23.—AURIGA.

Capella is comparatively near us. According to the measures of one of the highest authorities* its distance is 170 millions of millions of miles. Light occupies twenty-nine years in traversing this abyss. Were it as close as our sun, it would be sixty times as bright as he is.

Capella.

About half way from θ to β Tauri lies a fine compact cluster of small stars, which may be picked up with an opera-glass, in which it looks like a star enveloped in a cloud mantle.

A cluster.

Near β Tauri, on a line between it and β there

---

*Dr. W. L. Elkin, of Yale College.

Nova Aurigæ.

appeared in December, 1891, a new star. Professional astronomers, who usually have their eyes glued to the eyepieces of their telescopes, when observing, failed to see it. It was discovered late in January, 1892, by Dr. T. D. Anderson, a Scotch amateur. Its image was afterward found on photographic plates taken in December at the Harvard College Observatory. At the end of April it could scarcely be seen with the Lick 36-inch glass. But in the following August it was bright enough for a three-inch telescope, and had apparently turned into a nebula. A fuller history of the wonderful object and the theories of astronomers about it will be given later.

Mythology.

The mythological history of this constellation is very obscure. Perhaps the charioteer may be best regarded as Phaëton, the ambitious youth who requested his father Helios (the sun) to let him drive his chariot across the sky for one day. The horses ran away and came so near the earth that it was nearly set on fire. A thunderbolt from Jupiter, who occasionally did a sensible thing, ended the young man's career.

Queries.

What is the color of Capella? Is Capella brighter than Betelgeuse?

CHAPTER V.

THE CONSTELLATIONS FOR MARCH AND APRIL.

> " Starry crowns of heaven,
> Set in azure night!
> Linger yet a little
> Ere you hide your light."
>
> —*Procter.*

Gemini.

A LINE from Mizar (ζ Ursæ Majoris) carried down the handle of the Dipper and diagonally across the bowl to the two stars which lie in the front foot of the Bear, when prolonged 25°, ends near Castor and Pollux. They are the brightest stars in Gemini, and are respectively designated by the letters a and β (Fig. 24). Half way between Castor and the head of Orion is μ. Somewhat more than half way from Pollux to Betelgeuse is γ. a, β, γ, and μ are the four corners of a box-like figure resembling an end view of an upright piano. The keyboard projects from ζ to λ, and the pedals lie between γ and ξ. η, which is 2½° west of μ, is a variable, ranging from the third to the fourth magnitude. It is on a line from μ to ζ Tauri, at the top of one horn of the Bull. The heads of the twins contain Castor and Pollux respectively. γ and μ mark their feet.

Description.

The summer solstice, which is the point where the sun appears to be, when it is farthest north of the equator on June 21, is 2° west and a little north of η, close by a star of the fifth magnitude.

The summer solstice.

Castor is one of the finest double stars in the heavens;

Castor and Pollux.

so bright are its two components that both can be readily seen in daytime with a ten-inch telescope. Nearly one thousand years are consumed by one revolution of this majestic pair. Castor is approaching us at the rate of eighteen miles a second, while Pollux keeps almost at the same distance from us.

A little over one fourth of the way from μ to β Tauri

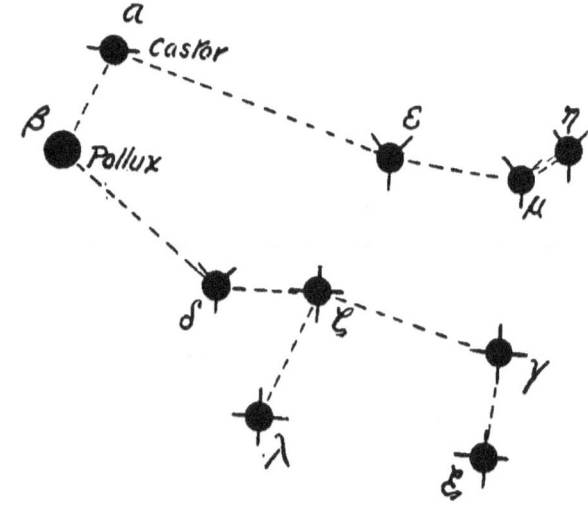

FIG. 24.—GEMINI.

is a splendid cluster, just visible to the naked eye. It is composed of hundreds of faint stars, and is roughly circular in form. The apparent diameter of the circle is two thirds that of the full moon.

Mythology.

The brothers Castor and Pollux were two mythological knights, whose chief deeds were the redressing of various wrongs. They were thought to be mighty helpers of men, and divine honors were paid to them both in Sparta and at Rome. The Romans believed that they received assistance from them, while fighting the

Latins at Lake Regillus. In Macaulay's "Lays of Ancient Rome" is the following reference to their appearance :

> " So like were they, no mortal
> Might one from other know ;
> White as snow their armor was ;
> Their steeds were white as snow."

According to one version of the story Castor was mortal, while Pollux was immortal. When Castor was dying Pollux prayed to be permitted to die with him. Jupiter did not wish to grant this request, but rewarded their attachment by allowing them both to spend alternate days on Mount Olympus and in Pluto's realm.

Which is the brighter, Castor or Pollux? What is the color of Castor? Is Capella whiter than Castor? *Queries.*

Perseus.

This constellation should be hunted up early in the month, as soon as it is dark ; at that time it is low in the northwest.

A little more than half way from Capella to γ Andromedæ, 3° north of the line joining them, lies α, which is at one corner of a small quadrilateral, the other stars of which are γ, ι, and τ. A line from Polaris through the center of this quadrilateral, when prolonged 11° further, meets β, which is commonly called Algol, the Demon Star. Its magnitude varies from the second to the fourth in less than three days. The rest of the constellation is best learned by a study of Fig. 25. The entire length of the figure from η to ζ is 27°. The head of Medusa, which Perseus carries in his hand, is formed of Algol and the stars near it. The constellation bears no special resemblance to a man, much less to a bear. It might be a fair model for a baboon. *Description.* *The Demon Star.*

Near the middle point of a line from γ to δ Cassiopeiæ

A cluster.

is a fine double cluster, distinctly visible to the naked eye, as a bright spot in the Milky Way. It is pretty in an opera-glass and fine in a small telescope. Here hundreds of suns are bunched together. This cluster is, for small telescopes, the finest visible in the United States.

Mythology.

Perseus belonged to Jupiter's numerous family of demigods. Polydectes, king of a little island, fell in love with Perseus's mother. The young man opposed the king's wishes in this matter, and was therefore sent to fetch the snaky head of the monster Medusa, who, with her sister Gorgons, was equipped with tusk-like teeth, brazen claws, and golden wings. So frightful was the aspect of a Gorgon that any one who looked on her was turned to stone. Equipped with winged sandals, a magic wallet, a helmet which made him invisible, a sickle, and a mirror in which he viewed the image of the monster, he accomplished his task. In his homeward voyage through the air he rescued Andromeda, the Ethiopian maiden, and married her.

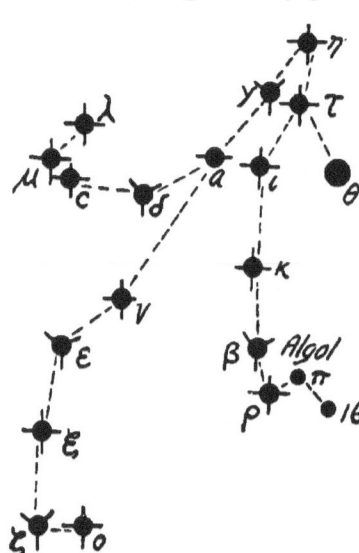

FIG. 25.—PERSEUS.

Queries.

Is Algol as bright as γ? Is Algol as bright as a? To what star in Perseus does a line joining the centers of the two clusters mentioned above point?

Cancer.

The principal stars of Cancer form an inverted Y (Fig. 26), which is on the meridian at 9 p. m., in the middle of the month. The total length of the ⅄ is 20°, and all the stars in it are of the fourth magnitude. A line from Polaris to *ο* Ursæ Majoris, when prolonged 40° further, ends near the center of the ⅄. Near the middle point of a line joining δ and γ lies the cluster of Præsepe, the Bee-hive, which falls an easy prey to an opera-glass. To the naked eye it is a hazy spot. Two degrees west of *α* is another cluster almost visible to the naked eye; a good opera-glass brings it out.

When Hercules was having a desperate battle with the nine-headed Lernean hydra, a gigantic crab came to the assistance of the hydra, and succeeded in wounding the hero.

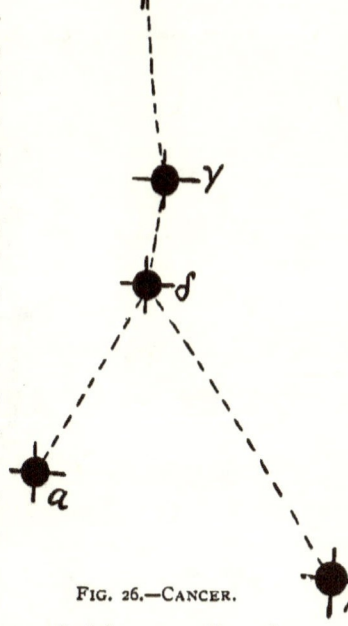

FIG. 26.—CANCER.

Canis Major.

The chief jewel of this group is Sirius, brightest of the fixed stars, which is readily found by prolonging the belt of Orion 20° eastward. The Dog sits upright, facing his master Orion (Fig. 28). Sirius burns in his head. The triangle formed by δ, ε, and η is in his haunches. β is at the extremity of his uplifted fore paw. He is evidently in the attitude of begging for a bite of the hare under Orion's feet. His hind legs stretch forward to ζ and λ. A fair cluster, barely visible to the naked eye, is situated near a point one third of the way from Sirius to ε. A small telescope reveals a red star in the center, which is brighter than its companions. δ and ζ appear double in an opera-glass.

Sirius.

Sirius is interesting not only from its brightness, which is seven times as great as that of Capella, but also from the fact that it is a remarkable double. A faint companion, fairly within the blaze of glory which surrounds the telescopic image of the bright star, is swung around once in fifty-three years. The distance of Sirius from us is fifty million million miles; light comes from it to us in eight years. The companion

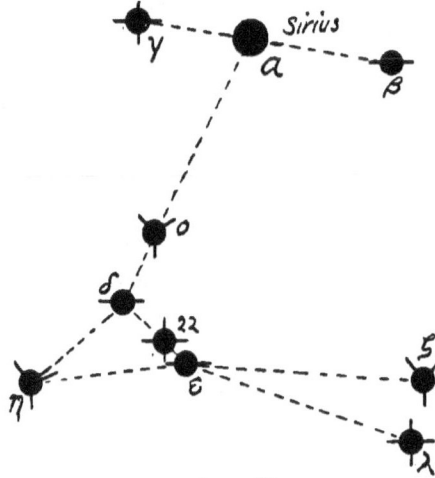

FIG. 27.—CANIS MAJOR.

Discovery of a companion.

was discovered by Alvan G. Clark, the optician.* When using Sirius to test the 18½-inch glass now at Dearborn Observatory, Evanston, Ill., he suddenly exclaimed, "Why, father, the star has a companion!" The real size of this splendid orb may be inferred from the fact that it radiates forty times as much light as the sun. A more complete history of it will be given hereafter.

* Of Cambridgeport, Mass.

Canis Minor.

There are but two bright stars in this asterism, *a* and *β* (Fig. 29). *a* is commonly called Procyon. Procyon is 27° east of Betelgeuse (*a* Orionis). These two stars and Sirius form an equilateral triangle. *β* is 4° northwest of Procyon.

Procyon is interesting for several reasons; it is one of the nearer stars, being but seventy million million miles away. It is moving quite rapidly, for a fixed star, along the face of the sky, requiring only 1,500 years to traverse a distance equal to the apparent diameter of the moon. This journey is not performed in a straight, but in a wavy line; hence it is supposed to be swung from side to side by the attraction of one or more companions, not yet discovered.

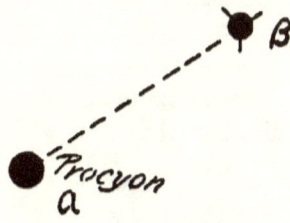

Fig. 28.—Canis Minor.

Lepus.

Lepus, the Hare, lies beneath the feet of Orion, a martyr to his proclivities for hunting. With a good opera-glass one may see γ double (Fig. 27). The most remarkable object in the constellation is the crimson star R, which can be seen with an opera-glass. A line from *a* through *μ*, when prolonged 3°, strikes it. Like most red stars it is variable, ranging in magnitude from 6.5 to 8.5 in a period of 14½ months.

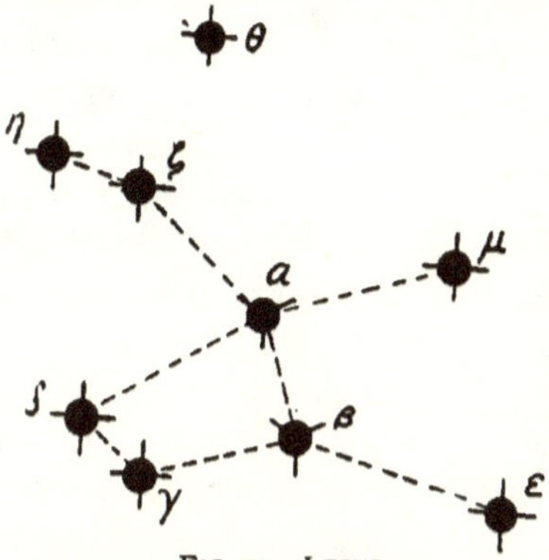

Fig. 29.—Lepus.

Leo.

Description.   This is a striking constellation, composed of a sickle and a large right-angled triangle (Fig. 30). It is just east of Cancer. A line drawn from Polaris to μ Ursæ Majoris, which lies in the forward hind foot of the Bear, prolonged 22°, meets γ, the brightest star in the blade of the sickle. A line from Polaris through the center of the bowl of the Great Dipper, when extended, passes through the large right triangle, which is east of the sickle. β, at one vertex of the triangle, is often called Denebola ; α, at the end of the handle of the sickle,

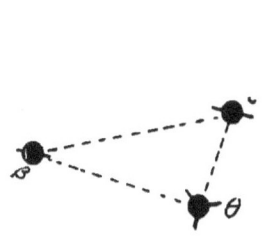
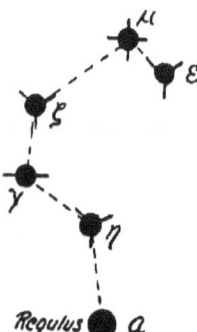

FIG. 30.—LEO.

is Regulus. The distance from Regulus to Denebola is 25°. The lion is crouching ; the handle of the sickle is in his breast, and the blade in his head. The triangle is in his haunches ; his tail and hind legs are represented by a few scattered stars south of the triangle.

Regulus.   The position of Regulus was determined by Babylonian astronomers 4,000 years ago. By its change in longitude* Hipparchus discovered the precession of the equinoxes 2,000 years ago. Regulus and Denebola
Double stars.   have each companions of the eighth magnitude, which

---

*Longitude is like right ascension, except that it is measured along the ecliptic, instead of the equator.

can be seen with a powerful field-glass. γ consists of a couple of bright revolving suns, which form one of the finest of such pairs. ζ is a double, which a fair opera-glass can handle.

This asterism is found in all the most ancient representations of the zodiac; the classic writers, however, have connected it with the story of the labors of Hercules. They state that it is the gigantic lion which ravaged the Valley of Nemæa. Hercules having found that his club and arrows were of no avail against this prodigy, gripped him by the throat and strangled him. King Eurystheus was so frightened, when Hercules returned with the dead lion upon his shoulders, that he ordered the hero thereafter to narrate his exploits outside of the city walls.

Mythology.

Is Regulus as bright as Procyon? Of what color is γ? A line drawn form γ to ε, prolonged 5°, meets a star of what magnitude?

Queries.

CONSTELLATIONS FOR APRIL.

Bootes.

The later in the evening one can observe Boötes, the better it will be seen. On April 1 at 9 p. m. it is low in the northeast, its principal stars forming a kite-shaped figure 25° in length (Fig. 31). The side from α to δ is lowermost. α is a star of the first magnitude, better known as Arcturus. A line from Polaris to a group of three fourth magnitude stars, which form a small triangle 5° from the end of the handle of the Great Dipper, prolonged an equal distance, strikes Arcturus. A line from Polaris to β Ursæ Minoris, the brightest star in the bowl of the Little Dipper, prolonged 35° meets β, which is at the summit of the kite. A line from Polaris to the star in the end of the handle of the Great Dipper, when pro-

Description.

longed an equal distance, ends near Arcturus at a small triangle composed of a third, a fourth, and a fifth magnitude star. These three stars form a tail for the kite. On the other side of Arcturus, at an equal distance, lies another small triangle, likewise composed of stars of the third, fourth, and fifth magnitudes. These two triangles mark the feet of the bear-driver. Arcturus is in his sword ; δ and γ are respectively in his right and left shoulders, while β marks his head. The little triangle near the end of the handle of the Great Dipper is in his uplifted left hand.

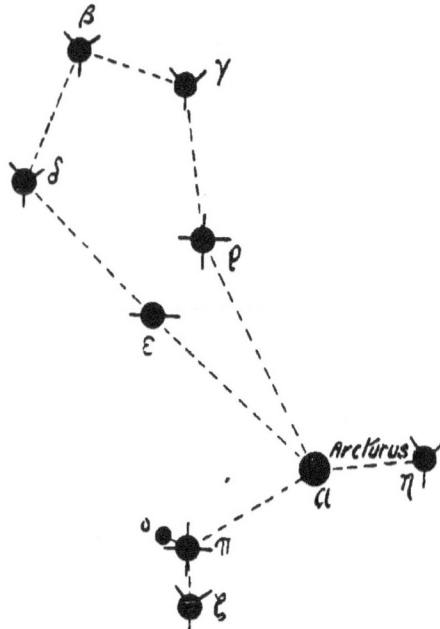

FIG. 31.—BOÖTES.

ϵ is a fine double, as seen with a glass four inches or more in aperture ; the colors of the components are golden yellow and blue. Its beauty has won the appellation of "pulcherrima." Over 1,200 years are occupied by one revolution.

A double star.

Arcturus is a star of amazing magnitude. So far is it away that it is impossible to measure its distance with any sort of accuracy. One of the latest measures makes its distance 1,000 million million miles. From this is derived an estimate that it is a million times as large

Arcturus.

as the sun. Its diameter is then 100 times that of the sun. The reason for this is readily grasped by considering two cubes, one of which has each edge a foot long, while each edge of the other is 100 feet in length. The second cube is 100 times as long, 100 times as broad, and 100 times as thick as the first. Therefore it is 100 x 100 x 100 times as great in volume. Arcturus is approaching us at the rate of five miles a second, but this is only one component of its motion. It moves along the face of the sky at the rate of 300 miles a second, if the preceding assumption about its distance is correct.

The mythological story usually accepted is that this constellation represents Arcas, the son of Callisto. When his mother was changed into a bear (Ursa Major) Arcas, not recognizing her, was about to slay her in the chase, when Jupiter prevented so unfortunate a deed by taking them both to the sky. The name Boötes is used by Homer, and signifies "a plowman." The Great Dipper has been often called a plow, though Homer calls it a wagon. It seems likely that Homer regarded Boötes as being either the driver of the wagon, or the guide of the plow. Mythology.

What is the color of Arcturus? What is the color of ε? Does Arcturus rise north of the east point of the horizon, or south of it? Queries.

Coma Berenices.

Only two stars in this little group are as bright as the fourth magnitude. There are sixteen stars of the fifth magnitude, and about seventy-five fainter stars, which can be seen with the naked eye. All these lie between the large triangle in the haunches of Leo and the kite in Boötes. The constellation contains many small neb- Description.

ulæ, but a large telescope is required to show them well. The most crowded part of Coma is a pretty sight in an opera-glass.

History. Berenice is an historic personage, the wife of Ptolemy III. When her husband went to war against the Syrians, she vowed to sacrifice her beautiful hair, in case he returned safely. The sacrifice was made, and the Alexandrine astronomer Conon commemorated it by establishing this constellation.

Virgo.

This constellation lies south of Coma Berenices and

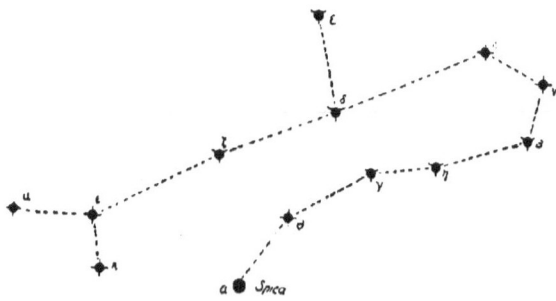

FIG. 32.—VIRGO.

Description. Boötes, and east of Leo. The principal stars can be so connected as to form an outline of the flowing robe of a virgin (Fig. 32). She is in a recumbent posture, lying nearly along the equator, her head being just south of β Leonis. α, a star of the first magnitude, has the proper name Spica, and forms an equilateral triangle with Arcturus and β Leonis. The right arm of the Virgin is extended to ϵ, and the left hand reaches down to grasp a spike of wheat at Spica. The celestial equator runs through the stars ζ and η on opposite sides of her body.

Spica. Spica is very remarkable in that it consists of two revolving bodies which occupy but four days in one revolution. It has never been seen double, but the periodic shiftings of the lines in its spectrum have shown its duplicity.

γ is a fine double, composed of two equal suns. It is now resolvable without difficulty by a three-inch telescope. The period of revolution is 175 years, a little more than that of Neptune about the sun.

Between Coma and the upper half of the Virgin's body is a remarkable region, which is thickly sown with nebulæ. Nebulæ.

In the Golden Age, when the gods dwelt upon the earth, Astræa was a divinity whom men especially reverenced for her pure life and kindly deeds. She was the last of the immortals to leave the earth at the close of the Golden Age. Mythology.

Does Spica rise south of the east point of the horizon, or north of it? Does a line from Spica to Polaris pass through the handle of the Great Dipper? How many degrees from δ to γ at the Virgin's girdle? Queries.

Corvus.

Corvus, the Crow, is further south than Virgo, and may be seen in the southeast at 8 p. m., any evening in April. The four brightest stars form an easily recognized quadrilateral (Fig. 33), the eastern side of which is 7° in length. A line from ι Virginis through Spica, prolonged westward 15°, passes through the two stars in the northern side of the quadrilateral. α, the lowest star in the diagram, is in the beak of the Crow, which stands upon the body of Hydra (yet to be described), pecking at it. Description.

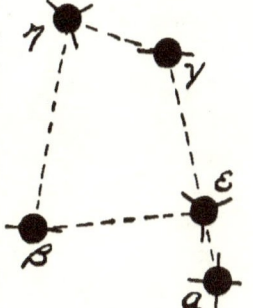

FIG. 33.—CORVUS.

92   *A Study of the Sky.*

Mythology.   Corvus was Coronis, a mortal princess, who was transformed into a crow by Minerva.

Queries.   What is the color of β? Which star is the brightest of the group? How far from δ is the nearest visible star?

Corona Borealis.

Description.   The Northern Crown is a very satisfactory group, because the eye at once recognizes a similarity to the object which it is supposed to represent (Fig. 34). The constellation is just east of the middle of the kite in Boötes. At the end of April it does not cross the meridian till 1 a. m. It is, at that time in the month, well up in the northeastern sky at 9 p. m. α, also called Alphecca or Gemma, is 10° east of ε Boötis.

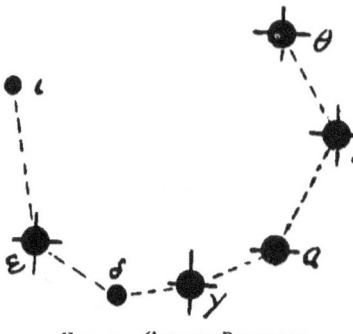

FIG. 34.—CORONA BOREALIS.

A temporary star.   1° south of ε is situated T Coronæ, one of the small number of temporary stars. In May, 1866, it blazed forth suddenly, equalling Alphecca in magnitude. After it was discovered it declined in brightness, and had sunk below the eighth magnitude by the end of the month. An opera-glass now shows it as a star of the ninth magnitude.

Mythology.   The crown belongs to Ariadne, whom Bacchus made his wife. He gave it to her at the time of the marriage, and afterward placed it among the stars.

Hydra.

Description.   Hydra is an immense snake, whose head is just south of the λ in Cancer; the end of its tail is south of the feet of Virgo. α, also called Cor Hydræ, is in its heart (Fig. 35). A line from Polaris running in front of the sickle in Leo (being 4° away from ε Leonis, which is at the point of the sickle-blade), when prolonged to a point 25° distant from α Leonis, meets Cor Hydræ. From Cor the snake's body winds eastward and southward, passing immediately beneath Corvus, and stretching 30° eastward to a group of small stars, which lies 20° south of μ Virginis. A line from δ Corvi to ε Corvi prolonged 13° meets ξ.

Chinese astronomers are said to have particularly observed Cor Hydræ over 4,000 years ago. Their records Cor Hydræ.

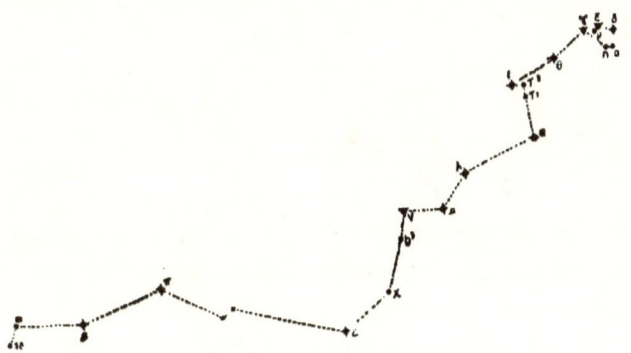

FIG. 35.—HYDRA.

show that in the reign of the emperor Tao it crossed the meridian at sunset, at the time of the vernal equinox (March 20 in the modern calendar).

ε is a fine double for a three-inch telescope; one component is yellow, the other blue.

Hercules was sent to kill a monster which was ravaging the country of Lerna, near Argos, and which has been called the Lernean hydra. It had nine heads, one of which was immortal. Whenever Hercules struck off a mortal head with his club, two others grew out to take Mythology.

its place. He finally burned the mortal heads, and buried the immortal one under a rock. As is fitting, we find the immortal head in the sky, close by Cancer, the Crab, which assisted Hydra in the fight and succeeded in wounding Hercules.

Queries.
What is the color of Cor Hydræ? A line from ε Corvi to ẞ Corvi, prolonged eastward 10°, strikes what star in Hydra? At the end of the tail of Hydra are two fifth magnitude stars 3° apart; how many faint stars can be seen between them?

CHAPTER VI.

THE CONSTELLATIONS FOR MAY AND JUNE.

"Awake, my soul,
And meditate the wonder! Countless suns
Blaze round thee, leading forth their countless worlds."
—*Ware.*

Lyra.

ONE who looks for this constellation early in May should observe it as late in the evening as is convenient. At 9 p. m. it is in the northeast, not very high up. It will probably be recognized at once because of the brilliancy of Vega, its leading star (Fig. 36). The parallelogram formed by β, γ, δ, and ζ will be below and at the right of Vega. The distance from Vega to β is only 8°. Vega is nearly equidistant from Polaris and the star at the end of the tail of the Great Bear, being over 40° from each.

Description.

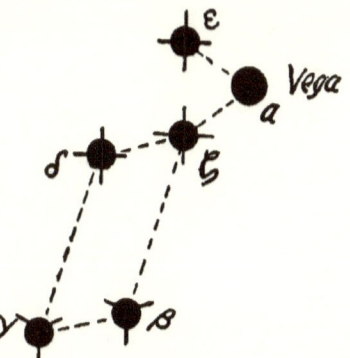

FIG. 36.—LYRA.

Vega is one of the most beautiful, as well as one of the brightest stars. It is 120 millions of millions of miles from us, and thirty times as bright as the sun. Light consumes twenty years in coming to us from it. It is approaching us at the rate of ten miles a second. It will be the pole-star 12,000 years hence.

Vega.

ϵ is one of the most famous of multiple stars. An

average eye perceives that it is oblong, and a good eye splits it into two. With a three-inch telescope each of the stars is again divided into two components. Both pairs revolve, one in a period of 2,000 years, the other in 1,000 years.

Epsilon Lyræ.

β is a variable star, which changes from magnitude 3.3 to 4.5, being alternately brighter and fainter than γ. Its period is nearly thirteen days. There are curious anomalies in its changes, for which astronomers have yet found no reasonable explanation.

A variable.

The only elliptical nebula which a small telescope will show is one third of the way from β to γ. In a large telescope it is an exceedingly beautiful object. Were the sun in the center of it, the planet Neptune would not lie outside of it.

An elliptical nebula.

Lyra is the golden harp given by Apollo to Orpheus: not only wild beasts were charmed by its sweet strains, but even trees and rocks, which moved from their places to follow the harper. With it Orpheus descended to Hades, stopped the sound of torment by its music, and won back his dead wife, melting stern Pluto's heart.

Mythology.

Is δ double to the naked eye? What is the color of Vega? Is Vega above the horizon more or less than twelve consecutive hours?

Queries.

Hercules.

A large part of Hercules lies between Lyra and Corona Borealis. It therefore appears to be above Lyra when seen low in the east. During May a better view of it can be obtained after 9 p. m. than before that hour. The giant is represented with his head toward the equator and his feet toward the north pole (Fig. 37). α is in the head; the shoulders are marked by β and δ; ε and ζ are in the belt. The positions of the limbs

Description.

The Constellations for May and June.   97

are indicated by dotted lines in the diagram. The entire length of the figure from α in the head to τ in the right foot is 35°. α is nearly 30° from both α Lyræ and α Coronæ. β is nearly half way from α to α Coronæ. The extremity of the left arm is marked by a small group less than two thirds of the way from α to α Lyræ.

α is a fine double star, which a two-inch telescope can resolve; the companion is blue. *A fine double.*

One third of the way from η to ζ is the finest globular cluster in the northern hemisphere. It is visible to the naked eye on a dark night. With a small telescope it looks like a nebula. A large glass resolves it into thousands of small stars, which are crowded together into one glowing mass in the center, from which streams radiate outward like the arms of a star-fish. When one reflects that each star is a sun, and that the distance of the cluster from us is so amazing that astronomers have not been able to measure it, or even to discover any changes in the relative positions of the stars due to their mutual attractions, the grandeur of the system fairly appals the imagination. *The great globular cluster.*

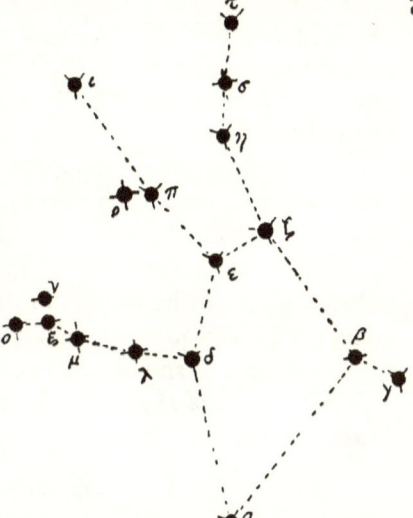

FIG. 37.—HERCULES.

The region of the heavens in which Hercules lies is of special interest, because several astronomers have shown *Our goal.*

that the sun with his attendant planets is moving in that direction.

Mythology.

Hercules is the giant whose marvelous strength was celebrated so often in Greek legends. The most famous of his exploits were the twelve labors, which he performed at the bidding of Eurystheus. The constellations of Leo, Draco, Hydra, and Scorpio are all connected with the stories of these exploits, which may be found in detail in a classical dictionary.

Queries.

What is the color of *α*? What is the appearance of the great globular cluster to the naked eye on a moonless night? Toward what star in Corona does the belt point?

Cygnus.

Description.

Cygnus lies east of Lyra; it is often called the Northern Cross, because the chief stars form an excellent Roman cross (Fig. 38). When seen low in the east the cross appears to lie on its side; the upright piece is over 20° long, and extends from *α*, also called Deneb, to *β*, or Albireo. The cross-piece runs from *δ* to *ε*. The bill of the Swan is at *β*, and the outstretched wings are shown by the dotted line from *κ* to *μ*. *γ*, at the intersection of the upright and cross-piece, is 18° east of *α* Lyræ, and a little nearer to Polaris. A line from *β* Lyræ to *γ* Lyræ, prolonged 8°, reaches *β*. The cross lies

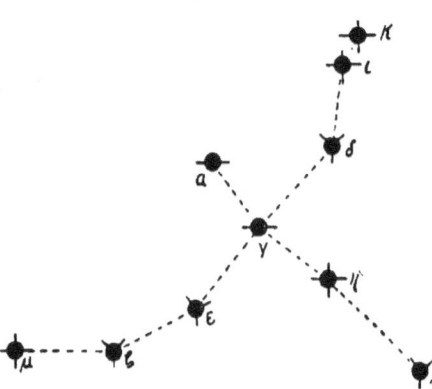

FIG. 38.—CYGNUS.

in a portion of the Milky Way which is rich in fields fine for an opera-glass. Some of the finest regions are within a few degrees of α; they appear to the unaided eye simply as bright portions of the Galaxy. There are also some dark rifts near by, which strikingly contrast with the glories all about them. *Fine fields.*

β is, for a small telescope, the finest colored double in the sky. A magnifying power of ten diameters splits it with ease. With larger telescopes the contrasted colors are seen finely by throwing the stars out of focus. *A colored double.*

61 is a star of magnitude 5.5, which is noted as the first star whose distance was measured. It is over 500,-000 times as far away as the sun; only two stars are known to be nearer. 61 is 6° from ε, and forms a parallelogram with α, γ, and ε.

A little less than one third of the way from α to κ, one degree north of the fourth magnitude star o^1, is o^2, which an opera-glass shows as a triple lying in a pretty field of smaller stars.

The Latin poet Ovid states that Cygnus was a friend of Phaëton, the unhappy youth with whom the horses of the sun ran away. The friend's grief was so poignant that Jupiter changed him to a swan. *Mythology*

A line from α to α Lyræ, prolonged an equal distance, meets what star in Hercules? A line from β to α Lyræ, prolonged 13°, meets what star in Hercules? A line from γ to α Lyræ points to what bright star in Hercules? *Queries.*

Draco.

The head of the Dragon is marked by a conspicuous quadrilateral formed of β, γ, ξ, and ν (Fig. 39). It lies just north of ι Herculis, which is the giant's left foot. The distance from γ to ξ is 5°. γ forms an equilateral triangle with Polaris and the star at the end of the handle *Description.*

of the Great Dipper. The convolutions of the Dragon's form can be best learned from the diagram, with the help of the following data. The first fourth of the body lies between Lyra and the pole. ε, where the body is coiled and turns sharply, is nearly half way from Polaris to δ Cygni. ι may be found by prolonging a line from Polaris to γ Ursæ Minoris 13°. λ, at the end of the Dragon's tail, lies between Polaris and the bowl of the Great Dipper, and is 8° from α Ursæ Majoris. α, which is about half way between ζ Ursæ Majoris (Mizar) and γ Ursæ Minoris, was the pole-star 5,000 years ago. Its brightness has probably diminished much during the past two centuries. It was previously rated as of the second magnitude.

FIG. 39.—DRACO.

Mythology.

There are two mythological stories with which this constellation is associated. The Thracian hero Cadmus slew a dragon which guarded a well from which he wished water. Minerva advised him to sow the dragon's teeth; armed men sprang up from them. Another dragon, Ladon by name, who guarded the golden apples of the Hesperides, was slain by Hercules and placed among the stars.

Sagitta.

Description.

Sagitta, the Arrow (Fig. 40), is a neat little figure, which lies south of Cygnus. α and β mark the butt of the arrow, and γ is at its point; the length of the arrow is 7°. A line from α Lyræ to β Cygni, prolonged 11°, meets γ, and is nearly perpendicular to the arrow. The constellation, though small, offers a fine field for a small telescope.

Two degrees southwest of the butt of the arrow lies ε, of the sixth magnitude, which is a pretty pair in a good opera-glass. Less than 2° beyond the point of the arrow a small telescope will pick up a pretty triple star, θ. Four degrees from the butt of the arrow, toward the belt of Hercules, lies a cluster visible with an opera-glass. A yellowish star of the sixth magnitude, 2½° south of γ, is the brightest of a group which shows nicely in an opera-glass, and contains a red star.

Pleasing objects.

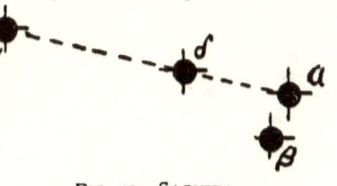

FIG. 40.—SAGITTA.

Scorpio.

In the latter part of May Scorpio is on the meridian in the south at midnight. The later in the evening one looks for it the better, for though many of the stars are very bright, the constellation being the most brilliant in the zodiac, they never get high in the heavens. The brightest star, α, is Antares (Fig. 41), and may be found by prolonging a line from Polaris to β Herculis, the prolongation being two thirds as long as the original line. The curve, composed of β, δ, and π, is 7° in length, and resembles the blade of a scythe, the snath of which extends down to ε; Antares is at one of the handles. Below ε the curve is U-shaped, and ends at the bright pair λ and υ, which lie in the Milky Way and mark the animal's sting. The sting is 17° southeast of Antares. The distance from Antares to β is 9°.

Description.

Antares.

Antares is a magnificent double, having a greenish companion fairly within the blazing aureole about the principal star. This was discovered in a curious way. Ordinarily a small telescope will not show the companion, because of the overpowering brilliancy of the large star. But on one occasion in 1819, when the star was emerging from behind the moon, the small star popped out first, and was seen for an instant before the large one appeared.

FIG. 41.—SCORPIO.

β is a fine double for a two-inch telescope. ν is 2° east of β, and is much easier to split than β. A large telescope divides each component of ν again, making it a quadruple star.

A rich cluster.

Half way between Antares and β lies a cluster, which Herschel described as the richest and most condensed mass of stars in the firmament. It is visible with a small telescope, but a large one is needed to bring out its beauty. In May, 1862, a star blazed out, apparently in the center of the cluster, almost extinguishing the latter by its brightness; in less than a month it faded into invisibility.

Mythology.

One of the mythological stories connects a scorpion with the story of Orion, stating that the mighty hunter boasted that he would kill all the wild beasts on the earth, whereupon the earth sent forth a scorpion which stung and killed him. When Æsculapius attempted to bring him back to life, Jupiter, knowing that Orion had already experienced his full share of life's sorrows, smote the physician with a thunderbolt.

Queries. What is the color of Antares? Which is the brighter, β or δ? At about what point of the horizon does Antares set? Is Antares above the horizon twelve consecutive hours, or fewer?

THE CONSTELLATIONS FOR JUNE.

Libra.

Description. The principal stars of this constellation form a rude square (Fig. 42), which lies half way between the feet of Virgo and the scythe-blade in Scorpio. The distance from α to β is 9°. α, which lies on a line from β Scorpii to α Virginis, appears elongated to a keen eye; it falls an easy prey to an opera-glass. Near the middle point of a line joining β to μ Virginis is δ, a star of the fifth magnitude, which is a very remarkable variable. In five and a half hours it sinks to the sixth magnitude; six and a half hours afterward it has regained its former brightness, and remains in that estate for forty-four hours, after which it fades again. Its entire period is fifty-six hours.

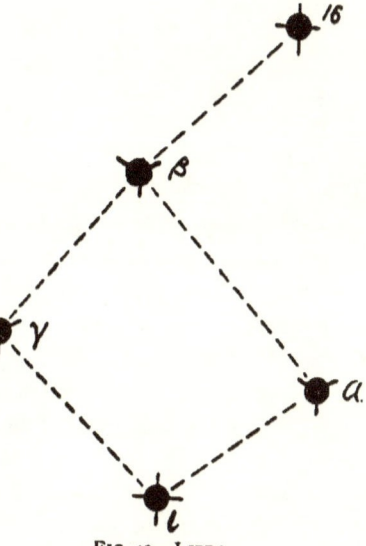

FIG. 42.—LIBRA.

History. Libra was originally a part of Scorpio, forming the claws of that venomous animal. The Egyptians are

Queries.

said to have formed it into a separate constellation as early as 300 B. C. In the time of Augustus Cæsar it was regarded as the balance belonging to Virgo, the goddess of justice.

What is the color of β? Where are sixth magnitude stars more thickly sown, northeast or southeast of the "square"? A line from γ to Polaris passes through what small but plain constellation?

Delphinus.

Description.

A line from Polaris through α Cygni, prolonged 30°, ends at a small diamond-shaped figure (Fig. 43), which contains three stars of the fourth magnitude and one of the third. The length of the diamond from β to γ is 2½°. Including ϵ we have a wedge-shaped figure which has been called "Job's Coffin."

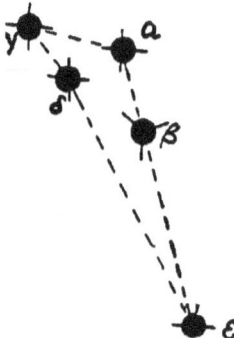

FIG. 43.—DELPHINUS.

γ has a bluish companion of the sixth magnitude, which a two-inch telescope will show.

A fish story.

The dolphin is supposed to be the fish upon whose back Arion, the ancient bard and musician, took his celebrated ride. When he was returning to Corinth from Sicily, where he had won a prize in a musical contest, the treasures which had been presented to him roused the cupidity of the sailors, who planned his murder. Obtaining their permission to play the cithara once more, he charmed a school of dolphins by his melodies; he then leaped into the sea, and was brought safely to land by one of them.

Aquila.

This constellation lies just south of Sagitta, and rises

near the east point of the horizon; in the middle of June it is on the meridian at 2 a. m. It will therefore be best not to look for it before 9 p. m. Altair, its principal star, may be located by a line from Polaris through δ Cygni; it is flanked by the stars β and γ (Fig. 44), which form with it a line 5° long, running athwart the Galaxy. This line prolonged southward 8° strikes θ. The rest of the figure, which bears not the remotest resemblance to an eagle, is easily found by the help of the diagram. Altair is a million times as far from us as the sun, its light taking sixteen years to reach us. η, which is 8° south of Altair, is a well-known variable, having a period of seven days and a fraction, in which it loses and regains over a magnitude. Its variations can be well seen by comparing it for a few nights with θ and ι, which are near by.

Description.

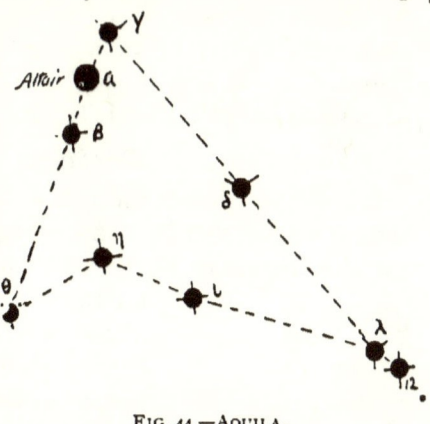

FIG. 44.—AQUILA.

Aquila is, according to one account, the eagle of Jupiter, which stood by his throne. Another story is that Merops, a king of the island of Cos, attempted suicide, wishing to follow his wife to the under world. Juno's proverbial kindness of heart led her to thwart this wish, by placing him among the stars, in the form of an eagle.

Mythology.

The line of three stars, in which Altair lies, when prolonged northward, passes through what brilliant star? What is the color of Altair? Does a line from λ to Polaris pass through α Lyræ?

Queries.

106   *A Study of the Sky.*

Serpens and Ophiuchus.

Description.   We treat these constellations together, since they form the one figure of a man grasping a serpent (Fig. 45). Ophiuchus, the serpent-bearer, is between Hercules and Scorpio. The head of the serpent is marked by the triangle formed of β, γ, and κ, in the upper right hand corner of the diagram; it lies 10° south of Corona.

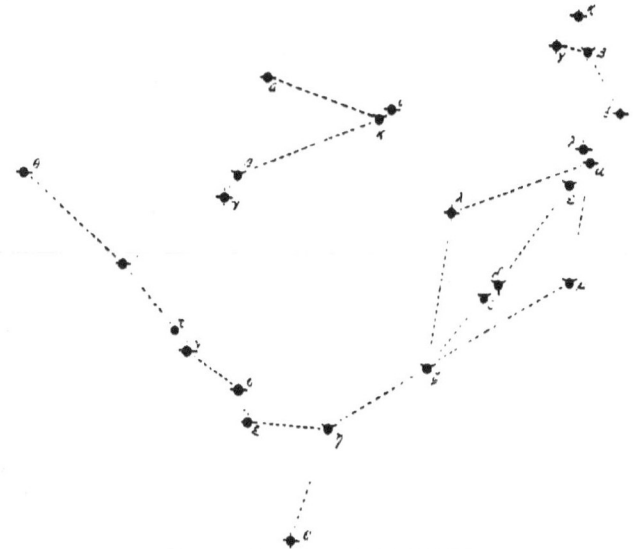

FIG. 45.—SERPENS AND OPHIUCHUS.

Thence the body of the serpent runs southward through α and ε Serpentis to δ and ε Ophiuchi, where one hand of Ophiuchus grasps the snake. The next two stars in it are ζ and η Ophiuchi. The distance from α Serpentis to ζ Ophiuchi is 22°. These two stars form with λ Ophiuchi and μ Serpentis a fine parallelogram.

The serpent turns.   From η Ophiuchi the snake's body goes eastward and northward, as shown in the diagram, ending at θ Serpentis, which is on a line from Polaris to γ Lyræ, prolonged 30° further ; θ is also 7° west of δ Aquilæ.

α Ophiuchi, which marks the man's head, can be found by drawing a line from Polaris to β Draconis, and prolonging it an equal distance. It may also be located by a line from α Boötis to the head of the serpent, prolonged as far again. α Herculis is but 6° from α Ophiuchi. β and γ are in the right shoulder of Ophiuchus, ι and κ in his left. His right knee is at η, and his left at ζ ; his right foot is at θ, and his left stands on Scorpio, close to α Scorpii. While Serpens is comparatively easy to learn, Ophiuchus requires some attention ; therefore we have entered into considerable detail.

One third of the way from θ Serpentis to α Ophiuchi an opera-glass will pick up a cluster. In the same line, Clusters. not far from α, is another cluster almost bright enough to be visible to the naked eye. There are many fine double stars and clusters in these constellations, but they are chiefly for good-sized telescopes.

Ophiuchus is supposed to represent Æsculapius, the god of medicine. Many temples were erected in his Mythology. honor in various parts of Greece, and were used as hospitals, as well as for worship. Tame serpents were kept at Epidaurus, the principal seat of his worship, and the god himself frequently assumed the form of a serpent.

Which is the nearer to α Herculis, the head or the left shoulder of Ophiuchus ? A small triangle of stars is Queries. 5° southeast of β Ophiuchi ; what are their magnitudes ? Two fifths of the way from α Ophiuchi to θ, the last star in the serpent's tail, is a double star 72 Ophiuchi ; what is its magnitude ?

Sagittarius.

This constellation is next to Scorpio, and east of it. In the middle of June it is on the meridian at 1 p. m. Description. It is best therefore not to study it till 10 p. m., or else to wait till the latter part of July, when it can be seen well at 9 p. m. The eye at once perceives the "milk-dipper" (Fig. 46), the bowl of which is upside down, and is defined by the stars ζ, τ, σ, and φ ; λ is in the end of the handle, and is 10° from ζ. Sagittarius is a Centaur, who is shooting at the Scorpion. The bowl of the milk-dipper is in his body. λ, δ, and ε represent the bow on which there is an arrow, whose tip is at γ.

FIG. 46.—SAGITTARIUS.

In the latter part of August, when the constellation is on the meridian, full in the south at 9 p. m., one may well explore the Milky Way in and above Sagittarius, with the help of an opera-glass or small telescope. There are several fine clusters and beautiful fields. Their whereabouts are indicated to the naked eye by bright spots in the Galaxy.

Cepheus.

Cepheus lies between Cassiopeia and Draco. The five brightest stars form a rude square surmounted by an isosceles triangle (Fig. 47). The entire figure is 20° long. γ is 12° from Polaris, nearly on a line from it to β Cassiopeiæ. α forms an equilateral triangle with Polaris and ε Cassiopeiæ. A line from γ to α, prolonged an equal distance, meets α Cygni. King Cepheus sits behind his wife Cassiopeia; his head is marked by ζ and two fainter stars close by it; his foot-stool is the tail of the Little Bear; γ is in his left knee; the rest of his figure may be supplied as one pleases. δ is a variable which has a period of 5⅓ days, and ranges in magnitude from 3.7 to 4.9. A good spy-glass reveals its duplicity; the two stars are respectively orange and blue. β is also a double, the large star being white, the small one blue; a two-inch telescope handles it nicely. μ, perhaps the reddest naked-eye star visible in the United States, is located 4° from ζ, toward α, but south of a direct line between the two. Its magnitude varies irregularly from 3.7 to 4.8.

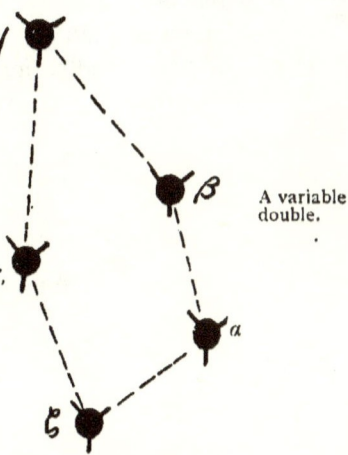

A variable double.

FIG. 47.—CEPHEUS.

Cepheus, like some men nowadays, was best known through his family. The "Classical Dictionary" says sententiously of him, "King of Ethiopia, son of Belus, husband of Cassiopeia, and father of Andromeda, was placed among the stars after his death."

Mythology.

Capricornus.

This constellation is east of Sagittarius. The line of α Aquilæ (Altair) and its two immediate comrades, extended southward, strikes into the heart of it. We shall not try to imagine that it is a goat, but rather the cross-section of a row boat (Fig. 48). The distance across the boat from α to δ is 22°. A line from Polaris to γ Cygni, prolonged an equal distance, ends at α, which the naked eye shows as a double. An opera-glass shows β to be double. By noticing that there is a pair

Description.

110 A Study of the Sky.

Pairs of stars. of stars at each corner of the figure, one will have no difficulty in picking out the outline of the constellation in the heavens.

A good view of Capricornus cannot be obtained during June until after midnight. In the latter part of

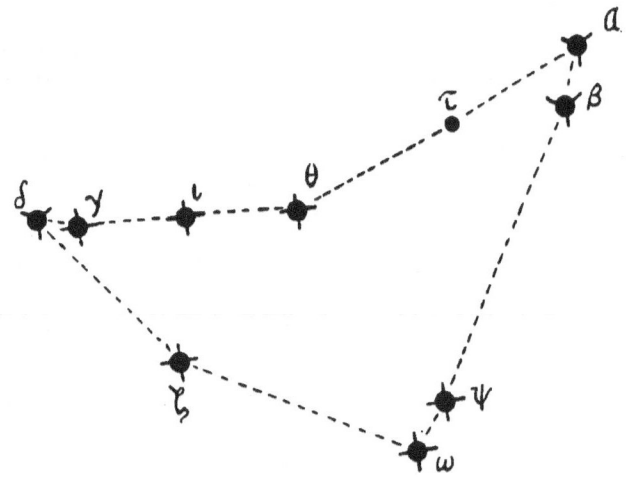

FIG. 48.—CAPRICORNUS.

August it reaches the meridian before 11 o'clock, and is well situated for observation at 9 o'clock.

Mythology. The mythology of this constellation is "confusion worse confounded." One who tries to study it up may be pardoned for wishing that Jupiter had given the goat a nice pasture in his back yard, and kept it out of sight of mortals.

CHAPTER VII.

THE ASTRONOMER.

" Priest-ministrant within this mighty Fane,
 Whereon thou standest now is holy ground ;
 Divinest gift is thine—to gaze the first
 On glories yet unseen by mortal eyes."
　　　　　　　　　　　　—*A. V. G.*

STUDENTS of English literature in our colleges are now encouraged, when studying the works of any particular author, to study the man as well, to become familiar with his daily life, to learn his personal history, to study his habits and his environment. In this way one is the better equipped to understand and to criticise his works, for the man is pretty sure to be reflected in his writings. Learning his point of view, we can the better appreciate the conclusions which he reaches, and can make allowance for his personal bias. If he be a thoroughly lovable man and an inspiring writer, we gain a greater uplift from unconsciously associating the man's character with his productions. *An author and his works.*

If this method is valuable in English literature, why should it not be in astronomy? Almost all of our knowledge of astronomy comes from the writings of men who state that they have perceived this and that, that they have made such and such measurements, that they have drawn certain conclusions. Why should we not inquire into the characters of these men? If some astronomer, who is noted for his powerful fancy, announces that he has found strong evidence that *Why not analyze astronomers?*

Specialists.

Jupiter has intelligent inhabitants, why should we not discount his statements because of the exuberance of his imagination? An astronomer, whose work is the observation of comets and asteroids, together with computation of their orbits, expresses an opinion on a recondite point in solar physics. Certainly his opinion should not have much weight in comparison with that of a special student of the sun. It may be that astronomers in general are altogether too conservative, and unwilling to welcome a piece of work which appears to overthrow some received theory.

No further illustrations are needed to show that the personality of the observer is a powerful factor in his scientific utterances. Let us therefore subject the average astronomer to a pretty thorough analysis, so that we may understand him and his work the better.

FIG. 49.—CHARLES A. YOUNG, PROFESSOR OF ASTRONOMY AT PRINCETON UNIVERSITY.

An astronomer defined.

Who, then, is the astronomer? Is he the long-haired man who stands upon the street corner and sells a peep through his telescope for ten cents? By no means. Is he the wealthy gentleman who is deeply interested in the science, and has a private observatory, in which he spends quite a little time surveying the wonders of the sky? Not at all. Is he the professor who has charge of an observatory, and uses its instruments for the instruction of the college students? Not usually.

The astronomer, whether in charge of an elaborate observatory, filled with costly instruments, or simply the possessor of a good opera-glass, or small portable telescope, is the man who by patient study of the sky adds to the sum total of astronomical knowledge. It is possible to be an astronomer if possessed of no optical instruments except a pair of good eyes, but the range of naked-eye work is extremely limited. The original investigator, then, is the man to whom we shall pay attention. *An original investigator.*

First as to his physique. He may be tall or short, broad shouldered or slim, thin or tolerably fleshy, but he is almost always possessed of a good constitution, which will endure rigors of cold or extremes of heat, and will not break down under a severe pressure of work, night and day, year in and year out. *His physique.*

His nervous system is well developed, his eyesight and hearing are fair, and his sense of touch is delicate. His hand is steady under trying circumstances. Nervousness is not a bane of his life, causing him to lose control of himself at moments when every faculty must be at its best, and every muscle obedient to his behest. *His nervous system.*

When observing a transit of Venus, a repetition of which will not occur during his lifetime, he is, at the critical instants, as cool and collected as if sitting in his office, looking over a new book. This self-control comes from long training; it finds a parallel in the steadiness with which a surgeon's hand, though previously trembling, executes the crucial part of a difficult *Self-control.*

Night work.

operation, when the life of the patient hangs in the balance. This ability to exercise self-control is enhanced by the astronomer's plain living and regular habits.

It is a mistake to suppose that he is ordinarily at work at all hours of the night, and tucks in bits of sleep partly by day and partly by night, under the direction of an alarm clock. For the majority of nights are cloudy, so that no observing is done; when the weather is clear he usually has on hand some work which comes during a certain portion of the night. He rarely works all night. Comet hunters are exceptions in the matter of regularity. They change their times of observing from night to night, working generally during those hours when the moon is below the horizon; the faint objects which they discover are not commonly readily visible in moonlight.

FIG. 50.—EDWARD S. HOLDEN, DIRECTOR OF THE LICK OBSERVATORY.

Education.

Astronomers are, on the whole, well-educated men, especially those who are the directors of large observatories. Very little can be done in their science without a sound knowledge of elementary mathematics. The principles of physics and mechanics come up continually. An American astronomer who cannot read scientific German and French with considerable ease is often seriously hampered in his work; for he must master the contents of many publications in those languages. Often he wishes to read Italian; a knowledge of Latin and Greek is not infrequently of service.

An astronomer may be very narrow-minded. The ceaseless round of computation by day and observation by night, demanding every iota of his time, has a strong tendency to keep his mind from expanding along any other lines. But if, as usual, he has been through an old-fashioned, now much berated, college curriculum, the liberalizing effect of the four years of study of various branches of knowledge keeps him from undue narrowness. It is noteworthy that men of only moderate mental caliber are the most likely to shrivel up. The mental giants have a many-sidedness, which leads them to explore other realms of knowledge to a moderate extent. One of the best text-books on political economy published in this country is the work of an astronomer, most of whose time is occupied with directing intricate calculations belonging to the strictly mathematical side of the science.

Narrowness.

FIG. 51.—SIMON NEWCOMB, SUPERINTENDENT OF THE "NAUTICAL ALMANAC" OFFICE.

Breadth of view.

116   A Study of the Sky.

Not a recluse.   The director of a large observatory is continually brought into contact with men who are prominent in other lines of scientific work, and with those who have won success in various non-scientific walks of life. He also looks after the business interests of the observatory, and sometimes raises funds for the enlargement of its work. These circumstances effectually prevent his becoming a recluse.

The value of time.   Astronomers have an inordinate sense of the value of time. A business man considers his own time very precious during business hours, and has no welcome for any one who consumes it needlessly. But after business hours are over he is at leisure, and whiles away much of his time in pleasurable occupations and social duties. All of an astronomer's waking hours, except when he is at meals, are business hours. So great is the volume of work which he would like to do, and so time-consuming are the laborious computations consequent upon his observations, that he is continually urged to work at his topmost speed. Every minute counts. The very clocks, chopping off second

Second after second.   after second, within his hearing, remind him that time flies, and that his mind must follow suit. By constant

FIG. 52.—BENJAMIN A. GOULD, EDITOR OF THE "ASTRONOMICAL JOURNAL."

practice in estimating small fractions of a second he gains a mental alertness which is carried into all his work. If he is explaining something, he expects the listener to grasp what he says instantly, and is well pleased if by any chance the hearer anticipates his explanation, and arrives quickly at the desired goal. *Alertness.*

The following incident will show how this mental quickening came to a college boy. He was a member of the junior class, and began a special course in practical astronomy by learning to take time observations. This work consists in observing the times that some clock or chronometer reads, when certain known stars, in passing through the field of view of a particular telescope, appear to cross a number of spider-webs placed at the focus of the glass. The construction of the instrument will be explained later.

FIG. 53.—EDWARD C. PICKERING, DIRECTOR OF THE HARVARD COLLEGE OBSERVATORY.

When a star's image crosses each spider-web, the observer is expected to note the reading of his timepiece. When observing by the "eye-and-ear" method he listens to the ticks of the clock, and tries to write down, to the nearest tenth of a second, the time indicated by the clock when the star crosses each web. Quickness of perception and rapidity of thinking are required for this. After the observations have been made, *Sharp work.*

certain easy computations enable him to find the error of the clock; then he compares this clock with the other timepieces of the observatory, to determine their errors.

What was the effect of this work on the college boy? He had been an easy-going young man, who was content with learning his lessons fairly, and spending the remainder of his time in recreation. When on the street he had been in the habit of sauntering along as became a gentleman of leisure. When set to do some bit of manual labor he had been apt to distinguish himself by the length of time which he consumed in the task. He played with his studies, as does a cat with a mouse, taking all the time he wished, and being satisfied if he was near the head of the class.

A lazy youth.

But now a change came over him. He set for himself a limited period of time in which each lesson must be mastered, if possible; he placed his Greek or Latin text-book and his lexicon on the study-desk in such positions that their leaves could be turned quickly. He ceased his careless sauntering, and began to walk more rapidly. He filled otherwise unoccupied chinks in the day by reading selections from the best authors. He began to speak with greater rapidity; when reading aloud, it was a mental strain for any one to follow him, for though the words were pronounced clearly, they were delivered like bullets from a machine gun; he could read 475 words a minute. He seemed to have become thoroughly imbued with a conviction that no moments should be wasted, and that as much work as possible must be crowded into each minute of the day.

A change.

If this was the effect of a few months of astronomical training on a college boy, what wonder is it that astronomers, after years of such work, gain special mental quickness?

Another characteristic without which no man can become an accomplished astronomer is perseverance. At times he plunges for weeks and months through mazes of figures, the sight of which fairly wearies the beholder. Then again he devotes himself to the study of some abstruse problem with such furiousness of application that he seems able for the time to think of scarcely anything else. Fits of prolonged abstraction seize him, and curious are the stories told of his actions when lost in contemplation.

FIG. 54.—WILLIAM H. PICKERING, OF THE HARVARD COLLEGE OBSERVATORY.

It is related of Sir Isaac Newton that he was once attracted by a fair lady, and paid court to her; in the course of an evening's visit he fell to musing. Reaching out his hand he took the young lady's and raised it gently toward his lips; he carefully picked out the little finger on which to bestow the evidence of his affection. About this time the lady also became lost in pleasant thoughts. Sir Isaac squeezed her finger a bit, and stirred the hot ashes of his pipe with it. The rest of the story is short; he remained a bachelor.

Perseverance.

Newton's courtship.

Accuracy.

Along with persistence goes a habit of unerring accuracy. The secret of this is chiefly that the whole of an astronomer's work tends to make him concentrate his attention on whatever is in hand. His whole mind is usually occupied with the particular work at which he has set himself. If he is in the midst of the computation of a preliminary orbit of a comet, a single incorrect figure may vitiate all the succeeding work and render his final results worthless. So well lubricated is his mental machinery that he goes through intricate calculations without becoming confused, or falling a prey to a haunting fear that some blunder has been committed. As there are certain methods of testing the answers of examples in arithmetic, so there are occasional check-formulæ, which the computer may use to test his work from time to time. The application of one of these formulæ rarely convicts him of error.

FIG. 55.—EDWARD E. BARNARD, OF THE YERKES OBSERVATORY.

Love of truth.

A habit of accuracy leads to love of accuracy, and love of accuracy leads to love of truth and hatred of error. One cannot converse long with an astronomer without noticing his love of accuracy and his evident endeavor to tell the exact truth. He despises untruth, and is a foe to prejudice of all kinds. If he hears a man putting forth argument after argument to bolster up some position, his mind naturally begins to search for facts which are opposed to the speaker's views. He has an inward contempt for any man who, instead of searching for truth, occupies himself with elaborating and defending some preconceived notion. He applies all reasonable tests to his own work, and attacks every important problem in as many ways as feasible, that he may obtain a series of independent results, from which the truth may best be wrought out. When he is engaged in original investigation, intellectual honesty is his king. Let us take a concrete illustration of this.

All sides of a question.

A student who has not gotten used to astronomical ways is measuring a certain angle. Each day he takes a set of observations. His first three sets yield the following values:

41° 51′ 27″.1
41 51 27 .9
41 51 27 .0

He measures the angle again and obtains 41° 51′ 25″.5. As this does not agree well with the previous results he feels disposed to reject it, and to tell no one about it, because it apparently proclaims him

FIG. 56.—JAMES E. KEELER, DIRECTOR OF THE ALLEGHENY OBSERVATORY.

A young man's quandary.

to be a poor observer. After thinking the matter over he asks the director of the observatory what he shall do with the discordant measure. The director inquires whether the observations seemed to be satisfactory at the time when he was making them, before he knew the result. The young man replies that while observing he thought he was doing accurate work, and that he does not believe that the instrument got out of adjustment during the observations. The astronomer informs him that if he has no reason for rejecting the last result, except that it does not agree with the former results as well as he would like to have it, he has no right to cast it out. Better to suffer the imputation of being an inaccurate observer than to sacrifice any honest work. The agreement of two or three observations does not prove that they are nearer the truth than some other observation, which disagrees with them.

<small>Rejection of observations.</small>

If any astronomer were known to be in the habit of giving a fictitious appearance of accuracy to his work by suppressing those observations which exhibited noticeable deviations from the others, all his work would at once be discredited by his scientific brethren, who would accuse him of "cooking" his observations. When one wishes to arrive at the truth he must take into consideration all the evidence, and not reject some of it, simply because it does not please him.

<small>Freedom from bias.</small>

If scientific men did nothing for their fellows except to impress upon them the necessity of bringing unbiased minds to the consideration of all important questions, and of being intellectually honest in their treatment of them, seeking the truth alone, their work would not be in vain.

<small>Independence.</small>

There is one more point in this matter of truth seeking, to which an astronomer pays special attention.

He strives to make measures of the same quantity independent of each other. Suppose, for example, that he is measuring a double star. He sees the two stars, and two parallel spider-webs. The spider-webs are fastened in a brass box, which can be turned. He wishes to make the spider-webs parallel to a line joining the stars. He sets the spider-webs as in Fig. 57, so that it is plain that they are not in the desired position. He then turns the brass box in a left-handed direction, until the desired parallelism has been attained, as in Fig. 58. A certain silver circle, which is carefully divided into degrees and fractions of a degree, the readings of which change as the box holding the spider-webs is turned, is next read. In Fig. 59 is given a view of the rotating box and the graduated silver circle. The box is then moved again till the spider-webs stand in the position shown in Fig. 60. From that position the astronomer brings them back to parallelism with an imaginary line joining the stars, as before, and reads the circle again. By observing thus in

A double star.

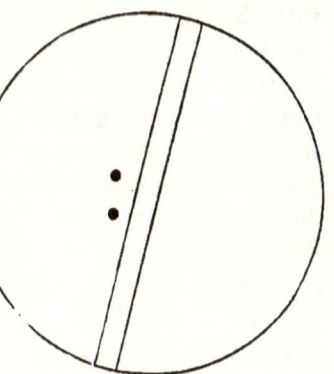

FIG. 57.—FIRST POSITION OF THE SPIDER-WEBS.

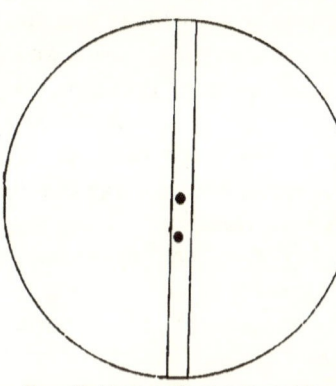

FIG. 58.—SECOND POSITION OF THE SPIDER-WEBS.

Another measure.

Elimination of bias.

two different ways he obtains more independent results than if he had moved the spider-webs in the same direction each time. By turning the box in two opposite

FIG. 59.—A MICROMETER.

directions, as he has just done, he also tends to eliminate a certain amount of personal bias, which would not be eliminated if he always turned the box in the same direction. He does not take many measures of the same double star on a given night, but prefers to take a few on each of several nights, thinking that he will thus secure greater independence, and consequently a higher degree of accuracy in the final result.

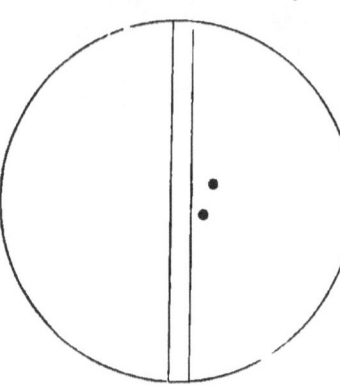

FIG. 60.—THIRD POSITION OF THE SPIDER-WEBS.

Practical astronomical work develops self-reliance.

Self-reliance.

A college student, who has been accustomed throughout his mathematical course to work examples with the expectation of obtaining answers which agree with those given in the text-books, finds that there are no ready-made answers to the problems which a course in practical astronomy presents for solution. Should he become an astronomer, it will only be after he has learned to say to himself, " This result is right because I have worked it out with care, and know what I am about."

Such words suggest conceit, but few classes of men are less conceited than original investigators. A sciolist may be extremely puffed up. A genuine man of science, whose investigations bring him to the frontiers of knowledge, finds so many unexplored lands lying before him and so many apparently impassable mountain ranges in his path that he is forced into an habitual attitude of humility. There come to mind the oft-quoted words of Sir Isaac Newton: "I know not what the world may think of my labors, but to myself it seems that I have been but as a child playing on the seashore; now finding some pebble rather more polished, and now some shell rather more agreeably variegated than another, while the immense ocean of truth extended itself unexplored before me."

Conceit.

FIG. 61.—SETH C. CHANDLER, OF CAMBRIDGE, MASS.

Finally, what shall we say about the personal habits of astronomers? Is an astronomer a good neighbor?

Personal habits.

Usually he is; in rare instances he is not. To be sure, he often comes home pretty late, but he has no difficulty in fitting his latch-key into the proper place; he has not been at a carousal. Sobriety is his habit. Bleared eyes and unsteady hands are not fit for astronomical work.*

Temper. He is usually quiet, and not easily roused. In the comparative seclusion of his observatory he gains a habit of calmness. To arouse whatever is evil in his nature you have but to interrupt him while he is intent upon some observation. On such an occasion he is likely to be short-tempered and sharp of speech. He reasons thus: "A business man would treat me with scant courtesy if I asked him to give up his business hours for my pleasure. Why should he not realize that I have business hours as well as he?" On occasions when he feels compelled to yield, he sometimes does curious things.

FIG. 62.—SHERBURNE W. BURNHAM, OF THE YERKES OBSERVATORY.

A literary ebullition. In one of the observing books in the archives of an American observatory is found this sentence, written at such a time: "Visitors who come on working nights and interrupt a series of observations

---

* It is related of an assistant in an English observatory that once, when on a visit to this country, he was found lying in a gutter, in a state of intoxication. A policeman shook him rudely, and asked, "What are you doing here?" "Observing, sir," was the sententious reply.

are undoubtedly parietosplanchnic Lamellibranchiates, afflicted severely with psittaceous psychopannychism." Such nonsense must have been an effectual safety-valve for the writer's feelings. On a similar occasion another astronomer rushed from the dome-room into an adjoin- *An attack.* ing apartment, seized a poker, and paced furiously up and down past the base-burning stove; a fresh hole gaped in the isinglass whenever he went by.

Ordinarily, however, the director of an observatory treats visitors who come at proper times with the utmost courtesy, and is best pleased if they rain upon him a shower of questions about his instruments or the celestial objects in view.

CHAPTER VIII.

A GREAT TELESCOPE.

" Through thee will Holy Science, putting off
Earth's dusty sandals from her radiant feet,
Survey God's beauteous firmament unrolled
Like to a book new-writ in golden words,
And turn the azure scroll with reverent hand,
And read to man the wonders God hath wrought."
—*A. V. G.*

Roger Bacon.

THE great telescope of to-day has been evolved during the past three centuries by a slow process of growth. Before its actual invention many men had ideas about the possibility of making an instrument which would make distant objects appear near at hand. Roger Bacon, who died in 1294, stated that transparent bodies could be made in such forms and placed in such combinations as to magnify objects. But he never constructed a telescope, for he ascribed to such an instrument some properties which it does not possess.

Hans Lippershey.

Galileo.

In 1608 Hans Lippershey, a resident of Middleburg, Holland, invented the telescope. During the ensuing year Galileo heard of the new invention, and reinvented the instrument. He made several small telescopes, the most powerful of which magnified thirty-three diameters, and revealed the spots on the sun, the lunar mountains, the moons of Jupiter, and the phases of Venus.

Failures.

Slight progress was made during the next hundred years. Men failed to get clear, sharp images of objects, no matter how accurately they ground the lenses of their telescopes. Even the immortal Newton was foiled. Newton foiled. When he discovered that white light was dispersed

FIG. 63.—THE YERKES TELESCOPE AT THE COLUMBIAN EXPOSITION.

into a number of different colors by being passed through a prism, he also found that passage through a Dispersion of light.

lens affected it in the same way. Believing that the dispersed rays could not be reunited, Newton gave up all hope of perfecting Galileo's form of telescope, and turned his attention to making concave mirrors, which reflected the light to a focus without dispersing it. Newton's first reflecting telescope was six inches long, and was equipped with a mirror one inch in diameter. So successful was the performance of this pigmy that he made a larger one, which is now in the possession of the Royal Society of London, and bears this inscription: "The first reflecting telescope, invented by Sir Isaac Newton, and made with his own hands."

FIG. 64.—ALVAN G. CLARK, OPTICIAN, OF CAMBRIDGE, MASS.

As the years rolled on, reflecting telescopes of larger and larger sizes were made, until at last Lord Rosse's leviathan, which has a mirror six feet in diameter, was mounted at Parsonstown, Ireland, fifty years ago. No other reflector of equal size has yet been constructed. Its mirror was made of polished metal. It is now customary to make the mirror of glass, and to coat it with silver.

Such telescopes offer special advantages for photographic and spectroscopic work, since the light which impinges upon a mirror suffers no dispersion, as it would if passed through a lens.

Since reflectors are little used in this country, we return to the history of the common form of telescope, which is called a refractor. The name refractor arises from the fact that rays of light, in passing through a lens, are bent, or "refracted." *A refractor.*

We have noticed that Newton thought it impossible to reunite the rays of various colors which were scattered in passing through his lenses. But early in the eighteenth century a well-to-do countryman of his, Mr. Chester Moor Hall, was struck with the fact that the human eye, which contains more than one refractive medium, produces images practically free from obnoxious color fringes. By combining two lenses of different kinds of glass he reunited the dispersed rays pretty well. Being a gentleman of leisure, he took no particular pains to follow up his discovery, and the credit of it was soon given to Mr. John Dollond, an optician, who experimented successfully along similar lines and published an account of his work in 1758. *Color fringes.*

A new difficulty of the first magnitude now arose. Good discs of glass more than three and a half inches in diameter could not be procured. In vain the French Academy offered prizes for larger discs; the best chemists were baffled. But the battle is not always to the strong. From 1784 to 1814, Guinand, a poor Swiss watchmaker, toiled with dauntless industry, overcoming one obstacle after another, until he succeeded in producing glasses eighteen inches in diameter. *A new difficulty.*

The manufacture of a large disc of optical glass* requires the utmost carefulness, as well as a high degree

---

*There are now only three firms in the world which have made very large lenses, Chance & Co., of Birmingham, Mantois of Paris, and Schott & Co., of Jena. Schott & Co. now produce a number of different kinds of glass, and a large amount of experimentation is going on, in an endeavor to find combinations of lenses which will give more satisfactory results than the time-honored combination of a lens of crown glass backed up by another one of flint glass. Professor Hastings, of Yale, has been successful in such researches.

of technical skill. Nineteen trials were made for one of the lenses of the 36-inch Lick object-glass, before success was attained.

The materials melted. — A pot made of very pure clay is heated to a high temperature, and gradually filled with a batch of the raw materials. After the batch seems to be thoroughly melted a portion of it is taken out and examined, to see if any unmelted particles of silica remain, or if there are minute air-bubbles, which have not been expelled by the heat.

The stirring. — Should neither of these defects be discovered, the melted glass is stirred with an iron rod, the lower portion of which is covered with clay. The stirring is continued for two or three hours, until the cooling glass resists further manipulation. The two workmen, who swelter in the furnace heat while executing this operation, must not allow the stirrer to touch the pot; for bits of clay might be ground off and mixed with the glass.

FIG. 65.—LUMP OF OPTICAL GLASS.

The furnace luted. — The glass is reheated, stirred a second time and even a third time, and returned to the furnace. Every open place in the furnace is stopped up, so that no air may gain admittance, and the whole is allowed to cool for several days, that it may not crack. A rapid cooling would cause it to be shattered into small fragments.

When the cooling is finished the glass is examined,

and any defects which may be apparent are ground away, or sawed off. An imperfect spot near the center of the disc may be sawed out, if the chunk of glass is not sawed clear through.

Imperfections cut out.

The accompanying figures show the block of glass from which the crown disc of the forty-inch Yerkes telescope was obtained. Fig. 65 is the original lump. Fig. 66 shows it

FIG. 66.—THE LUMP CUT DOWN.

after some imperfections have been sawed off. The lump is now to be molded into the shape shown in Fig. 67. The glass is put into a mold, which is placed in a special furnace and heated very slowly. At last the glass softens and adapts itself to the shape of the mold. The temperature is lowered to about 1,200° Fahrenheit, and every opening in the furnace stopped up; after an exceedingly slow and careful cooling the ten-

A forty-inch disc.

FIG. 67.—THE LUMP MOLDED.

sided block is removed and examined. Fresh imperfections are discovered and cut away, as Figs. 68 and 69 testify. The defects may be of such a nature that the disc must be reheated and molded again, but if too many annealings are attempted, the glass may lose its transparency. After months of labor the original shapeless mass is reduced to a beautiful circular disc.

A few small bubbles, or bits of grit, while they mar the appearance of a disc, have no perceptible deleterious effect in a finished lens. They prevent the passage of a certain minute quantity of light, and theoretically injure the perfection of the image of an object seen through the lens.

Bubbles.

FIG. 68.—THE LUMP AFTER FURTHER CUTTING.

When a careful test is made "striæ," or veins, may be found in the interior of the lens; should these be numerous or pronounced the lens must be rejected.

Striæ.

The glass may have passed through all these tests and yet be worthless. If the process of cooling was not conducted with sufficient care the glass may have solidified in a state of dangerous internal strain. To test for this the glass is laid upon a piece of dark

FIG. 69.—THE LUMP CUT DOWN STILL MORE.

Internal strain.

cloth, in some place where there is suitable light, and examined by a Nicol's prism. If a pronounced dark cross is seen in the glass, the internal strain is too great, and the glass must not be used for a telescope.

The glass-founder has now finished his part of the work, and the disc, if sufficiently perfect, is turned over to the optician, who is to fashion its curves so accurately that the rays of light from a distant star may be converged by it to a point which can be covered with a spider's web.

FIG. 70.—MACHINE FOR POLISHING LENSES.

The optician's work.

The rough grinding is done with a cast-iron tool, similar in appearance to the one lying on the floor in the illustration (Fig. 70). If a convex surface is to be produced on the glass, the tool is hollowed out and made of the proper degree of curvature. The usual grinding material is emory, which is placed between the tool and the glass. A better material is obtained by driving a blast of air into melted iron. A cloud of minute particles of iron is blown out; being chilled by contact with the air they settle down as a very fine powder.

The grinding.

After the lens has been brought nearly to the proper shape it is placed upon the machine shown in Fig. 70 to be brought to its proper form by polishing. The tool, which lies upon the lens, is similar to the former one, except that its face is composed of squares

The polishing.

of pitch, instead of squares of cast-iron. The lens lies on a table which turns slowly. The tool is moved by two wooden rods, each of which is driven by a crank at its further extremity; the cranks are of different lengths, and turn at widely different rates. So complicated is the motion that the tool never describes the same path twice. When the surface has been brought to a brilliant polish, the lens appears to be finished.

The testing. But the most difficult part of the process is yet to come. The surface, which looks perfectly spherical, is

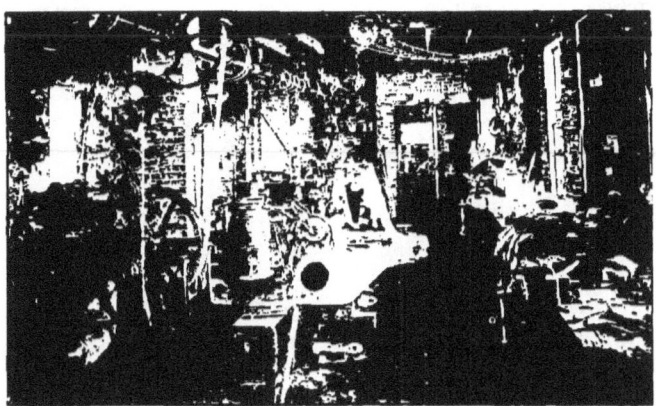

FIG. 71.—ALVAN CLARK'S WORKSHOP.

probably too high in certain regions and too low in others; these inequalities must receive attention. A spherometer which will measure $\frac{1}{50000}$ of an inch is too rude to measure them. The lens is set up on edge in a special testing room, where the temperature is not subject to sudden variations; light from a lamp shining *An artificial star.* through a small hole is sent through the lens, and impinges on a mirror, which reflects it back again through the glass to the eye of the optician. To him the entire lens appears to be aflame with light. If it is

A Great Telescope.

not uniformly bright all over, its shape is not perfect. Imperfect portions cause dark spots in the midst of the general brightness. Perhaps some part of the surface is too high and must be polished down; perchance it is too low, and the rest of the surface must be brought down to it. From the testing room to the polisher and back again the lens must go, till the optician is satisfied with its performance. At times the operator rubs down some protuberant portion with his hand.

Inequalities.

If the lens is touched with one finger for a few seconds, during the process of testing, the heat thus communicated to the lens raises an intolerable lump in it, which will not disappear till that portion of the glass has cooled again.

FIG. 72.—JOHN A. BRASHEAR, OPTICIAN, OF ALLEGHENY, PA.

A zone which is elevated three or four millionths of an inch must not be neglected.

The final shaping of the lens ordinarily involves the expenditure of so much time that the cost of rubbing off a given quantity of the material is one thousand times as great as the cost of taking off an equal quantity by the first process of rough grinding.

Final touches.

138   *A Study of the Sky.*

Placed in a cell. The finished object-glass is put into a cast-iron cell; the edges of the two lenses composing the object-glass do not touch the cast-iron; each of them rests against a silver surface on the inside of the cell; otherwise a little corrosion of the iron might damage the glass. The cell is then ready to be fastened to the steel tube of the telescope.

The mounting. The instrument maker has an important work to perform before the great lens can be set

" Like a star upon earth's grave and cloud-encircled brow."

He must make such a mounting that the telescope can be readily directed to any point in the sky; furthermore, the telescope must move automatically in such a way that a star may be kept in the field of view for hours.

FIG. 73.—THE TWO LENSES OF AN OBJECT-GLASS.

Since the earth rotates, and carries the telescope with it, the

The earth's rotation counteracted. latter, if directed toward a given star, at any instant, will point in quite a different direction a minute afterward. The mechanician must therefore counteract the rotation of the earth.

An odd axis. For purposes of explanation it is best to consider the earth as fixed and the celestial sphere as rotating about an axis drawn from the north celestial pole to the south celestial pole. This conception has already been presented in Chapter II. Imagine this axis to be a wooden shaft six inches in diameter, rotating steadily, making one turn in twenty-four hours, and carrying the celestial sphere with it.

If a lath be nailed to this shaft in such a position that it points to Sirius, it will continue to point toward Sirius day after day, as the shaft and sphere rotate together. This is the fundamental idea upon which the mechanician seizes. He quickly perceives that he can set up a short shaft of steel, which shall point to the north celestial pole, and resemble a section of the wooden shaft which we have been considering. By suitable mechanism he can rotate the steel shaft once in twenty-four hours. Then if he can attach the telescope to this shaft in such a way that it can be pointed in any direction, the problem is solved.

A steel shaft.

The fundamental shaft which points toward the celestial poles, and is parallel to the earth's axis, is called the *polar axis*, and is shown on top of the pillar in Fig. 74; it is below the telescope and parallel to it. To the upper end of the polar axis is fastened a long "sleeve," at right angles to it. Inside this sleeve turns another axis, called the *declination axis*, at the lower end of which a

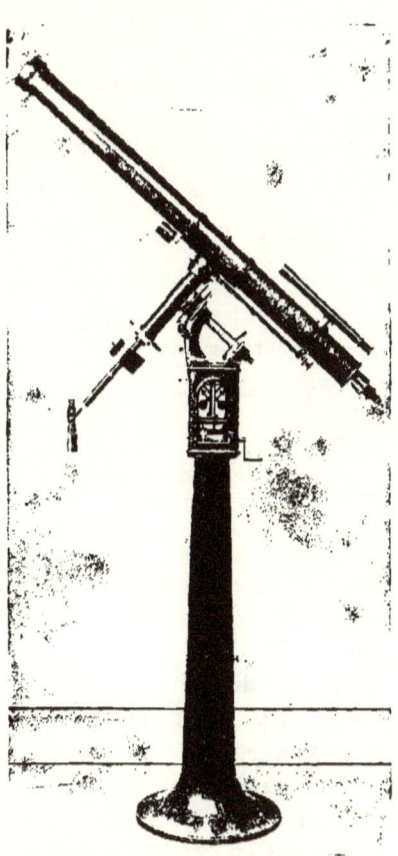

FIG. 74.—AN EQUATORIAL TELESCOPE.

An equatorial mounting.

lamp is shown in the figure. The declination axis carries a heavy weight, to balance the weight of the telescope, so that the entire structure may be nicely poised on the polar axis. The telescope is fastened to the declination axis, and is at right angles to it. On each axis there is a graduated circle; by these the astronomer sets the telescope so that it points toward any object whose right ascension and declination are known. The clock-work for rotating the polar axis lies under it, and is driven by a weight concealed in the hollow pillar which supports the instrument.

Ingenious contrivances. A large instrument of this kind is very complicated, and fairly bristles with ingenious contrivances to facilitate the work of the exacting individual who is to use it. When an astronomer's eyes first rest upon a great telescope, with which it is to be his good fortune to storm the sky, his sensations are of the liveliest character. The mass of steel, iron, and brass which confronts him speaks eloquently of the patient ingenuity of the mechanician who calculated the form and dimensions of each of the hundreds of pieces of metal which are joined in the intricate mechanism, and subordinated them all to one great purpose.

Accurate workmanship. It also tells of the painstaking care of many skilful workmen, who have toiled thousands of hours perfecting the teeth of the gears, polishing the pivots and bearings, making the various screws true, and fitting all together, to form a harmonious whole.

Various materials. Not only must the different parts be correctly proportioned, but each must be made of the proper material. Steel of various degrees of hardness, cast-iron, wrought-iron, brass, copper, lead, phosphor-bronze, silver, German silver, nickel, hard rubber, wood, carbon, glass, vegetable fiber, and even spider-webs all occupy their proper places. At some points friction is relieved by ball-bearings; at others by friction rollers; at still others friction must have full play. *Friction.*

FIG. 75.—THE CHAMBERLIN TELESCOPE OF THE UNIVERSITY OF DENVER.

The tons of metal which compose the moving parts of the great Yerkes telescope are moved in any direction, swiftly or slowly, by means of electric motors. The *Electric motors.*

astronomer presses the button, the motor fulfils his bidding.

Fig. 75 shows a large telescope ready for work. The pillar goes through the floor without touching it, and rests on a stone pier below. Near the bottom of the pillar are two hand-wheels, by means of which the telescope can be moved quickly into any desired position. Above them is a box containing clock-work which indicates the right ascension and declination of any object at which the telescope is pointing. Through a glass door in the uppermost section of the pillar one may see the driving clock. The declination axis is behind the tube. The observing platform, which slides up and down along an inclined runway, is shown at the left. The overarching iron dome rests upon antifriction wheels, which are on top of the stone wall.

A telescope in its home.

CHAPTER IX.

THE ASTRONOMER'S WORKSHOP AND SOME OF HIS TOOLS.

> " Go to yon tower, where busy science plies
> Her vast antennæ, feeling thro' the skies ;
> That little vernier, on whose slender lines
> The midnight taper trembles as it shines,
> A silent index, tracks the planets' march
> In all their wanderings thro' the ethereal arch,
> Tells through the mist where dazzled Mercury burns,
> And marks the spot where Uranus returns."
> —*Holmes.*

AN astronomical observatory is conspicuous among surrounding structures by its unusual appearance. One or more domes surmounting it catch the eye at once. There are long narrow doors in the walls and shutters on the roof, which arrest attention. Fig. 76 is a representation of an observatory. *An observatory.*

First as to the site. The location is usually not a matter within the astronomer's control ; he is fortunate if he is even allowed to plan the building, so as to adapt it to the purposes to which it is to be devoted. If he had his choice of location, he would be likely to choose a considerable elevation. *Its site.*

A mountain top would seem most suitable were it available ; but experience shows that such is not usually the case. The advantage is that the observer is above quite a thickness of atmosphere, so that the stars shine out more clearly, and faint objects are more distinctly visible. But the disadvantages are many. On a moun- *A mountain.*

tain top the air is almost always in motion; warm currents rush up the sides of the mountain, and cooler air descends. The expansion of the warm and vapor-laden air, which comes from below, chills it, and pro-

FIG. 76.—THE YERKES OBSERVATORY.

duces mists, or even clouds, which hang about the summit.

Obtrusive currents of air. Even when no mist forms, whirling currents come between the telescope and the celestial object toward which it is pointed. The light from the object, in passing through these changing currents, is bent hither and thither, so that the object appears to dance, and to be distorted; no satisfactory view of it is possible. Furthermore the wind shakes the telescope itself, and renders accurate observations out of the question. It is generally admitted that an ideal site is an elevated plateau; the farther it is from a mountain range the better; a dry atmosphere is also considered advantageous.

The environs of a city. Where circumstances limit the location to the neighborhood of some city, a study of the prevailing winds is made, so that the evil of the city's smoke may be minimized. A spot of ground embracing a few acres, so that other buildings may not be built too near the observatory, and commanding a fair sweep of the horizon, is sought. It is advisable to avoid proximity to railroads, because of the earth tremors caused by the passage of heavy trains.

When the site has been chosen and the instrumental equipment determined upon, the building is so planned as to furnish a suitable home for the instruments, and working quarters for the astronomer. The building shown in the illustration (Fig. 77) faces southward because the large telescope under the dome is chiefly used for observing objects in the south, east, or west, and is not often pointed northward. Were the building turned around, the observer would have to look over some portion of the roof most of the time. From the roof, which has been heated during the day, arise currents of warm air which would disturb telescopic vision.

The building.

FIG. 77.—THE CHAMBERLIN OBSERVATORY.

To avoid these as much as possible the wings of the building are set back.

The meridian circle, the instrument next in importance, is now to be provided for. Shall it be in the east wing or in the west? If it is put in the west wing,

The transit room.

which is heated up by the afternoon sun, observations in the early evening will be vitiated by the currents of warm air rising all about it. The east wing, on the other hand, is largely protected from the sun in the afternoon, being in the shadow of the rest of the building. This instrument is therefore installed in the east wing ; a continuous slit is cut in the roof and in the north and south walls, so that the telescope may survey the entire meridian from the north point of the horizon up to the zenith, and down to the south point. When the instrument is not in use the slit is closed by doors.

The clocks. The clocks are next to be suitably housed. Shall they be put in the west wing? By no means. For the heat of the afternoon sun would cause them to change their rates. Fine clocks are supposed to be so constructed that changes in the temperature will not cause them either to gain or to lose. But no clock has yet been made which will not change its rate under variations of temperature. Why, then, shall they not be placed in the deep basement underneath the tower, below the surface of the ground, where the thermometer

Temperature and humidity. will probably not vary 5° a day, in ordinary weather? In that location there will be another foe to fight ; for a cellar, even though it be surrounded by a stone wall two feet thick and have a cement floor, is damp. The delicate mechanism of the clocks will suffer from this cause. The clocks must not stand on the floor or be hung upon wooden partitions. Special piers must be

Special supports. built to support them, unless there is some other adequate provision for them.

In order to avoid changes of temperature a portion of the round tower is partitioned off, on the main floor. The space shown in Fig. 78 is so selected that no wall of the clock-room, except a very short length, where two windows are, is an outside wall of the building. These two windows are made double, and covered with wooden shutters. Thus both the sun's rays and the storms of winter are guarded against. If the clocks were hung on the stone wall which partly bounds the room, the turning of the dome, which rests on this wall, *The clock-room.*

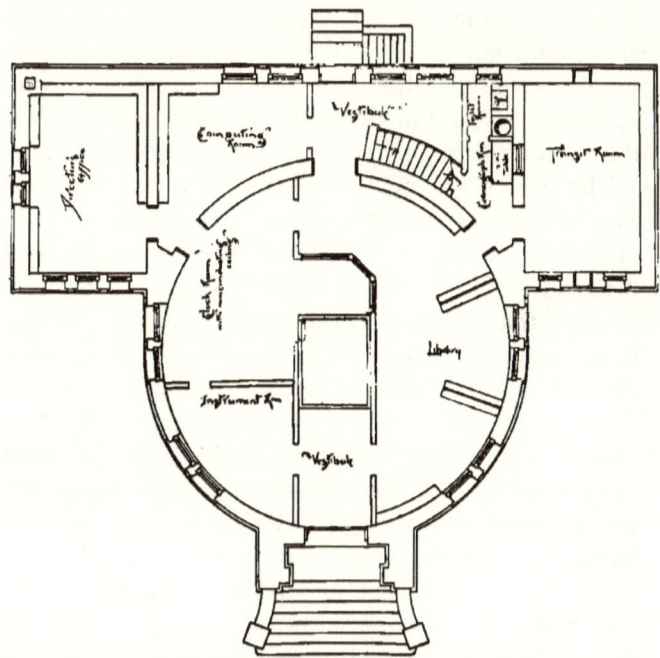

FIG. 78.—MAIN FLOOR OF THE CHAMBERLIN OBSERVATORY.

might jar them a trifle. Therefore the great pier in the center of the tower is utilized. Stout beams are built into the pier, and project through the thin partition into the clock-room; the beams do not touch the partition, for in that case the vibrations of the floor, as people walk about on it, would shake the clocks.

The west wing contains the study of the astronomer. *The study.*

148   *A Study of the Sky.*

The basement.
He does not care for the heat of the long summer afternoons, if the instruments are protected from it.

In the basement arrangements are made for the heating plant, which, if one has plenty of money to spend, is a hot-water system ; also for a photographic dark-room, battery-room, janitor's quarters, storeroom, and workshop. A good carpenter's bench and a small kit of tools are needed. If the observatory is a large one, a lathe and other machines for working metals are a part of the equipment. Quite a little of the basement is occupied by the piers on which the instruments rest.

Foundations and floors.
The foundations of these are sunk pretty deep, the depth depending upon the character of the soil. A gravel bed makes an excellent foundation ; rock or hard clay is also satisfactory, except that they readily transmit vibrations arising from the passage of railroad trains within half a mile, or heavy traffic in a neighboring street. The floors must not touch any of the piers, for, in that case, the vibrations caused by human footfalls will be communicated to the piers and thus to the instruments.*

The upper story.
In the upper story of the observatory the principal room is the dome-room, the home of the great telescope. On a level with the floor of this room is an extensive balcony from which one can glance at all parts of the sky. Two or three small rooms adjoin, where various attachments of the telescope are kept, and where the observer may occasionally warm himself on a bitter night.

No heat.
It is not practicable to heat the dome-room, for the

---

* Before the telescope of the Chamberlin Observatory was installed, the floor of the dome-room was shored up on the great pier, so that it might not sag when the various parts of the telescope were laid on it, preparatory to being put together. After the telescope was mounted, the props were forgotten for a time, and every star under observation danced about in a most disheartening manner, as people walked about the room. In a few days the props were remembered and knocked out. The trouble ceased at once. The stone pier which had been so shaken weighs 320 tons.

heated air would escape through the slit, when the dome shutter was rolled off. Nor is it allowable to experiment in this direction, because a current of warm air rising in front of the large glass would cause the stars to appear blurred and to dance about in such fashion that no satisfactory views of them could be had.

Domes more than thirty-five feet in diameter are built of iron. They are made as light as is consistent with a proper degree of rigidity, and are covered with heavy galvanized iron. Great care is taken to mount them in such a manner that they will rotate with ease. An astronomer whose strength has been exhausted by turning an unmanageable dome is in no physical condition to manipulate a delicate instrument, the smallest reading of which corresponds to a distance of $\frac{1}{50000}$ of an inch.

Domes.

Where a good current of electricity and a small electric motor are available, the observer has but to touch a push button, and the dome revolves. For very large telescopes, the floor of the dome-room is made of iron, and is raised or lowered by powerful machinery, which may be started and stopped by pressing a button.

A rising floor.

Some of the astronomer's tools are so important and so common that we must examine them. The great telescope which was described in the last chapter is much too cumbersome to be used in the most refined investigations for determining the right ascensions and declinations of "fundamental stars." The instrument used for this purpose is comparatively small, extremely rigid, and so mounted that it can view a celestial object only when the latter is near the meridian.

Some of the astronomer's tools.

Fig. 79 shows that the instrument consists of a telescope, which is perpendicular to a horizontal axis. The axis points east and west and terminates in two cylindrical steel pivots, each of which rests in a wedge-shaped metal bearing called a V,* from its resemblance to that letter. These bearings are fastened very securely to two substantial piers, generally of stone.

The graduated circles. Upon the axis are mounted two circles, one, at least, of which carries a band of silver, on which fine marks, technically called "divisions" or "graduations" have been cut with the utmost accuracy. If each division represented a degree there would be 360 of them around the entire circle. Usually there is a graduation for each five minutes of arc; as five minutes constitute one twelfth of a degree, there are 12 x 360, or 4,320 graduations on the circle.

FIG. 79.—A MERIDIAN CIRCLE.

Measurement of angles. If the telescope, which is now pointing upward, were turned so as to point downward, the graduated circle would turn with it, and the angle through which the telescope was turned could be measured by means of a suitable fixed pointer placed close to the silver graduations. If the pointer were opposite the 10° mark on the circle when the telescope was pointing directly upward, it would be opposite the mark for 190° when the telescope pointed

---
* This bearing is commonly referred to as a "wye."

straight down, the circle having been turned just half way round. Instead of one pointer there are usually four ; the silver graduations are so fine that they cannot be well seen without a magnifying glass ; the pointer must therefore be very fine, and the spider is called upon to furnish it.

The spider-web, which is to serve as a pointer, is placed inside of a microscope, which is sighted at the silver circle. To insure great accuracy in reading the circle four microscopes are frequently employed. They are shown in Fig. 79, being fastened to a metal drum, which rests on top of one of the piers. On looking through one of the microscopes one sees the spider-web, and also the magnified divisions on the circle. At the outer end of each microscope a little box is placed ; this contains a measuring instrument called a micrometer. If the spider-web does not appear to coincide with one of the graduations on the circle, its distance from the nearest graduation is measured with the micrometer. The silver circles are usually read to the nearest tenth of a second of arc. If such a circle be ninety inches in circumference, a tenth of a second is only $\frac{1}{111000}$ of an inch. *The reading microscopes.*

Standing upon the horizontal axis of the instrument is a metal frame which supports a delicate level, the sensitiveness of which is astonishing. Suppose that two points on the level tube, one eighth of an inch apart, are in the same horizontal plane at a given instant. If by some movement of the instrument one of the points is raised a millionth of an inch above its neighbor, the level bubble will move. *The level.*

A peep through the eyepiece of the telescope reveals a forest of black lines ; at night, when lit up by a special lamp, they appear as a system of golden wires. In Fig. *The reticle.*

80 are nine parallel wires, and one at right angles to them. Eight are arranged symmetrically with respect to the middle wire. They come from the spider's loom; woe to the luckless wight who accidentally touches them, or blows upon them! They are in the focus of the telescope, close to the observer's eye, inside of the tube. If the telescope be directed to the heavens on a clear night, star after star will pass through the field of view, marching across one vertical wire after another, moving parallel to the horizontal wire.

The celestial meridian. When a star is just crossing the middle wire, it is on the celestial meridian of the place of observation, if the instrument is in perfect adjustment. Let us stop a moment and think out the reason why a star is on the meridian when it is on this middle wire.

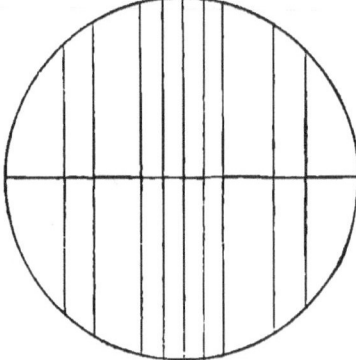

FIG. 80.—THE SPIDER-WEBS.

Consider a surveyor's transit which he carries about and sets up on its tripod whenever he wishes to make any measurements. In it there are two cross wires, one horizontal, the other vertical. If he wishes to sight at the top of a church spire he moves his telescope until the tip of the spire appears to lie on the intersection of the cross wires. *A surveyor's transit.* At that instant a straight line drawn from the top of the steeple through the center of the object-glass of the telescope strikes the point where the two wires cross each other. This line is called the sight-line of the telescope.

Returning to the meridian circle we see that its sight-line, which is a line drawn from the center of the object-glass* to the point where the horizontal and central vertical wires meet, is perpendicular to the horizontal axis. Let us point the telescope at some house miles away to the southward. Since the horizontal axis points east and west, the sight-line, which is perpendicular to it, must be pointing due south. If a chimney of the house appears to lie upon the middle wire the chimney is due south of the instrument. Passing by the house we prolong the sight-line to the celestial sphere, which it strikes at the south point of the horizon.

The meridian circle again.

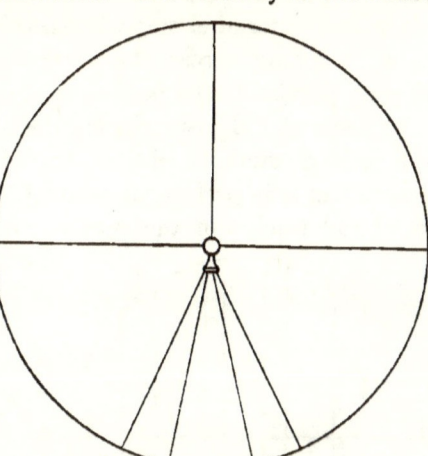

FIG. 81.—THE SPIRE ON THE CROSS WIRES.

We gently take hold of the telescope and pull the eye-end down ; as it turns on the horizontal axis the object-glass rises, and the sight-line traces a line on the celestial sphere. Farther and farther upward the line is traced on the sky till it reaches the zenith. As we go on, the circle which we have been tracing runs down from the zenith to the north point of the horizon. The telescope is now horizontal, and pointing northward. We continue revolving the telescope in the same direction ; the eyepiece rises and the object-glass falls, while the sight-line is cutting into the earth's surface, tracing upon it the terrestrial merid-

The telescope is revolved.

---
* The large glass at the upper end of the tube.

ian of the place of observation. When the telescope finally reaches its original horizontal southward-pointing position, the sight-line has traced the celestial meridian on the sky, and the terrestrial on the earth. If the celestial meridian were visible as a fine gold thread lying on the celestial sphere, and one tried to look at it with the meridian circle, it would be concealed from view, being behind the central spider-web. Therefore, at the instant when any star appears to be crossing the central spider-web, it is on the meridian.

<small>Mechanical perfection sought.</small>

Thus far we have considered the meridian circle as an ideally perfect instrument. True it is that the mechanician has exhausted the resources of his art when he has made a first-class meridian circle. He has striven to make the pivots at the ends of the axis of the same size and exactly round. The telescope has been set at right angles to this; the object-glass and spider-webs have been inserted with the utmost care. Upon the graduations of the silver circle weeks of the most painstaking labor, coupled with the most scrupulous care, have been lavished. The microscopes with which the circle is read have been constructed with an eye to perfection. The interior of the glass level-tube, which is to test the horizontality of the axis, has been ground to the proper curvature, and fastened to its supporting frame in such a way that changes of temperature will not cause the tube to be pinched or sprung. The mason has endeavored to set the supporting piers so solidly that nothing short of a miniature earthquake will disturb their positions.

<small>Perfection impossible.</small>

The astronomer views the finished work with the admiration which every one must have for any piece of mechanism which represents the utmost of human skill. But the instrument, which is to the eye of the body a thing of beauty, is to the mind a mass of imperfections.

Fig. 82.—The Lick Observatory.

The pivots on which the instrument revolves are of unequal sizes, and neither of them is round. For this reason alone the sight-line, instead of tracing a perfect circle on the sky, traces a gently waving line. The axis, which is apparently amply able to support the light telescope, bends a trifle under its weight; perchance one half of it bends more than the other half.

Flexure. The telescope tube flexes under the weights of the object-glass and of the eye-end. Changes of temperature and other causes alter the position of the object-glass in its cell, and change the direction of the sight-line, which passes through its center.

Errors of graduation. The exquisite silver circle will cost the astronomer many a month of arduous toil. For if he assumes that one of the graduations is exactly in the right place, almost all of the remaining 4,319 are so far out of their true positions that he must determine their errors. As we have before stated, he wishes to read as small a quantity as $\frac{1}{144000}$ of an inch, and most of the circle-divisions are in error as much as $\frac{1}{50000}$ of an inch; some of them are over $\frac{1}{30000}$ of an inch out. The little micrometers on the microscopes cannot do their small duties with sufficient precision. The inner surface of the level tube, which has been ground so smooth, is embellished here and there by a miniature mountain, which arrests the free movement of the level bubble.

Level errors.

Movements of the ground. The solid foundation on which the instrument has been set is continually in motion, shifting the positions of the piers by small amounts. Earthquakes are only the big brothers of the many small disturbances of the earth's crust which are noticed by astronomers alone.

A difficult task. The observer with a meridian circle has therefore a difficult task; he must manipulate the instrument with exceeding care, and must study many of its errors from night to night, because they continually change in inexplicable ways. His occupation is largely an unrelenting chase after errors, which must be determined and taken into account.

A chronograph is considered an indispensable part of the instrumental equipment of an observatory. It is used, as its name indicates, for noting time. At any instant when an observer wants to note the time he touches a telegraph key, and the chronograph records the time. The large cylinder shown in Fig. 83 revolves once a minute. If the pen-carriage stood still the pen would

A chronograph.

FIG. 83.—A CHRONOGRAPH.

draw the same circle over and over again on the paper which is wrapped around the cylinder. But the mechanism is so arranged that the pen-carriage slides slowly from one end of the cylinder to the other. The pen therefore traces upon the paper a long spiral line, like a screw-thread. When a telegraph operator presses his telegraph key the sounder by his side clicks. If a pen were suitably attached to the sounder, the pen would make a mark on paper. In a similar fashion a notch is made in the line which the pen draws on the chronograph sheet, whenever an observer presses the key.

The pen-carriage slides.

158 *A Study of the Sky.*

The record of the clock. The clock is equipped with a little device which acts like an automatic telegraph key, causing the pen on the chronograph to make a notch whenever the clock ticks, with the exception of the fifty-ninth second of each minute, for which there is no record on the chronograph. The omission of this second is a matter of convenience, to identify the beginning of each minute. If the observer notices the time when one of the clock notches

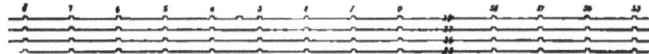

FIG. 84.—A PORTION OF A CHRONOGRAPH SHEET.

was made, he can easily tell what the clock read when any other notch was made.

The time noted. When he sees a star cross a spider-web in the meridian circle and touches his key, a notch is made which usually comes between two of the clock notches. If it is between the notches for $9^{hr.}\,28^{min.}\,3^{sec.}$ and $9^{hr.}\,28^{min.}\,4^{sec.}$, the fractional part of a second is estimated from the relative distances between the notches. One of the notches shown in Fig. 84 was evidently made at $9^{hr.}\,28^{min.}\,3.4^{sec.}$ It is much easier for an observer to touch a telegraph key at the proper instant than to estimate the required time by listening to the ticks of a clock, while his eye is occupied at the eyepiece of the telescope.

The micrometer. The micrometer is used on all kinds of astronomical instruments wherever small distances are to be measured accurately. It aids in reading the silver circle on a meridian circle; the diameters of planets, the heights of mountains on the moon, and the distances of the stars are all measured by its help. It is beyond our present province to explain how the minute fractions of an inch which a micrometer measures are transmuted into miles in the celestial spaces, by the alchemy of the mathematician's art. But we may at least see what the great micrometer which is screwed on at the eye-end of the Lick telescope looks like, and get a little insight into the method of its manipulation. Looking through the eye-piece, we shall not be confronted by a forest of spider-webs, as in the meridian circle. It will suffice if there are but two fixed wires crossing each other at a right angle, just as in the surveyor's transit. Besides the fixed

A great micrometer.

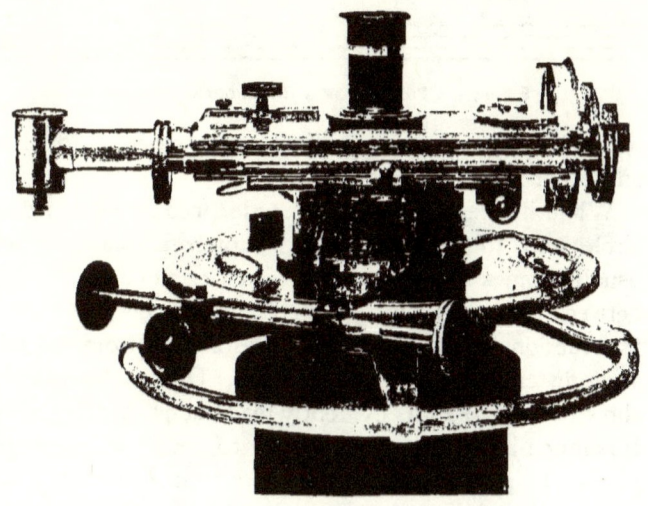

FIG. 85.—THE LICK MICROMETER.

wires there must be one **movable one**, which is parallel to one of the fixed wires. The concealed frame, which holds the movable wire, is driven by a fine screw, the large head of which is visible at one end of the box. This head is graduated so that thousandths of a revolution of the screw can be read. If the screw has fifty threads to the inch, an entire revolution of it will cause the movable spider-web to move $\frac{1}{50}$ of an inch. One hundredth of a revolution will cause a motion of $\frac{1}{5000}$ of an inch.

A fine screw.

A planet's diameter.

If the diameter of a planet is to be measured, the movable spider-web is driven, by turning the screw, until the image of the planet in the field of view is neatly embraced between the two parallel spider-webs. The reading of the graduated head of the micrometer screw is taken, and the solution of the problem is then a mere matter of a little simple figuring, which the astronomer does at his leisure.

When the apparent distance between two stars is to be measured, the micrometer box, containing the spider-webs, is turned till the two parallel webs stand perpendicular to a line joining the stars.

Distance between stars.

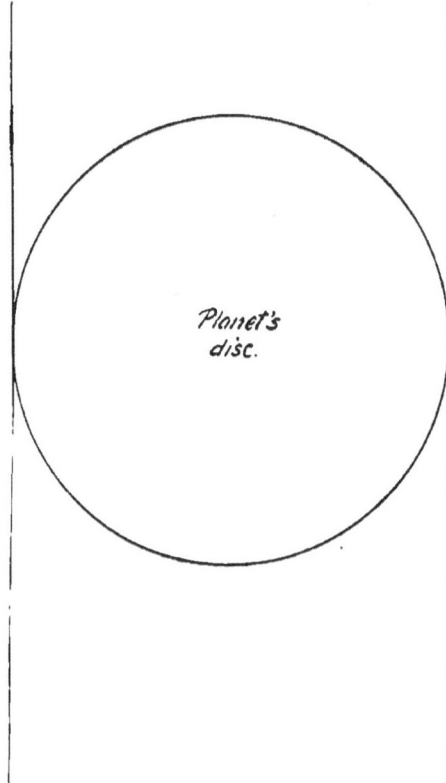

FIG. 86.—MEASUREMENT OF A PLANET'S DIAMETER.

At the completion of the measure the spider-webs are bisecting the images of the stars, as shown in Fig. 87.

In reducing observations made with the micrometer

no such tantalizing chain of errors is encountered as with the meridian circle. If the micrometer screw were of even pitch throughout its length, so that each revolution of it advanced the spider-web just $\frac{1}{50}$ of an inch, all would be well. When the irregularities in the screw-pitch, which are always very small, have been determined, the battle is won.

Errors.

If, however, one of the spider-webs is accidentally broken, the insertion of a new one demands a little skill. The astronomer cannot sweep down one of the cobwebs in the observatory to get a suitable wire. House-spiders are too effeminate; their webs are not sufficiently tough, and are covered with dust. A big field-spider, which successfully copes with an unwary grasshopper, binding his struggling victim by weaving a shroud about him, produces a web that is elastic and tenacious. The cocoon, in which are stored hundreds of yards of gauzy fiber, is captured. By the exercise of a little dexterity a piece of web three or four inches long is pulled out and placed under a magnifying glass. It proves to be too thick, and is rejected. Another piece is examined; curious little knots are strung along it. The next piece, when held up to the light, is too transparent. Soon a fine, smooth, opaque bit of web is discovered; it is submerged in a basin of water and stretched out, while soaking, so that it becomes finer yet. Inside of the micrometer are two fine grooves. One end of the web is laid in its groove, with the aid of a magnifying glass, and a drop of shellac is dropped upon it; the

FIG. 87.—BISECTION BY SPIDER-WEBS.

A broken spider-web.

162   *A Study of the Sky.*

shellac hardens and holds it. It is now stretched taut with the utmost care, and the other end fastened in its groove ; if it be not pulled with sufficient force, it will be baggy and useless. If pulled a trifle too hard, all is over in an instant, and the cocoon is explored for a new web.

The spectroscope.   One more instrument demands attention. It is the wonder-working spectroscope, with which substances which exist in distant stars are detected, and motions otherwise unknown are brought to light.

A shower.   White light is a combination of many different colors. When the sun shines through a shower of rain, his light

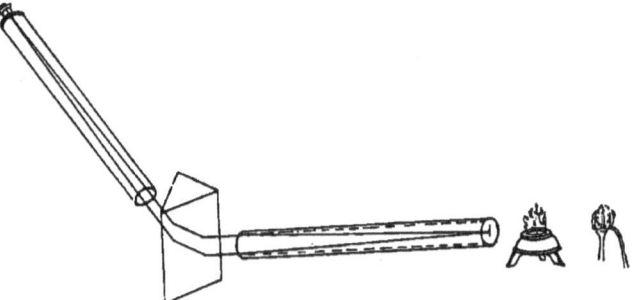

FIG. 88.—ESSENTIALS OF A SPECTROSCOPE.

is split up in passing through the raindrops, and a rainbow is produced. Many an old lamp, once the glory of grandfather's parlor, is surrounded by prismatic pieces of glass, which are rich with varied hues, as the light shines through them and is dispersed into its component colors.

Construction of the spectroscope.   The spectroscope is a beautiful instrument, in which the light is dispersed, and by which it is studied. Fig. 88 shows a triangular prism of glass, on each side of which a telescope is placed. The eyepiece of the telescope at the right has been supplanted by a brass cap, in which there is a long narrow slit. The light from an ordinary lamp enters at this slit, impinges upon the prism, is dispersed by the prism, enters the telescope at the left, and emerges into the observer's eye.

The light which entered the narrow slit has been spread out into a ribbon which is red at one end and violet at the other. Between these colors lie orange, yellow, green, cyan-blue, and ultramarine blue. The ribbon is called a spectrum. *Spectra.*

Let us now replace the lamp by a spirit lamp, and lay some common salt on the wick. The previously colorless flame becomes yellow, as the salt burns. Looking into the spectroscope we see no longer a colored band, but simply a yellow line. When the salt has been burned up we try chloride of lithium in the same way; a carmine line appears. A salt of thallium will produce a green line. Burn all the substances together, and all the lines are visible simultaneously. *Experiments.*

Again let us look at the yellow line, as the salt is being turned from a solid into a gas, in the hot flame of the spirit lamp. Behind the spirit lamp is put a very bright white light, which will shine through the hot gas into the slit. In place of the bright line produced by the glowing yellow gas there is now a dark line, and on either side of it the spectrum stretches in all its beauty, violet at one end, red at the other. The dark line lies in that part of the spectrum which is of a yellow color. If the spirit lamp be now removed, the dark line in the yellow of the spectrum disappears, and the spectrum is, as at first, a variously colored ribbon, in which there are no dark lines. What caused the dark line, which has now vanished? The bright white light is composed of all sorts of colors, among which is yellow. When this *Further experiments.*

light shone through the hot yellow gas in the spirit-flame, the gas absorbed some of it, so that there was a dark place in the yellow of the spectrum.

Three principles.
By numerous experiments the following principles have been established :

Principle I. An incandescent solid or liquid, or a glowing gas which is made dense by the application of pressure, produces a spectrum, which is a ribbon of light of various colors, as previously described. This is a *continuous spectrum.*

Principle II. A heated gas, which is composed of only one chemical element, gives a spectrum consisting of one or more bright lines. This is a *bright-line spectrum.*

Principle III. A white light shining through a gas produces a spectrum which would be continuous if it were not crossed by dark lines. The dark lines correspond in position to the bright lines in the spectrum of the gas. This is a *reversed spectrum.*

The principles applied.
How does an astronomer apply these principles? He takes off the eye-end of his telescope, and attaches the spectroscope instead. The instrument is directed at a nebula ; the light from the nebula enters the spectroscope slit, passes through the prism, and produces a spectrum of bright lines. The nebula is therefore a glowing gas. By comparing the spectrum of the nebula with the spectrum of hydrogen, for instance, it is proven that hydrogen is present in the nebula.

The spectrum of the sun is a reversed spectrum crowded with thousands of dark lines. White light coming from the sun's interior passes through the heated gases in his atmosphere, and suffers absorption, according to Principle III. A spectroscope can be so constructed that the spectrum of the vapor of sodium will be shown in the field of view, just below the solar spectrum. The prominent lines in the sodium spectrum are just below certain dark ones in the solar spectrum. Sodium is therefore in the sun.

What would the observer conclude about the nebula in Andromeda if its spectrum were continuous?

Powerful spectroscopes are provided with more than one prism, and are too complicated to be explained easily.

For certain classes of work prisms are rejected, their place being taken by a diffraction grating, which is a *A grating.*

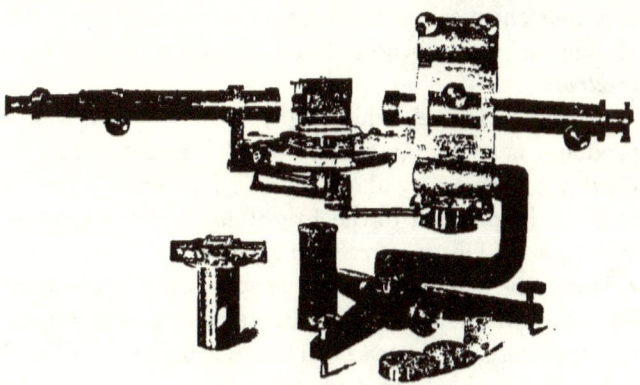

FIG. 89.—A SPECTROSCOPE.

metallic mirror on the face of which thousands of fine lines have been ruled. Sometimes 40,000 lines are ruled side by side in a space an inch wide. White light is dispersed into its different colors by being reflected from the surface of the grating.

There are many other astronomical tools, descriptions of which are forbidden by the limitations of this book. Mention must however be made of the photographer's camera, which is so common a piece of apparatus that a description of it is unnecessary. Many special photo- *Photography.*

graphic telescopes have been built, which have revealed objects too faint to be seen with the most powerful visual telescopes. To the results of photographic work in various astronomical lines, reference will be made from time to time. Very many departments of observational astronomy have been invaded by the sensitive plate, which, despite its imperfections and limitations, is now admitted to furnish results superior to those obtained without its aid.

Superior results.

CHAPTER X.

TIME.

> "Old Time, in whose bank we deposit our notes,
> Is a miser who always wants guineas for groats ;
> He keeps all his customers still in arrears
> By lending them minutes and charging them years."
> —*Holmes.*

IN this busy age, when more progress is made in a minute than was formerly made in an hour, and the exacting demands upon men in all walks of life make them more chary of hours than their forefathers were of days, the importance of accurate time is realized as never before. The piercing whistle of the factory or machine shop wakes the echoes of the early morning at the exact moment when some steady clock reads seven, and hundreds of working people take their places promptly, to begin the day's toil. The railroad conductor, with pocket chronometer in his hand, stands beside the palatial through train, while the engineer holds the panting locomotive in check, till the signal is given to open the throttle and speed the waiting passengers on their way. *[Importance of accurate time.]*

"Thirty seconds too late," says the depot clock, as the belated traveler hurries to the platform, only to find that the train has pulled out. "Our clock at home was five minutes slow," says the blushing schoolgirl, when called to account for her tardiness. "The school clock must be a minute and a half too fast," says the boy who played marbles two minutes too long. The *[Tardy people.]*

business man paces impatiently to and fro in his office, waiting for friends who were to come precisely at three. The electric car has just gone by, and the mistress of the house, arrayed for an afternoon's shopping, stands on her doorstep in a pet; the kitchen clock was two minutes slow. The careful mariner, feeling his way along the coast, through a fog, feels a shock which shows that the good ship has struck a rock. The trusted chronometer has gone wrong, and the ship must go down in the seething floods.

A wreck.

Scientists dispute about tenths of seconds, quibble over hundredths, and take still smaller fractions into account, while the world wonders how they contrive to measure intervals of time so minute.

Small fractions.

Though all the daily doings of the civilized world are governed to a large extent by the timekeepers which are to be found everywhere, few stop to inquire into the authoritative source of standard time, and the methods of its dissemination. People generally have vague notions that astronomers observe the sun when it is on the meridian, regulate their clocks accordingly, and then telegraph the time about for the benefit of railroads and jewelers.

Standard time.

Let us go to the bottom of this matter, by visiting an observatory and seeing just what the astronomer does; we must not go at mid-day, for he does not use the sun to get time by. In the evening we may find him at work, and fortunate shall we be if he permits us to sit down in the room where he is observing, and silently watch his operations. In the center of the dimly lighted room is the meridian circle, which we have described in Chapter IX. The roof shutters have been opened, and we may see the stars trooping past on their way to the western horizon. On a table near the

Time observations.

instrument stands a chronometer, ticking off each half second; by its side lies a book, containing a list of stars. The book gives the right ascension and declination of each star. The astronomer glances at his chronometer and sees that its reading is about $8^{hr.}$ $53^{min.}$ In the list he finds a star whose right ascension is $8^{hr.}$ $56^{min.}$ $4.93^{sec.}$ The star therefore will cross his meridian about $8^{hr.}$ $56^{min.}$, and will come into the field of view of his instrument a few seconds before that time.

Looking at the declination he mentally figures out the reading of the silver circle, when the telescope has the proper slant to the horizon. In a minute he has turned the telescope on its horizontal axis till the circle has the proper reading, and has applied his eye at the eyepiece. Faint stars come drifting through the field of view, shying past the golden spider-webs, as if they wished to escape from the astronomer's gaze as quickly as possible; but he pays no attention to them. *The circle is set.*

In a short time the expected bright star appears on the edge of the field of view, glowing like a little sun. The observer glances quickly at the chronometer, and begins counting the readings of the second-hand; "four, half, five, half, six, half," he says to himself, as he resumes his place at the eyepiece. The star moves onward; it has leaped across the first spider-web, and the astronomer hurriedly writes in his note-book the figures 13.1. *The star comes.*

He has estimated that the star crossed the first spider-web one tenth of a second after the chronometer ticked the thirteenth second of some minute. Hurriedly glancing at the chronometer's face he again counts, and after a few seconds he makes another record, perchance 24.7. Thus he continues till the star has crossed the last spider-web; having gotten the seconds and fractions of *Accurate estimates.*

a second as correctly as he can, he writes down the minute and the hour more leisurely. The record stands as follows :

$$13.1^{sec.}$$
$$24.7$$
$$33.6$$
$$42.4$$
$$8^{hr.}\ 55^{min.}\ 54.1$$

The average of these five times, obtained by dividing their sum by 5, is $8^{hr.}\ 55^{min.}\ 33.58^{sec.}$ That is the time, as nearly as the astronomer could estimate it, which the chronometer read when the star crossed his meridian. The book on the table states that the star really crossed the meridian at $8^{hr.}\ 56^{min.}\ 4.93^{sec.}$

The chronometer's error. The chronometer must therefore be in error ; by subtracting the chronometer time from the time given in the book, we get the remainder $31.35^{sec.}$ Shall we not say that the chronometer is $31.35^{sec.}$ slow? If the observer could estimate the time when the star crossed each spider-web accurately, and the instrument were perfectly adjusted in the meridian, one star would be sufficient. But the instrument has many errors, which must be taken into the reckoning, and the observer cannot do anything as accurately as he wishes. He therefore observes several stars, and applies the refinements of mathematical analysis to the problem in order to determine the errors of the instrument, and make allowance for them. From the observation of each star he obtains a value of the error of the chronometer; these he combines, taking their average as the final result.

Personal equation. When the utmost obtainable accuracy is desired, the "personal equation" of the observer must be taken into account. It takes time for men to think ; the more complicated the operation, the greater the time. In the case of eye and ear observations, such as have just been described, one impression reaches the brain through the eye, when the star crosses the wire. Another impression comes from the chronometer, and is transmitted by way of the ear. The brain is occupied with the process of counting, but when the two impressions arrive, it compares them, pronounces judgment, and directs the hand to make a certain record. If a man is especially trained he can do all this without losing his count of the chronometer-beats. He can even observe the times of transit across two or three wires without removing his eye from the eyepiece, or stopping to write anything down.

In the case of chronographic observations, which have been described in Chapter IX., and which are now generally used, the brain has much less to do. As before it receives an impression by way of the nerves of sight, and sends a mandate to the finger to touch the telegraph key. The mandate is obeyed, and the time is recorded almost instantaneously on the chronograph sheet. The personal equation for eye and ear observations is usually greater than for chronographic work, because of the greater complexity of the process. *Chronographic observations.*

A machine has been invented for determining the personal equation of a time observer. The observer looks through a little tube, resembling the eyepiece of a telescope, and sees an artificial star, which is driven by clockwork across a system of wires. The machine automatically records the time when the star crosses each wire; the astronomer presses his telegraph key, as usual, and thus records the time when he thinks that the star crosses each wire. *Personal equation machine.*

Such tests have demonstrated that the average

observer is between one and two tenths of a second behind time. Sometimes he has a habit of touching the key a few hundredths of a second before the star reaches the wire ; he probably estimates the rate at which the star is moving, and starts his mental machinery ahead of time, endeavoring to get the nervous impulse down to his finger at the time when the star arrives at the wire. In the case of eye and ear observations a discrepancy of over a second was once found between two noted astronomers ; the cause of so large a difference can only be guessed at. Apart from personal equation,

Probable error. the probable error of a time determination derived from a dozen stars is two or three hundredths of a second.

Time, like money, is easier to get than to keep. After the error of a clock has been found, its rate must be sought. If on January 8, at 7 p. m., a clock is $10.93^{sec.}$ fast, and on January 11, at 7 p. m., another series of observations makes its error $10.42^{sec.}$ fast, it has lost $0.51^{sec.}$ in three days and is therefore losing $0.17^{sec.}$ a day. This rate is used in predicting the error for a few days ahead. If one wishes to know the error on January 13 at 7 p. m., he computes that the loss in two days is $2 \times 0.17^{sec.}$, which equals $0.34^{sec.}$; since the

Error and rate. clock was $10.42^{sec.}$ fast on January 11, and has since lost $0.34^{sec.}$, it must be only $10.08^{sec.}$ fast. But the rate can be relied upon for only a few days ; the clock may be as fine as the maker can produce ; it may be enclosed in an air-tight case, so that variations in the pressure and humidity of the air have no appreciable effect upon it ; it may be put upon as solid a base as can be found, and in a room kept at as constant a temperature as possible ; it may be wound by an electric motor, so that the case need not be opened—yet its performance will not satisfy the astronomer. Week after week its rate will change by small amounts, from obscure causes, which the astronomer cannot even foresee. Over and over again must observations be made, and calculations be carried through, that the time may be well kept.

No endeavor is made to keep a standard clock right, for the constant changes which would be necessary would introduce intolerable disturbances into the clock's performance. It is therefore permitted to go on month after month, without alteration, its errors and rates being determined from time to time by observations of the stars.

We have seen how an astronomer gets time, and how he endeavors to keep it. We shall now see how he disseminates it for the benefit of the country at large. *Time disseminated.*

Here electricity comes into play; as a telegraph operator by touching his key can make any sounder on the line tick, so a clock may be arranged to accomplish the same end. While the second-hand is flying from one second to the next one, a tooth of a wheel mounted on the same arbor as the second-hand strikes a miniature telegraph key, and the signal is sent. One of the clocks at the United States Naval Observatory at Washington sends a signal over the Western Union wires to distant cities day after day, and thousands of telegraphic instruments tick as the signal passes.

The sending of the signal is but a small part of the work of disseminating the time. In some cities a time ball is hoisted to the top of a pole a few minutes before noon, and released at noon by an electrical impulse. In others the fire bells are rung at the same hour. The Western Union Telegraph Company controls a system of clocks, which are set automatically once a day, when a signal is sent to them. Thus a business man may have reasonably correct time in his office, if he is willing *Special devices.*

174   *A Study of the Sky.*

Standard meridians.

to pay the small rental charged by the company.* The system conduces to the accurate running of trains, for every important railway station contains a telegraph office.

The system of standard meridians, which has been adopted by the railroads and by the most important municipalities, is a great convenience. The trains in the eastern portion of the United States are governed by Eastern Standard time, which is five hours later than Greenwich time, and is not far from local time at Philadelphia. Central Standard time is six hours later than Greenwich time, and is used in the Mississippi Valley and adjacent states. It is nearly the same as local time at St. Louis. Mountain time differs from Greenwich time by seven hours, and dominates the semi-arid region formerly known as the Great American Desert. The seven-hour meridian passes through Denver. Pacific time, one hour slower still, is the standard for the Pacific coast. The eight-hour meridian passes centrally through California.

Improvements in the plan.

Two further improvements upon this plan may yet be made. There should be no insurmountable difficulty in having the time the same throughout any given state. The fact that the meridian by which Central time is governed runs near the Mississippi River much facilitates the grouping of the states in such a way that the time which should be adopted in each one is easily remembered.†

---

* The clocks furnished are of a fair grade, and are expected to vary only a few seconds a day. They are set just right by the signal, and if they do not get out more than twenty seconds during the ensuing twenty-four hours, the next signal sets them right again. A rate of twenty seconds a day is rare. The system has therefore a high efficiency.

† Central Standard time should be in force in all the states which border on the Mississippi, and the three great lakes, Superior, Michigan, and Huron, together with Alabama. These states are Michigan, Indiana, Kentucky, Tennessee, Alabama, Wisconsin, Illinois, Mississippi, Missouri, Arkansas, and Louisiana.

Eastern time should be the standard in all states east of the preceding ones. These are Maine, New Hampshire, Vermont, Massachusetts, Rhode Island,

A further desirable change, which would be more difficult of accomplishment, because of the conservatism of even so progressive a people as Americans, is counting the hours continuously through the day from one to twenty-four. The designations, a. m. and p. m., would then be unnecessary. This system has already been tried upon the Canadian Pacific Railway, and is in force in Italy. Its advantages are simplicity and accuracy. Astronomers already have a twenty-four-hour day, which begins at noon. *A twenty-four-hour day.*

The business man prefers to have the date change at midnight, when he is usually asleep. The astronomer finds it inconvenient to change the date at midnight, when he is frequently engaged in observation. The astronomical day begins twelve hours later than the civil day; January 5, 10 a. m., is January 4, 22 hours, by astronomical reckoning. March 16, 8 p. m., is March 16, 8 hours, astronomically reckoned. Astronomers have of late years discussed the advisability of making their day begin at the same time as the civil day, viz., at midnight, but they have not yet made the change. *Astronomical and civil date.*

Europe is much in advance of America in the matter of time distribution. The city of Paris is supplied with a system of electrical clocks, and also with a system of pneumatic clocks, which, as their name indicates, are driven by compressed air. The standard clocks are so numerous that any one may learn the time accurately, with little trouble. Many small municipalities have extensive systems of electrical dials. *Time in Europe.*

Connecticut, New Jersey, Maryland, the Virginias, the Carolinas, Georgia, Florida, New York, Pennsylvania, and Ohio.
  Mountain time should prevail in the first double row of states and territories west of the states which have Central time. These are the Dakotas, Nebraska, Kansas, Indian Territory, Oklahoma, Texas, Montana, Wyoming, Colorado, and New Mexico.
  Pacific time should be adopted by all the remaining states. These are Idaho, Utah, Arizona, Washington, Oregon, Nevada, and California.

One of the most elaborate systems of time distribution is to be found in Great Britain. The Royal Observatory at Greenwich is the source of accurate time, which is telegraphed over the United Kingdom. A time ball is dropped at Greenwich, for the use of ships in the Thames. Another at Deal serves the shipping in the Downs. The great clock at Westminster Palace is regulated in accordance with the telegraphic signals. Through the post-office department are sent signals which are utilized in various ways, such as the regulation of clocks, the striking of bells, and the firing of guns.

Time distribution in Great Britain.

However elaborately accurate time may be distributed in a given city, business men rely upon their watches, which are compared from time to time with some timepiece supposed to be a standard. The price of a watch movement is, in general, a good indication of its quality; so excellent are the products of American makers, that one need not buy a foreign watch in order to get a good timepiece. In purchasing a watch of moderate price one may get an approximate idea of its excellence by paying attention to certain details. The more jewels the better. The hair-spring should be composed of a number of closely packed coils; if the end of the outermost coil comes in toward the center, overlying the other coils, the hair-spring is a "Breguet," which is the best form. The rim of the balance wheel should be made of two metals, the outer one brass and the inner one steel. This combination is of no use unless the rim has been cut through at two opposite points.

Watches.

The Breguet spring.

A fair compensation for changes of temperature is obtained by using this form of balance. All modern American movements, unless very cheap, have compensation balances. When hot weather comes the hairspring loses strength, and the balance must become

Compensation for temperature.

smaller in diameter, if it is to be driven as rapidly as before. The brass in the rim expands in the heat more than the steel does; thus each half of the rim is bent inward, and the diameter of the balance grows less. When the watch is exposed to cold the hair-spring acquires more vigor, and the watch tends to gain; but the outer brass portion of the rim contracts more than the inner steel portion, and each half of the ring bends outward, increasing the inertia of the wheel, and thus preventing the gain which would otherwise ensue.

To test the running of a watch one should compare it with a standard clock every day, or even more often, until a satisfactory knowledge of its performance has been obtained. A watch which is set right today and found nearly correct a month afterward may meanwhile have wandered off two or three minutes, and come back again. *The rate of a watch.* Sometimes a watch exhibits a large daily variation, gaining a considerable fraction of a minute during the first few hours after it is wound, and losing it during the remainder of the day.

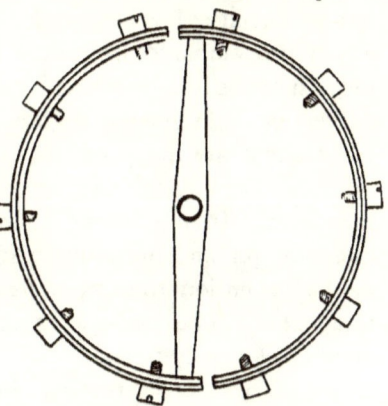

FIG. 90.—A WATCH BALANCE.

It is needless to say that a watch must be treated well, if it is expected to do good work. It must not be handled carelessly, nor be permitted to run down; if it runs down, it rarely starts again with the same rate that it had previously. Unless a watch is expensive, and "adjusted for heat, cold, and position," it is likely to *Good treatment.*

exhibit considerable variations of rate, if it is not kept in nearly the same position at night as in the daytime. It is not a good plan to put a watch under one's pillow.

Ladies culpable. — Ladies are especially culpable in the matter of handling their watches. They do not wind them regularly, and they let them lie around in bureau drawers or handkerchief boxes, or other places where they are considered safe for the time being. For these reasons ladies' watches rarely keep good time.

The regulator. — A young man is likely to move the regulator too often. If his watch suddenly begins to gain a few seconds a day, the regulator is moved backward at once. The less one alters the regulator the better, for a watch, like a human being, is subject to spells of irregularity, from which it recovers if left to itself.

Miscellaneous facts. — If the minute-hand is once set exactly over a minute mark, when the second-hand is at 60, and the two hands do not keep together, either the face is poorly engraved, or the pinion on which the minute-hand turns is not in the center of the face. If either of these hands slipped, which is rarely the case, the same effect would be produced.

Occasionally a watch gains a minute or so in an hour; this indicates that the hair-spring is caught, so that it does not vibrate freely; a jeweler will loosen it in a moment. A watch may stop because it has been wound too tightly; a little shaking for a few minutes in such a way as to make the balance wheel vibrate will relieve the difficulty.

In general, the possessor of a watch does his full duty by it if he winds it regularly, handles it carefully, keeps it in the same position as much as possible, and has it cleaned once in two years.

CHAPTER XI.

THE SUN.

"See the sun!
God's crest upon His azure shield the heavens."
—*Bailey.*

OF all the heavenly bodies the sun is of the greatest importance to man. Without its steady gravitational pull on the earth our planet would fly away to unknown regions of space, and the chill of death would settle down upon it. The oceans would stiffen into glass : the rivers would halt in their courses. All the higher forms of vegetable life would wither and die, and humanity, having struggled in vain against inevitable fate, would perish of hunger and cold. For the human race is dependent upon the energy which the sun radiates so lavishly. *Its importance.*

The sun stimulates the growing plant to disengage carbon from the embrace of oxygen, feeding on the carbon and leaving the oxygen, which is necessary for the life of men and animals. Its heat evaporates the waters of the oceans, which rise, form clouds, and descend again as rain or dew, quenching the longings of the parched earth, nourishing vegetation, coursing in majestic rivers to the sea, refreshing the bodies of men and animals, and giving delight to all intelligent spirits. *Oxygen and carbon.*

The energies of the sunbeams were stored ages ago in primeval forests : the forests were overwhelmed by the mighty deep and buried in a sepulcher of stone. To-day men dig up the mummified sunbeams and burn them in their furnaces and fireplaces. The genial light of the grate fire is due to those ancient sunbeams which are now released from their prison house. The flying locomotive, beneath whose impetuous rush the earth trembles, gets its speed from the sunbeams. The white-hot glow of a Bessemer converter comes primarily from the sun. The water which flows into our houses has been purified by the sun's rays, and has been forced through the pipes by great engines which derive their power from solar energy stored in coal. The electric car is driven by a current generated by a dynamo, and the dynamo in turn by a steam engine which is fed with the sunbeams of bygone ages. The electric light, which turns night into day, is stray sunshine. Nearly all the heavy work of the civilized world is done by the sun.

Bread, which is the staff of life, comes from wheat which has been stimulated in its growth by the sunbeams, and moistened by water lifted by the sun. If the mill which reduced the wheat to flour was driven by the wind, we find the source of the wind in heat produced by the sun's rays. If the mill was driven by water power or by steam, we still say that the sun supplied the power which turns the millstones. Even the final process of baking the bread is an application of heat originally derived from the sun. A man's muscles obtain their strength from the food which he has eaten : in the food has been stored the energy of the sun.

In fine, we owe to the sun the sustenance of our bodies, the maintenance of our physical energies, the comforts which we enjoy, the cooling breeze, the gentle shower, and the manifold beauties of nature. We proceed therefore to a short study of this wonder-working body, and shall endeavor to gain some notions about its

The Sun. 181

distance, its size, its motion, its changes of appearance, its make-up, its energies, and its future.

The distance of the sun from the earth is nearly 93,000,000 miles. If a straight road were built from the earth to the sun, and the earth, rotating at its present speed, were to start along this highway, like a rolling wheel, more than ten years would elapse before it would reach the sun. For in one day it would travel a distance equal to its own girth, which we will call 25,000 miles. In forty days 1,000,000 miles would have been left behind; over 3,700 days would therefore be consumed in the entire journey. An express train, traveling fifty miles an hour day and night, without intermission, would require over two centuries to traverse the same distance. *The sun's distance.*

There are many ways of finding the distance of the sun, most of which involve complicated mathematical operations. But one of them is easily understood. By a series of beautiful and accurate experiments physicists have measured the velocity of light, which they place at 186,330 miles a second. Astronomers have found that light takes 499 seconds to come from the sun. Therefore the distance of the sun is obtained by multiplying these two numbers together. This is the mean distance of the earth from the sun. Since the orbit of the earth is not a perfect circle, but an ellipse, its distance from the sun varies. It is nearest to the sun at the beginning of the year; six months later, on July 1, it is almost 3,000,000 miles further away. *How the distance is found.*

When the distance of the sun is known its diameter is easily computed. It is 866,500 miles; this is nearly 110 times the earth's diameter. The sun is therefore over 1,300,000 times as large as the earth. If the earth were magnified until it became as large as the sun, and *The diameter.*

the sizes of its inhabitants were increased in like ratio, a man originally 5 feet 11 inches in height would become 650 feet tall. If the force of gravity were no stronger than at present, his original weight would be multiplied by 1,331,000. But, according to the principles of mechanics, the earth's attraction for a body upon its surface would be 110 times as great as before ; hence our unfortunate human being would weigh over 10,000,000 tons, if his former weight was only 140 pounds.

Use of a telescope. When the sun is viewed with a telescope especial precautions are taken to diminish the intense light, so that the eye of the observer may not be ruined. A very dark glass held in front of the eye will furnish the needed protection, but it may become too hot and break. Special forms of eyepieces have been devised, which allow most of the light and heat to escape, reflecting only a small part of it to the observer's eye.

Spots. A cursory examination with even a small telescope reveals the existence of small black spots upon the solar surface. Each spot is surrounded by a lighter border, which appears to be composed of a large number of filaments, like the fringe around a table-mat. The dark portion of the spot is called its umbra ; the surrounding border is the penumbra.

Rotation. If an observer makes a drawing showing the positions of the spots on the solar disc, and looks at them again in a day or two, he sees that they have moved. A watch of a few days will convince him that they are being carried around at a pretty regular rate, and that the sun, like the earth, turns on an axis, making a complete rotation in three weeks and a half.

Spots near the solar equator revolve in twenty-five days and a fraction ; those which are nearly midway between the poles and the equator consume twenty-

The Sun.   183

seven days in making one revolution. Spots are never
seen more than half way from the equator to the poles, *Distribution of the spots.*
and are much less numerous near the equator than a few
degrees away from it. This strange distribution of the
spots, together with the curious irregularity in their

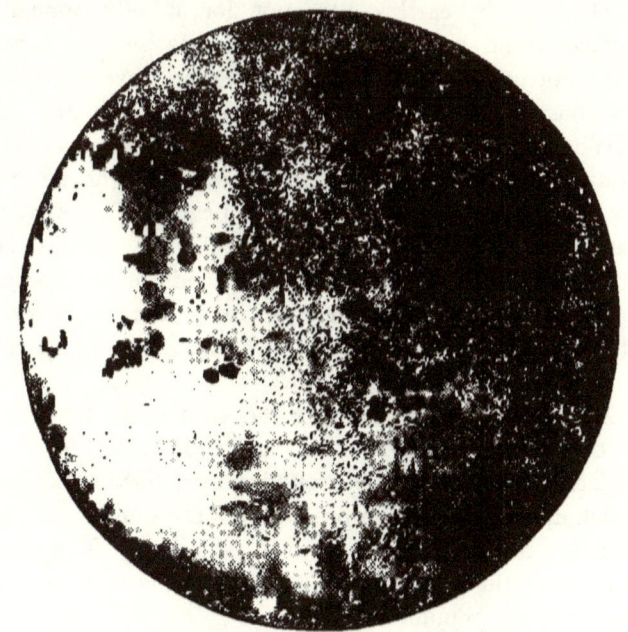

FIG. 91.—SUN-SPOTS.

times of revolution, constitutes the first of a number of
unexplained mysteries concerning the solar surface.

When a large spot is on the edge of the sun's disc,
one may see that it makes a slight notch in the sun's *A spot is a depression.*
limb (as the edge of the disc is called). Therefore
the spot must be a depression below the grayish-white
surface of the sun. The shape of the spot is like that of
a dinner plate, the bottom of the plate corresponding to

184   *A Study of the Sky.*

Sizes of spots. the umbra, and the gently sloping rim to the penumbra.
Spots vary in size from the merest black points, just visible with high telescopic power, to immense objects,

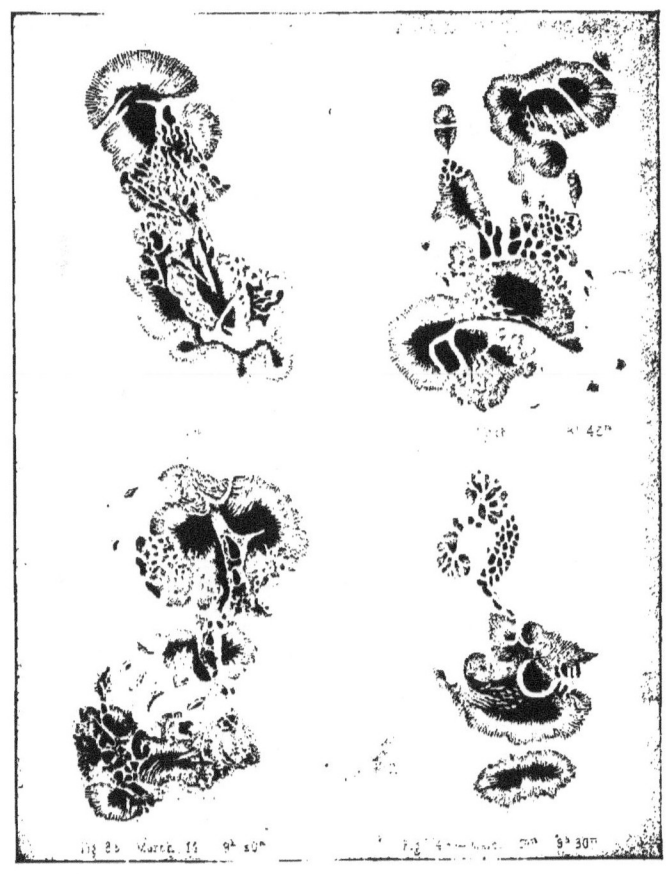

FIG. 92.—CHANGES IN A SOLAR SPOT.

A large spot-group. covering thousands of millions of square miles. One of the largest spot-groups on record had a diameter of 150,000 miles. The central spot of a large group, which appeared in February, 1892, measured 100,000 miles by 50,000 miles. Such enormous objects are easily visible to the naked eye if it be protected by a dark glass.

Sun-spots change their appearance from day to day, and frequently from hour to hour. At times a white bridge may span the black gulf of the umbra; at other times the umbra may be almost entirely hidden by a grayish veil similar in appearance to terrestrial clouds. The filaments of the penumbra, which are usually nearly straight, may become violently curved and distorted. Occasionally the appearance of the filaments indicates that the spot has a rotary motion, like that of a terrestrial whirlwind. A spot frequently breaks up into a multitude of smaller ones. A group of small ones may coalesce into a single large one.

Their changes.

In July, 1892, a double sun-spot, consisting of two umbræ, separated by a bright bridge, and surrounded by a common penumbra, experienced a very rapid change of appearance. A bright jet of white matter shot out over one of the umbræ, and when photographed presented the appearance of a gigantic fish-hook, carrying at its extremity a huge ball of light. This was but the precursor of a terrific commotion, for, after half an hour, it was found that a multitude of outbursts had taken place, so that the spot was completely hidden. This solar storm, which extended over billions of square miles, was not in the sun-spot, but high above it. Sometimes, when our atmospheric conditions are peculiar, a clear sky is converted into a cloudy one in the course of a few minutes, and the clouds pass away again in a few hours. The solar disturbance behaved in a similar fashion; in two hours after the disappearance of the spot it was again in view, unscathed by the tempest.

A solar tempest.

Duration and death.

A sun-spot usually lasts a few weeks; one is on record which was observed for eighteen months. The death of a sun-spot is a short process. The surrounding material rushes pell-mell into the cavity, and all is over.

Periodicity.

One of the most remarkable facts about sun-spots is their periodicity. At times the sun is almost free from them for a number of successive weeks. At other times they are to be counted by tens and even run up into the hundreds. When the first quarter of the nineteenth century had been rounded out, a persevering German, Schwabe by name, who was a magistrate in the town of Dessau, being possessed of a telescope and a large fund of patience, resolved that he would watch the sun day by day and count the number of spots. So it came to pass that the sun found Schwabe continually on the alert for over forty years.

An examination of his record books, after he had been at work nearly twenty years, revealed something quite unexpected. He quaintly said that, like Saul, he went out to seek his father's asses, and found a kingdom. His discovery was that there was a certain regularity about the number of spots visible. If spots were decidedly scarce in a given year, the next year the number was larger, the next year larger still, and so on, until the fifth or sixth year, when the number was greatest; during the ensuing year they were fewer, and after that their number diminished until it became a minimum again. Eleven years and a fraction elapse between one minimum and the next one. The period of eleven years is subject to irregular variations of a year or more.

The photosphere.

Considerable light is thrown on the nature of sun-spots by a knowledge of the medium in which they reside. It is called the photosphere, because it is the light-giving surface directly visible to us. It is analogous to the crust of the earth, but is far from being solid. The heat of the sun is so intense that any known solid would be quickly melted and vaporized, if dropped

Photosphere not solid.

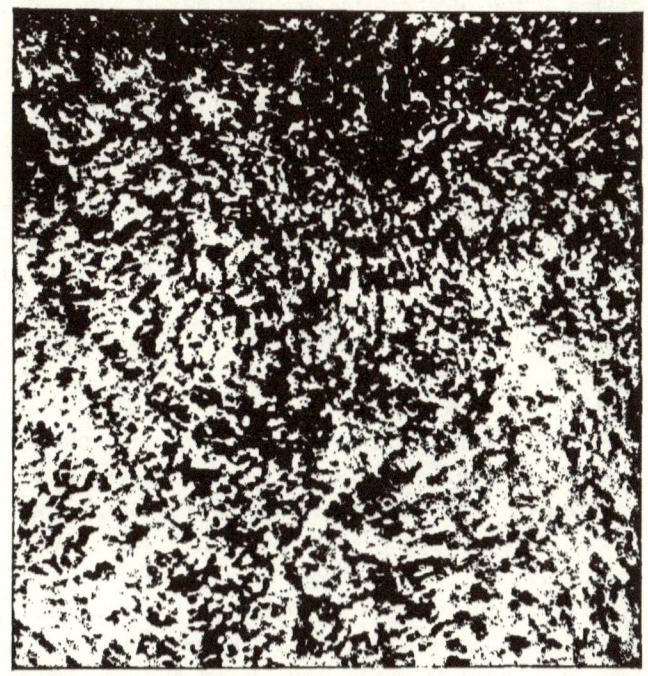

FIG. 93.—A PORTION OF THE PHOTOSPHERE.

into its fiery bosom. The photosphere is a sheet of luminous clouds, floating in an intensely heated gas, as terrestrial clouds float in our atmosphere. It is not of uniform brightness, but consists of a grayish background, plentifully besprinkled with comparatively small masses of greater brightness. If great things may be compared with insignificant ones, the photosphere may

A sheet of clouds.

be said to resemble a plate of rice-soup. The solar "rice-grains" average 500 miles in width, and are themselves composed of smaller "granules," compacted together.

Three quarters of the sun's light is derived from the rice-grains, which cover about one fifth of the entire surface. They are by some supposed to be the upper ends of ascending currents, rising from the intensely heated interior; the dark spaces between the spots, according to this view, mark the terminations of streams of matter which have been cooled somewhat and are descending. The penumbræ of sun-spots contain long-drawn-out rice-grains.

The solar interior. The interior of the sun is thought to be mainly gaseous, because of the intense heat which must prevail there. Near the center the gases may be changed to liquids because of the enormous pressure of the superincumbent fluids. A heat, the intensity of which no man has the temerity to estimate, strives to expand the gases imprisoned beneath the overlying photosphere.

From time to time outbursts occur at weak places in the photosphere; the pressure from below is temporarily relieved in the locality of the outbreak, and the photosphere in that region sinks a little, forming the shallow basin of a sun-spot. The uprushing gaseous matter, like a stream of water thrown by a fire engine, rises to a certain height, and falls back again upon the solar surface.

Origin of a spot. But why is the umbra of a spot so dark? Since the umbra is depressed below the general level, and is overlaid by a greater depth of cooler vapors than the adjacent regions, it looks darker than they. For the light from the umbra, coming up through the vapors, is partially absorbed; the umbra therefore looks dark in contrast with the surrounding portions of the photosphere. However, the darkest portion of a spot is brighter than a calcium light. When the force of the eruption has expended itself and hot gases are no longer thrown up to great heights, to be cooled and precipitated upon the solar surface, the spot ceases to exist. *A calcium light.*

Such, in brief outline, is the most reasonable theory concerning the nature of sun-spots. Many other theories have been put forth from time to time, but they all seem open to very serious, if not fatal, objections.

No satisfactory explanation has yet been advanced for the periodicity of spots, or for their absence from the polar regions. The paucity of our knowledge concerning these solar storms is not astonishing, in view of our ignorance about the whirlwinds and cyclones which stir up limited portions of our own atmosphere.

While the photosphere is depressed in the locality where a sun-spot lies, it is elevated in numerous other places. The elevations are called *faculæ*, and are specially numerous in the neighborhood of spots. The agitations to which the photosphere is subject seem to raise its outer surface in mountainous ridges and isolated crests like the waves of a choppy sea. These elevations of photospheric matter sometimes rise to a height of several hundred miles, and look much brighter than the surrounding regions, as there is less gas above their summits to absorb their light on its journey to our eyes. Recent photographs show that the fainter *faculæ* extend in a network over the entire photosphere, as shown in Fig. 94. The sensitive plates bear mute witness to the photospheric tumults. *Faculæ.*

When the moon causes a total eclipse of the sun by coming between that luminary and the earth, it covers up the dazzling photosphere, and permits less brilliant *The chromosphere.*

190   *A Study of the Sky.*

A scarlet envelope.

gases in its vicinity to be seen. The photosphere is thus found to be covered by a scarlet envelope called the chromosphere (color sphere). Its depth is 5,000

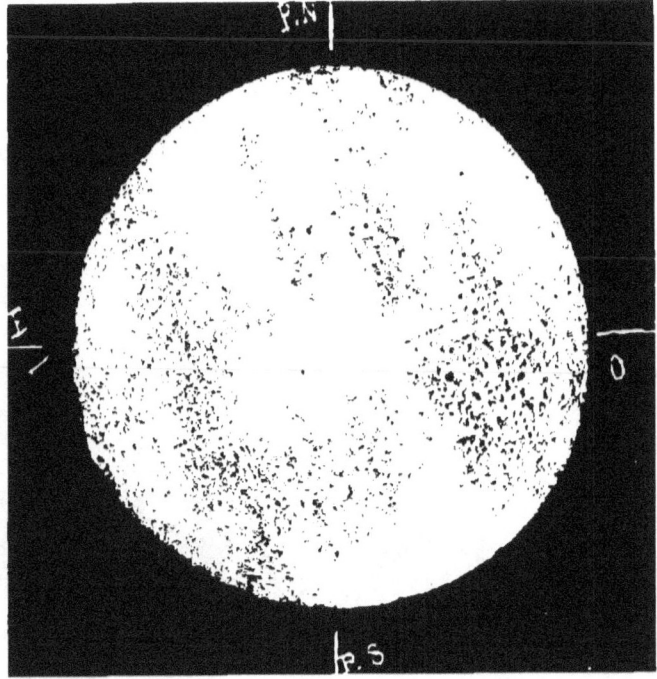

FIG. 94.—FACULÆ.

miles, and it, like the photosphere, is agitated by tremendous forces.

Prominences.

Rising from it are beautiful scarlet forms of various shapes, which have been named protuberances, or prominences. Some of them look like huge trees, with trunks thousands of miles in diameter, and tops spreading out to great distances. The top of such a prominence is often connected with the chromosphere by smaller trunks, so that the whole resembles a huge banyan tree. Some look like jets of fiery liquid, and remind one of the streams of water thrown by fire engines. A few resemble huge billows of flame. Sometimes cloud-like masses of chromospheric matter float above the chromosphere, having no apparent connection with it. One has been noticed which was 475,000 miles above the solar surface. Thanks to the spectroscope these beautiful objects may now be observed any clear day when the sun is shining in its full strength. Fiery jets.

The most interesting prominence ever seen was ob-

FIG. 95.—PROMINENCES.

served in the fall of 1871 by Prof. Chas. A. Young.* One day at noon he was looking at one of these objects, which was a long, low, red cloud, connected by four or five stems with the chromosphere. It was remarkable A remarkable prominence.

---

* Director of the observatory at Princeton, N. J.

only for its size, being about 100,000 miles long and half as broad. At 12:30 p. m. he was called away, having noticed nothing special, except that below one end of the prominence a small bright lump had developed on the solar surface. In twenty-five minutes he returned, but the prominence was gone. The small bright lump had apparently become a surging flame, rising to a height of 50,000 miles. The prominence had been blown into shreds by some tremendous explosion, and the débris of its wreck was rising 400

An explosion.

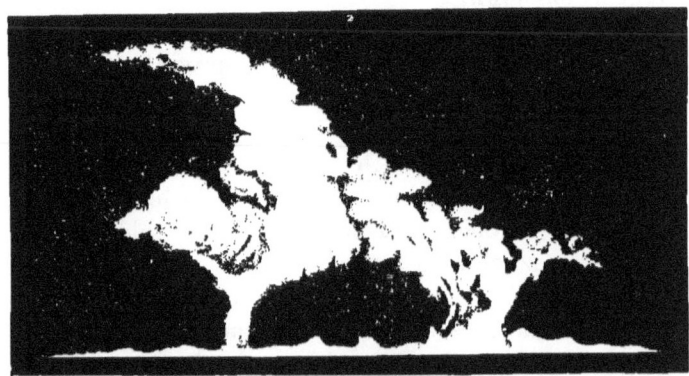

FIG. 96.—A QUIESCENT PROMINENCE.

times as swiftly as a rifle bullet flies. In ten minutes it had reached a height of 200,000 miles. At 1:15 p. m. only a few shreds of the prominence were visible.

Prominences are divided into two classes, the *quiescent* and the *eruptive*. The former are the cloud-like forms which have been already mentioned; they are composed mainly of hydrogen and helium.* The latter are fiery fountains which sometimes rush forth with veloci-

Two classes of prominences.

---

* When helium was named it was supposed to be found in the sun alone. But it was discovered along with argon, and has since been found in rare minerals. It also rises from particular springs in the Black Forest and elsewhere.

ties exceeding 300 miles a second. Since the velocity is never measured at the start, when it is greatest, before it has been diminished by the resistance of the gas through which it flies, and by the backward pull of the sun, which is nearly twenty-eight times as great as the pull at the earth's surface, its original value may be as great as 500 miles a second. Some of these eruptions hurl masses of heated gas so swiftly that the sun's attraction cannot hold them back, and they escape into space, are condensed into solid bodies, and fly away to regions unknown.

The lightning-girt cyclone strikes terror to men's hearts, as it plows through a town, uprooting the sturdiest trees, and tearing in pieces structures of solid masonry. But how insignificant it is compared with a jet of glowing gas, which travels further in a second than the cyclone does in an hour, and which, if it should strike the continent of North America, would turn its surface into a glowing cinder in a minute.   *The fury of an eruptive prominence.*

Such a storm, "coming down upon us from the north, would in thirty seconds after it had crossed the St. Lawrence be in the Gulf of Mexico, carrying with it the whole surface of the continent in a mass, not simply of ruin, but of glowing vapor, in which the vapors arising from the dissolution of the materials composing the cities of Boston, New York, and Chicago would be mixed in a single indistinguishable cloud." A terrestrial volcano may bury a city and cause the waters of an adjacent sea to boil. But many a solar eruption could fuse the earth into a misshapen lump.

What is found beyond the chromosphere? At the instant when a solar eclipse becomes total, and the moon hangs in mid-heaven, a black ball, fringed with the rosy prominences, it is surrounded by sheets of soft, pearly   *The corona.*

Fig. 97.—The Corona of July, 1878.

The Sun.

light, which form an aureole of surpassing beauty. The aureole has received the name "corona," as it is a crown of light upon the king of day. Its form varies. At times it is small in extent and roughly quadrangular in form. At other times it extends out in great streamers, as if the sun had wings. Streamers nearly 9,000,000 miles in length were observed in 1878 from the summit of Pike's Peak. Close to the sun the corona is bright, in marked contrast with the filmy streamers; the inner corona is composed of fine filaments, closely packed together, which a small telescope shows beautifully. They closely resemble the finest of human hair.

The corona is not to be considered as a solar atmosphere. Were that the case, it would decrease in density with a certain regularity the further it extended from the sun; it would also extend to about the same distance on all sides of the sun. When examined with the spectroscope it yields two different spectra. There is a faint continuous spectrum, which may come from sunlight reflected from the materials composing the corona, or may be caused directly by white-hot solid or liquid particles scattered through the corona. The other spectrum is a bright-line spectrum coming from a glowing gas. The most prominent line in it is not identical with the spectral line of any substance found on the earth; the name "coronium" has been proposed for the unknown sub-

Not a solar atmosphere.

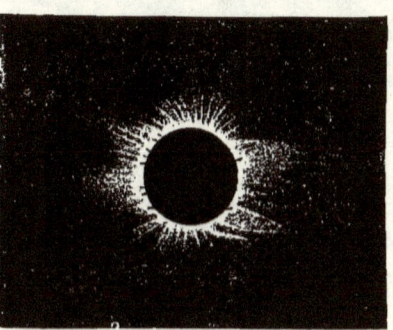

FIG. 98.—THE CORONA OF JANUARY, 1889.

The spectra.

stance which causes it. Other lines reveal the presence of hydrogen and helium.

Filaments.

Whence are these curious interlacing filaments of the inner corona, and the outstretched wings of the outer

FIG. 99.—THE CORONA OF APRIL, 1893.

Dark rifts.

corona? Why are dark rifts seen in certain places, as if the corona had been cleft by a gigantic cleaver from its outermost boundaries straight down to the solar surface? How are the materials composing the corona upheld against the gravitational pull of the sun? To these and other similar queries astronomers reply frankly that their knowledge is inadequate.

That the coronal matter is excessively rarefied in its higher regions is proven by the fact that several comets have passed through it without any perceptible change in their motion. This rarefied matter may be upheld by an electrical repulsion originating in the sun.

Rarefied matter.

The fine filaments are due, perchance, to streams of gas, which the sun is continually ejecting. Their curved forms and apparent interlacings are thought by Professor Schæberle* to be due to the sun's rotation.

Cause of the filaments.

Let us recapitulate what has been stated concerning the make-up of the sun:

I. The interior of the sun is supposed to be mainly gaseous, the expansive power of the gases being held in check by the grip of gravitation.

The sun's make-up.

II. As the film of a soap-bubble confines the air within it, so the photosphere, which is the home of the sun-spots, strives to confine the imprisoned gases. It is composed of vapors which have been somewhat condensed by their proximity to the cold of outer space.

III. Certain light gases which do not condense so readily as those of which the photosphere is composed form a shallow layer covering the photosphere. The layer is of a scarlet hue, nourishes the prominences, and is called the chromosphere.

IV. Beyond the chromosphere, and to a certain extent mingled with it, is the pearly corona, whose mysterious filaments and vast extension furnish food for much speculation.

Bright as full sunshine is, it may be compared with the light of a candle. Light screens are placed over

An experiment with sunlight.

---

* J. M. Schæberle, of the Lick Observatory.

the windows of a room so that it is completely darkened. A small hole is made in one screen and a lens inserted in it. By manipulating a mirror outside, a horizontal beam of sunlight is thrown through the lens, which spreads out the beam of light, so that it illuminates a large circle on the opposite wall. If the diameter of the circle is 200 times the diameter of the lens, the area of the circle is 200 x 200, or 40,000 times as great as that of the lens. Therefore the beam of sunlight, when thus spread out, has only $\frac{1}{40000}$ of its former intensity. A pencil is held in the enfeebled sunlight, close to the wall, so that its shadow is cast there.

A standard candle. A standard candle is lighted and held in such a direction from the pencil that the shadow which it casts on the wall is near the shadow cast by the sunlight. The candle is placed at such a distance from the pencil that the two shadows appear of equal intensity. In this manner the enfeebled sunlight is compared with the light of a standard candle.

The moon and an arc light. The intensity of the light of the full moon may be estimated in the same way; it is found that sunlight is 600,000 times as bright as the light of the full moon. An arc light approaches sunlight in intensity more nearly than any other artificial light. Yet if we view with a dark glass an arc light which is directly in line with the sun, it appears as a dark spot on the solar surface. It is about one third as intense as sunlight.

The sun's heat. The amount of heat which the sun sends to the earth is determined by allowing a beam of sunlight to shine upon a quantity of water, and measuring the rise of temperature thus caused. In this way it has been found that if the earth were entirely covered with a blanket of ice 165 feet thick, and the heat sent us by the sun were uniformly distributed over the ice, it would be melted in a year. An ice blanket of equal thickness, covering the sun, would be melted off in three minutes. If the solar heat was dependent upon the combustion of coal, a chunk of the best anthracite as big as the moon would have to be fed to the sun every forty-five minutes.

The earth receives but a small fraction of the light and heat radiated by the sun. Imagine a hollow sphere of crystal, the center of which is at the sun, the surface of the crystal shell being 93,000,000 miles from the sun. Let the earth be set, like an emerald, in the crystal shell. The amount of heat received by the shell in one second equals that emitted by the sun in the same time. Remove the emerald, leaving the hole in which it was set. Knowing the diameter of the earth, calculate the area cut out of the crystal shell by the hole; it is about 50,000,000 square miles. Also find the area of the surface of the crystal sphere. The earth's portion of it.
An emerald in a crystal sphere.

As the area of the hole is to the area of the sphere, so is the amount of heat received by the earth in one second to that radiated by the sun in the same time. Substituting the proper numbers in this proportion we find that the sun radiates 2,200,000,000 times as much light and heat as the earth receives.

If a javelin of ice forty-five miles thick were hurled directly at the sun by some Titanic arm, with the velocity of light, and the entire outpour of solar heat were concentrated upon it, the threatening weapon would be melted as fast as it advanced. A javelin of ice.

Not only do light and heat come from the sun, but electrical influences as well. In various parts of the world are magnetic observatories, where delicately suspended magnets swing gently to and fro in obedience to changes of magnetic force, and vibrate violently when thrilled by magnetic storms. In years when sun-spots Electrical influences.

are numerous, the magnetic needles are subject to numerous large oscillations, and the glimmering auroras coruscate in greatest splendor. When sun-spots are few the needles and auroras have a comparative rest.

There are several instances where solar disturbances were observed at times of derangement of the earth's magnetic condition.

A notable magnetic storm. On September 1, 1859, a remarkable magnetic storm was in progress. Earth currents played havoc with telegraphic communication, and were at times sufficiently strong to work lines without the aid of batteries. At a station in Norway the telegraphic apparatus was set on fire. In this country the electric fluid established private lines in the nervous systems of operators without going through the formality of getting a franchise. The pen of a recording telegraph in Boston was followed by a flame. The shimmering auroras of the north made forays into the tropics.

A chromospheric disturbance. Late in the forenoon of that day an English astronomer, who had devoted many years to a study of sun-spots, was engaged in observing a large group ; he was startled by the appearance of two brilliant flashes, which dazzled his eye, though it was protected by a dark glass. In five minutes they had faded away, having apparently traveled a distance of 35,000 miles along the sun's disc.

Professor Charles A. Young, when observing in the Rocky Mountains in 1872, saw, on the morning of August 3 at 8:45, 10:30, and 11:50, special disturbances of the chromosphere, caused by eruptive prominences of great brilliancy. At the same time the magnets in English observatories twitched. Professor Young's assistant, who was making magnetic observations, was obliged to desist, because the magnet swung clear off the scale.

In the face of these and other similar coincidences.

one can scarcely doubt that solar disturbances bear some relation to magnetic storms. The nature of the connection is not known, and some physicists doubt whether the electrical influences at work on the sun are of sufficient intensity to cause such violent terrestrial disturbances as are on record.

Various attempts have been made to determine the effect of sun-spots upon the weather. Meteorological records have been diligently compared with those of sun-spots to see whether years when spots are plentiful are hotter or cooler than those when spots are few. The results obtained by different investigators are so conflicting that the question cannot be decided. An exhaustive study of the amount of rainfall in different years has shown that fluctuations probably exist resembling those of sun-spots. But much further research has yet to be made before conclusions which command confidence can be reached. *The weather.*

If sun-spots had any marked effect upon meteorological conditions, the commerce of the world would be affected. Commercial crises have been investigated from this point of view, but nothing conclusive has been determined. As the years roll on, and both solar and meteorological phenomena are more diligently observed than in the past, some investigator may cause light to shine where darkness now reigns; but enough has already been done to show that commotions on the sun's surface have very little, if any, effect upon meteorological conditions on the earth.

The problem of the maintenance of the sun's heat is before us. During historic time the heat received from the earth has been practically constant in amount. In the main, plants grow to-day just where the same species flourished in the days of Pliny. Men needed fires to *The maintenance of the sun's heat.*

No observed changes.

warm their bodies in ancient times just as now, and were oppressed by the heat of midsummer as they are to-day. There is no trustworthy human record of any great migration of animals, which might be due to changes of temperature. The rocks, to be sure, tell of great changes in the remote past, epochs when high northern latitudes experienced tropical temperatures, and other epochs when the temperate zones were encased in ice. But no one knows whether these conditions were due to variations in the earth's distance from the sun or to changes in the intensity of the solar heat or to a combination of both causes. Amazing as is the daily outpour of solar heat, there is no evidence from observation that it has changed in quantity or quality since human history began.

Combustion.

The supply cannot be infinite; how, then, is the radiation maintained? Not by combustion, for in that case the solar fires would have burned out ages ago. If the sun were a mass of the best hard coal, burning in oxygen, it would be consumed in sixty centuries. If combustion is excluded from the list of possible causes, what shall we say about the impact of bodies from without?

The meteoric theory.

If a projectile from a rifled gun strikes the armor-plate of an ironclad, the shot is not only deformed but heated. If the earth should fall to the sun from its present distance, as much heat would be developed by the impact as the sun radiates in ninety-five years. The fall of giant Jupiter would cause an accession of heat equal to the amount now given off in over 30,000 years. Why may it not be that meteoric bodies fall upon it in sufficient numbers to keep up the supply of heat? We reply that if there were any such aggregation of meteors in the sun's vicinity it ought to have a marked effect upon the motion of some comets which come near the sun, and would encounter it. Doubtless the sun receives some heat from such a source as this, but only a fraction of its heat can be thus accounted for.

The theory generally accepted is called the contraction theory. When a body falls from any elevation to the earth's surface, heat is produced when it strikes. If the same body be attached to a rope and made to turn a machine with badly oiled bearings, at least a portion of the energy of the descending body is converted into heat. In the first case energy is converted into heat suddenly, at the instant when the body strikes; in the second case a portion of the energy of the descending weight is being gradually converted into heat.

<small>The contraction theory.</small>

Without going more deeply into details we may say that if the sun be slowly contracting in size, so that the particles of matter which compose it are falling toward the center, heat is being produced by this contraction.

If the sun's diameter diminishes five feet a week the total radiation of the sun is explained. Such a shrinkage is so slight that it would not be certainly detected by our present means of astronomical measurement in 10,000 years. The contraction theory is considered the most reasonable which has yet been advanced.

If all the heat which the sun gives out comes from its contraction, and if the amount of heat radiated yearly is practically constant from age to age, it is possible to reason backward to a time when the sun was inconceivably vast, and to reason forward to a time when it will probably cease to give sufficient heat to maintain human life on the earth. Upon these hypotheses the sun would consume 18,000,000 years in radiating away the heat which would be developed by its contraction from a size inconceivably great to its present dimensions. Five mil-

<small>The sun's past and future.</small>

lion years hence it will, upon this hypothesis, have only half its present diameter, and the matter composing it will be crowded into one eighth the space now occupied.

Contraction. The compression will probably turn most of it into a liquid or solid form. Further contraction being then very difficult, the temperature of the sun will probably fall so rapidly that its function as a life-giver to the earth will cease before another 5,000,000 years have rolled away.

Our reasoning has been based upon unverifiable hypotheses and the conclusions may be far astray. They simply represent the best guessing that scientists can make with reference to the past and future of the sun. There is at any rate no reason for alarm at present.

Mark Twain has well satirized scientific speculations which involve millions of years in the following passage :

Now, if I wanted to be one of those ponderous scientific people, and "let on" to prove what had occurred in the remote past by what had occurred in a given time in the recent past, or what will occur in the far future by what has occurred in late years, what an opportunity is here ! Geology never had such a chance, nor such exact data to argue from ! Nor "development of species," either ! Glacial periods are great things, but they are vague, vague. Please observe : In the space of 176 years the Lower Mississippi has shortened itself 242 miles. That is an average of a trifle over one and one third miles per year. Therefore, any calm person, who is not blind or idiotic, can see that in the old Oölitic Silurian period, just a million years ago next November, the Lower Mississippi was upwards of 1,300,000 miles long, and stuck out over the Gulf of Mexico like a fishing rod, and by the same token any person can see that 742 years from now the Lower Mississippi will be only a mile and three quarters long, and Cairo and New Orleans will have joined their streets together, and be plodding comfortably along under a single mayor and a mutual board of aldermen. There is something fascinating in science. One gets such wholesome results of conjecture out of such a trifling investment of fact.

Amusing speculations.

CHAPTER XII.

THE MOON AND ECLIPSES.

> " That orbed maiden, with white fire laden,
> Whom mortals call the moon,
> Glides glimmering o'er my fleece-like floor,
> By the midnight breezes strewn."
> —*Shelley.*

THOSE who speculate about the origin of celestial bodies have a fine field of thought in connection with the moon. It is an undoubted fact that the moon raises tides in our oceans. The wash of the tides against continents and islands tends to retard the rotation of the earth by a trifling amount. If this retardation is not offset by other causes, as, for instance, a shrinking of the earth from its progressive cooling, the length of the day must be gradually increasing. The increase must be very slow, because it has not yet been brought to light by observation. The action of the moon upon the earth is accompanied by a reaction of the earth, which expresses itself in allowing the moon gradually to move farther and farther away. _{Tides retard the earth's rotation.}

Reversing the process, we look back through geologic ages to a time when the earth whirled much faster than at present, and the moon was close to its surface, both bodies being hotter than now. How did these bodies come to be in such close companionship? Does it not seem probable that they were originally one? A grindstone which rotates too rapidly bursts asunder. Is it not then entirely possible that when a mass of heated _{Looking backward.}

matter in a fluid state rotates rapidly, a piece of it may fly off?

Looking forward.

If we have hit upon a correct theory of the moon's origin, let us follow up the clue. The moon has disengaged itself from the earth, but is still held in check by the attraction of gravity, so that it is describing an orbit about the earth. Both bodies are in a fluid condition and rotating. They are so close together that the attraction of each raises large tides on the other. The tide on the earth checks the swiftness of its spinning. If the moon is rotating swiftly its tides put a brake upon it. If, on the other hand, it is rotating very slowly, the friction of the tides quickens its rotation.

As previously mentioned, one result of this tidal action is that the two bodies separate. They grow cooler and more rigid; the powerful tides raised upon the moon by the earth, keeping it continually egg-shaped, have had such an effect upon the original rotation that the moon has now solidified as a slightly elongated body, the longest axis of which points toward the earth. So it has come to pass that the moon keeps the same face turned toward the earth.

The moon's rotation.

If this be true, does it rotate at all? Certainly; while it is making one revolution about the earth it also makes one complete rotation on its axis. This may be illustrated very simply.

In the center of a circle one hundred yards in diameter a man is standing; he watches a boy who runs at a uniform rate around the circle; the boy keeps the left side of his head continually toward the man. At one instant the boy is facing the north; in a few seconds he has run one fourth of the way around the circle, and faces westward; in a few seconds more he faces southward, then eastward, and finally northward again, when he has completed the circuit. Since the boy has faced all points of the compass successively he must have turned once around; but the man has seen only half of his head.

A complete rotation.

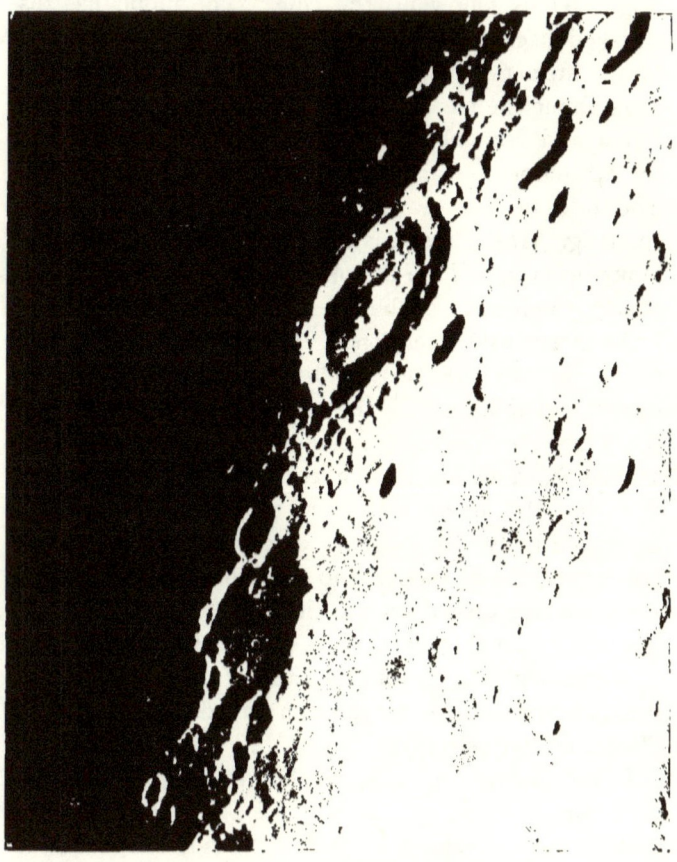

FIG. 100.—LUNAR FORMATIONS.

If the boy had slackened the speed of his running at any time, *but kept on turning* at the same rate as before, the man would have seen a little more of his face in

Why we see more than half the moon.

consequence. If the boy had quickened his pace at any time without changing the rate of his turning, the man would have gotten a view of a little more of the back of his head.

<small>Various reasons.</small>

The moon is not moving in a circle around the earth, but in an ellipse; when it is nearest to us it moves more swiftly than when further away. But it rotates on its axis with a constant speed: thus we are enabled to see a little more than half of its entire surface. Furthermore the moon does not stand upright; that is, its axis is oblique to the plane of its orbit. Consequently we sometimes see beyond its north pole, and sometimes beyond the south pole. Also, as the earth turns, it carries the observer along and changes his point of view, so that he can see a trifle more of the moon than otherwise. Fifty-nine per cent of the moon's entire surface is thus presented to our view. The visible area is slightly more than double that of Europe.

<small>Some data.</small>

The moon's diameter is 2,163 miles, and its average distance from us is 238,840 miles. It is $\frac{3}{11}$ as large as the earth, but only $\frac{1}{80}$ as heavy.

<small>The moon's phases.</small>

The moon's apparent changes of form result from its revolution around the earth, which is accomplished in $27\frac{1}{3}$ days. If it is to-day nearly on a line between the earth and the sun, it will not be in line again at the expiration of this period of time. For the earth has moved on meanwhile and altered the direction of the line. Thus it comes to pass that $29\frac{1}{2}$ days elapse before the moon crosses the line again.

Why then is not the sun hidden from view once every $29\frac{1}{2}$ days by the interposition of the moon's dark mass? The moon's orbit is tilted in such a way that the moon usually passes apparently above or below the sun, instead of in front of him. When the moon is nearly in line between the sun and us, the sun lights up that half of it which is turned away from us, and the dark side is toward us. Besides this, the sun blinds our eyes, so that we can see nothing in his immediate neighborhood unless it be intensely bright. The moon is "new."

But in a couple of days our vision will be charmed by the sight of the young moon hanging low in the west in the evening twilight. Its position with reference to the sun has so changed that we can see a part of its bright hemisphere, as a graceful crescent.

Most of the dark hemisphere of the moon is also visible. The earth plays the part of a mirror, and reflects back a portion of the sunlight which it receives. Some of this reflected sunlight lights up the dark side of the moon, so that we can see it. *Earth shine.*

On the next night the moon is east of its former position, and sets later; its crescent is larger. A week after new moon comes the phase of first quarter, when the moon is a bright semicircle off in the south at sunset. On that evening and the three following its telescopic appearance is the most interesting. *First quarter.*

From night to night the illuminated disc grows larger, as the moon moves eastward, till it becomes a complete circle, and the moon is full. It then rises about sunset and sets about sunrise. *Full moon.*

During the next week the moon wanes and shrinks to a semicircle. One may then see it in the south at sunrise, and in the southwest during the forenoon; it is at the last quarter. The half moon changes to a diminishing crescent, and is lost in the sun's rays, as it becomes new again. *Last quarter.*

When the moon is full, large dark brown areas are seen upon its face with the naked eye. According to Alexander von Humboldt the people of Asia Minor see *The face of the full moon.*

210   *A Study of the Sky.*

in these markings a resemblance to terrestrial seas and continents, and say that the moon exhibits a reflection of the earth as though it were a mirror. In the minds of many a human figure is outlined ; it has been super-

Judas Iscariot. stitiously asserted that it is the figure of Judas Iscariot, whose sin has led to his being thus pilloried before the eyes of mankind for all generations. The casual onlooker perceives a human face, the eyes, nose, and mouth being fairly conspicuous. Even children notice it.

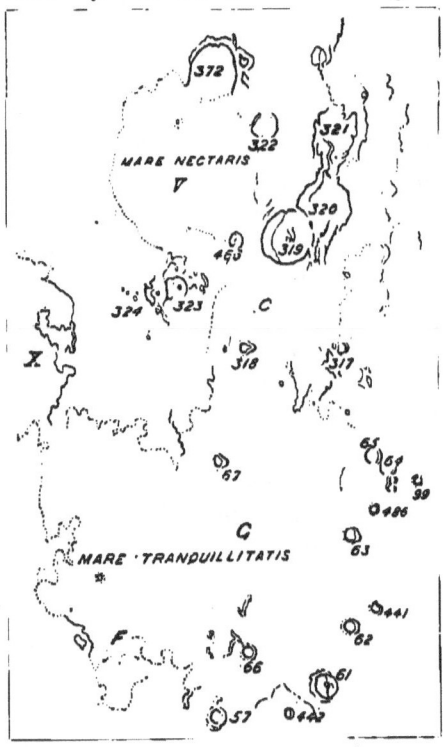

FIG. 101.—LUNAR PLAINS, CALLED SEAS.

An opera-glass shows that the bright portions of the lunar surface are covered with rugged formations, while the dark portions are smooth.

The plains. When Galileo's telescope revealed these smooth regions they were supposed to be seas, which soon received such names as the Sea of Serenity, the Ocean of Tempests, and the Lake of Death. More powerful instruments show minute pits sunken all over the supposed seas ; they are therefore vast plains.

The Moon and Eclipses.

Great hopes were originally entertained that with increase of telescopic power would come evidences that the moon was inhabited by intelligences, whose works would become manifest. It is doubtful whether any telescope that has already been constructed, or ever will be, can show the moon's surface better than it would be seen with the unassisted eye at a distance of 200 miles. A structure as large as the Liberal Arts Building at the World's Fair would be readily made out, if of a different color from the soil on which it was built. No details of the architecture could be distinguished, and one would never know whether it was a formation of nature or a structure erected by intelligent beings. Herschel once used a magnifying power of 7,000 diameters, which would theoretically bring the moon within thirty-five miles, but he could not see as well as if he had used a much lower amplification, because of ever-present atmospheric disturbances. *Increase of optical power.*

Despite this atmospheric handicap a vast amount of lunar detail has been studied out, so that the topography of the side of our satellite which is turned toward us is much better known than that of vast areas of the earth's surface. *Accuracy of lunar maps.*

For the geographical explorer has to press his way through deadly swamps, and across torrid deserts, scorched to the marrow by the sun, smitten by nameless fevers, tormented by insects, menaced by wild beasts, and ambushed by savages. The astronomer, on the other hand, sits in the seclusion of his observatory, in the quiet of a beautiful evening, making his measurements with inoffensive spider-webs, and recording them with a harmless pencil.

The chief classes of lunar formations are craters, mountain ranges, isolated peaks, plains, rays, clefts, and rills. *A summary.*

A drop of water falling from the eaves of a house upon soft moist earth below makes a depression surrounded by a little wall of mud; this resembles a lunar crater.

The crater Copernicus.

One of the finest, situated not far from the center of the full moon, is named Copernicus (Fig. 102); it is fifty-six miles in diameter. To compare Vesuvius with it is to compare a pin-prick with a silver half dollar. In the center of the ring lies a rugged hill half a mile high, lifting its six heads up into the sunlight. The surrounding ring is beautifully terraced, as if there had been successive elevations and subsidences of lava in ages past. The summit of the ridge is a narrow ring, the top of which is over two miles above the floor of the crater. The surrounding region is thickly dotted with minute craterlets. When the sun rises upon this magnificent crater the highest parts of the ring catch the sunbeams and outline the majestic circle. Within all is dark; the sun rises higher and its light begins to creep down the inner wall of the further side of the crater. Yet all is dark within, and the central hill is invisible. Presently the six central peaks emerge one by one from the surrounding darkness, and one can dimly descry the floor of the crater still enveloped in shadow, but rendered faintly visible by the light reflected from the illuminated portion of the inner wall. Hours wear away, and the interior is bathed in sunshine, except where short shadows hug a portion of the crater wall and nestle at the foot of the central hill.

Other craters.

A few of the largest craters are over one hundred miles in diameter. In some cases the floors of craters are depressed below the general level of the surface; in other cases the floors are elevated. It may be quite smooth, or it may be pitted with tiny craters and ornamented with rugged hills. The walls may be precipitous in the extreme, or magnificently terraced and cut

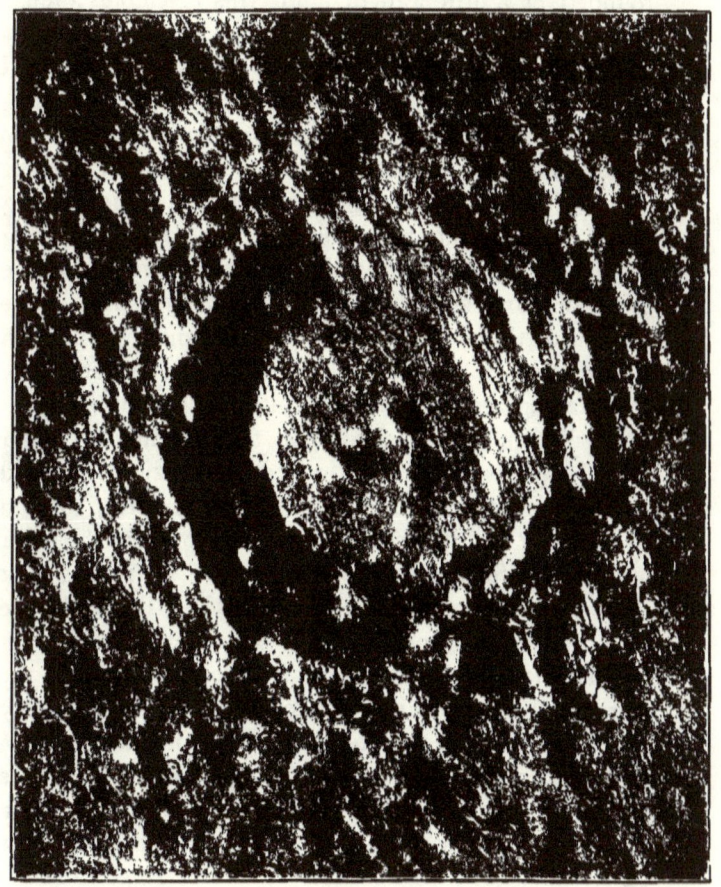

Fig. 102.—Copernicus.

up by yawning ravines. A man standing in the center of Schickard could not see the rampart surrounding him, though it is over 10,000 feet high; so rapidly does

Schickard.

the moon's surface curve, because of its small diameter, that the top of the rampart would be below the man's horizon. One of the peaks within Clavius rises nearly five miles above the bottom of one of the craterlets at its foot. Sunlight never reaches the bottoms of some of the pits near the moon's poles.

The Apennines. The finest mountain range is the Apennines (Fig. 103). It is only 450 miles long, but the summits of its peaks rise to altitudes which rival those of the Andes. The loftiest peak lifts its head to the proud height of 18,500 feet. On one side the entire range rises gradually from the plain; on the other side it descends precipitously to the border of a "sea." The shadows cast by some of these peaks when the sun shines upon them are over 75 miles in length. The heights of mountains and of crater-rims are found by measuring the lengths of their shadows.

Pico. Isolated mountains are rather rare. One of the finest is named Pico. Like the spire of some buried cathedral it rises abruptly from a level plane to a height of a mile and a half. A most imposing spectacle it would be to a man standing near its base.

The plains. The great lunar plains, which have already been partially described, and which look quite smooth when viewed with a small telescope, lose their unruffled appearance when examined with a high magnifying power. The surface is covered with low ridges, and minute pits abound.

Rays. Several of the larger craters are surrounded by fine systems of diverging rays, which are distinct at full moon. Tycho, a noble crater, the wall of which is 17,000 feet high and fifty-four miles in diameter, is the center of the most conspicuous system of rays to be seen on the moon. It looks like the hub of a wagon wheel, from which the spokes radiate in all directions. The rays are whiter than the general surface and are often hundreds of miles in length.

Clefts are cracks which appear in various regions. They are half a mile or so in width, and run in some instances hundreds of miles across plains and through craters, never halting at any obstacle. They are of unknown depth. Such a chasm upon the earth would strike terror to the heart of a traveler who found it lying across his path. *Clefts.*

Rills resemble the beds of ancient water courses; they are, however, small, and not likely to catch the eye of the casual gazer. *Rills.*

A body which was once hot and has cooled may well exhibit most of the peculiar formations which have just been described. Most of them have counterparts upon the earth. The neighborhood of the terrestrial crater Vesuvius is similar in appearance to many a portion of the lunar landscape. The craters cannot be closely likened to terrestrial volcanoes. The latter have small throats, and are surrounded by outpourings of lava. The former frequently embrace hundreds and even thousands of square miles within their walls, and do not appear to have deluged the surrounding country with the products of fiery outbreaks. The systems of rays can scarcely be due to overflows of lava. For in that case a ray would spread out, the further it got from the parent crater; it would also be deflected when it encountered another crater, and would be either heaped up, or would flow around it. But the rays are unchanged in width as they take their way across mountains and through craters. *Origin of the formations.*

The general appearance of the lunar crust may be reproduced on a small scale by pouring the tap-cinder *Tap-cinder.*

FIG. 103.—THE APENNINES.

from a smelting furnace into a stout receptacle. At first a thin crust forms where the mass is exposed to the cooling action of the air. The crust is broken open in various spots by the action of the heated fluid. Some of the molten matter exudes through the holes ; a little ring is built up, or a cone-like structure. The contracting material within leaves the crust without adequate support and it cracks in weak places. Thus the work of solidification proceeds, and the final appearance of the crust bears a resemblance to the lunar surface.

The question of changes in lunar topography during the past hundred years is a mooted one. Certain it is that there have been no marked changes. But there may have been minor ones, such as the falling of a portion of the wall of a crater, or the crumbling of some pinnacle. There is no trustworthy evidence of any volcanic outburst, great or small. Such an eruption as that at Krakatoa, which in 1883 gave rise to the red glows which persisted for many months, could not have escaped the scrutiny of astronomers. Craters change their appearance greatly as the sun rises upon them and causes their shadows to shift; hence very careful and prolonged study, comparing the old maps with present appearances, is needed to establish any claim of change. Now that photography has entered the field, and the sensitive plates make a record which is free from bias, it may be possible in the future to attain a good degree of certainty in this matter. *Changes.*

When the moon parted company with the earth, ages ago, it is probable that both masses were enwrapped in a gaseous envelope. The lion's share of this atmosphere naturally fell to the earth, because of its superior attractive power. The moon may have started away with quite a scanty covering of air. It is natural then to *The lunar atmosphere.*

suppose that the moon's atmosphere is now very rare. So clearly are the lunar mountains defined, so black are their shadows, so sharp is the dividing line between the illuminated and unilluminated portions of the moon, that there cannot be a dense envelope of air, which behaves as ours does, scattering the sunlight in every direction from the motes which float about in it, and causing twilight as the sun rises or sets. But a more delicate test is at hand.

A star is hidden. As the moon performs its monthly journey around the sky it passes between us and countless stars which seem to bestrew its pathway, but are really far beyond it in the depths of space. So well is the moon's rate of travel known that astronomers can predict accurately the time when it will hide any particular star from view. If there were a lunar atmosphere a star's radiance would be dimmed just before it disappeared; it would also change color as the sun does at sunset, when it shines through a greater thickness of air than at noon.

Effect of refraction. The mention of sunset brings to mind the fact that the air has a refractive power and bends rays of light which pass through it. On this account we see the sun after it is really below the astronomical horizon, and it appears again the next morning before it would, were there no air to bend its rays out of a straight course.

A lunar atmosphere would therefore bend the rays of light from a star, and delay the time of its disappearance just as our air delays the time of sunset. It would also cause the star to reappear before it would otherwise. Thousands of occultations of stars by the moon have been accurately observed. The stars disappear and reappear on time.

A vacuum. The vacuum at the lunar surface is believed to be as complete as under the exhausted receiver of an air-pump.

What has become of the original aërial endowment which the moon probably possessed? Several theories have been given to explain its disappearance. The best of these is based upon observations on terrestrial rocks; a rock which is heated expels gases which it had previously absorbed; when cooling, it has the power to take them up again. It may be that the lunar atmosphere entered into chemical combination with the cooling rocks, and our satellite was thus stripped of its aërial vesture.

Where has the air gone?

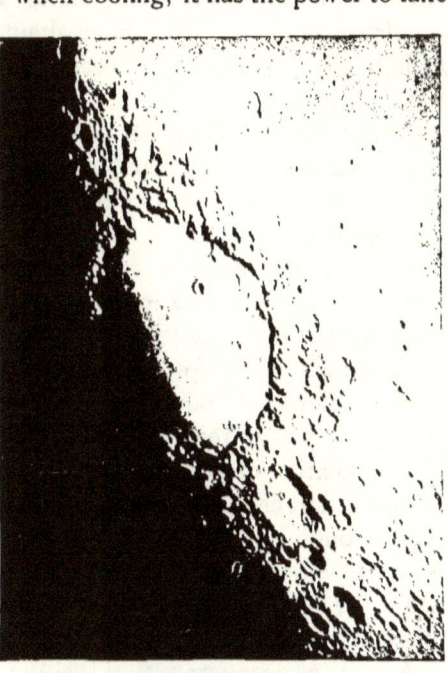

FIG. 104.—THE MARE CRISIUM.

No water is directly revealed by telescopic search; if it existed the sun would evaporate it, and a slight lunar atmosphere, composed of water vapor, would be formed. Since observation has pronounced against the existence of a lunar atmosphere of appreciable density, it has also negatived the existence of water upon the moon's surface. Small bodies of ice may be there undetected, but there is no cogent reason for believing in their existence. Any water which the moon possessed originally may have

Water.

been taken up by the rocks as they crystallized, or may have sunk into cavernous depths in the interior.

A hot-bed.

The absence of air has a marked effect upon the temperature at the moon's surface. The gardener's hot-bed illustrates this matter. The sunlight pours through the glass cover of the bed and warms the soil within. The soil in turn strives to radiate off the heat which it has received, but the glass is a barrier to the returning heat. For heat from an intensely heated body passes through glass quite readily, while heat from a body at a low temperature, like the earth, finds difficulty in passing through glass. Therefore the gardener's bed becomes considerably warmer than the exposed ground round about it.

Air as a blanket.

In the same way our atmosphere keeps in the heat which the sunbeams have brought to the earth's surface; the earth is kept warm by its blanket of air. For this reason the mean temperature on the top of a high mountain is much lower than that at its foot; the top is covered by a scantier blanket of air than the foot. Aëronauts ascending to great heights experience bitter cold. Twenty miles above the earth's surface the temperature must be appallingly low. Were the atmosphere to be taken away, the sun would beat upon us more hotly than at present, but the beneficent heat would be quickly radiated off, and eternal winter would reign.

The temperature.

Many attempts have been made to determine the temperature of the moon's surface by measurement of the heat which it sends to us. The moon's rays, condensed at the focus of a large mirror, fall upon a delicate instrument for measuring changes of temperature. Though the results of various experiments differ, it is considered quite certain that the warmest portions of the lunar surface never rise above the temperature of freezing water. When some point has been in darkness for a week or more, the lunar nights being over two weeks in length, its temperature can scarcely be above —200° Fahrenheit. It has been estimated that the sun sends to the earth as much heat in a minute as the full moon would give could it shine upon us for three years without change of phase.

The moon is a land of death, the sepulcher of any life which may once have existed upon it. If an astronomer could establish his telescope upon the rim of some great crater during a lunar night, and could endure the rigor of the cold, as well as the absence of air, what glories would rivet his astonished vision! The sky, blacker than the deepest velvet, is inlaid with jewels unmatched by the gleam of a Koh-i-noor, or the splendid glow of the precious ruby. Each of the familiar constellations shines forth with a brilliancy before unknown. Not a star scintillates; all shine serene, as though some high behest were upon them. A crowd of smaller stars, never before revealed to the unaided eye, besprinkle the sable folds of the garment of night. The Milky Way enchants the beholder by its splendor. Surely the chariot of the Almighty has been driven along it. *A visit to the moon.*

Amid this unchanging calm there is one magnificent panorama. Yonder glows a mighty orb, which moves with majestic pomp amid the hosts of heaven; star after star is quenched before it, and reappears in its wake. Steadily the sunlight creeps over its surface, changing it from a crescent to a full-orbed circle. While this change is taking place what a panorama rolls before the astronomer's eye, and is eagerly viewed with his telescope! Great masses of white cloud, tinged with golden orange, vast expanses of ocean, dull continents relieved here and there by a dash of color, snowy masses at the *The earth is a panorama.*

poles—all these roll before him, now glowing in the light, now lost in the darkness.

The day comes. But what is the soft radiance which appears yonder upon the horizon? Higher and higher it rises; more and more is the lunar landscape lighted up. The ghostly shapes of distant mountains are dimly outlined. Long, black fingers stretch themselves across the plains; thousands of dark pits dot the ashen landscape. The sun's long coronal streamers are heralding the dawn. Thoughtlessly he watches for the twilight, and expects to see the Milky Way veil its glories before the coming of the king of day; but it shines on, with undiminished splendor. Behind him, on the opposite side of the crater, towers a precipitous pinnacle. Its rugged summit catches a ray of direct sunlight and is bathed in its effulgence. Yonder glows another peak and still another against the jet black sky. No rosy tints melt into amber, and suffuse the heavens. No lark soars to greet the rising sun, or to pour out his soul in ecstatic song. The silver-rimmed crater, standing on the dividing line between the world of light and the world of darkness, is filled with the shadow of its own wall. Deep down in its rugged depths are descried the heads of its central mountain, which are soon to be kissed by the sunlight. No laughing brook leaps down the mountain side; no morning zephyr plays among the rugged battlements; no flower turns its charming face toward the sun.

The day declines. The day wears on; the somber shadows move over the desolate wilds. The rocky sentinels keep their grim and silent watch over the dead planet. Stray meteors dash against the beetling crags, or bury themselves in the plains beneath. The life-giving sunbeams find no life responsive to their subtle touch. The shadows turn and lengthen; the glowing sun sinks beneath the horizon, and the dread chill of the long lunar night comes on.

The moon is of service to man in many ways. Its light relieves the darkness of the night, and this adds to his safety and happiness. As it moves across the face of the sky it becomes a timekeeper by which the mariner may determine his longitude, in case he is on a long voyage and fears that the error of his chronometer

The moon's worth to man.

The mariner.

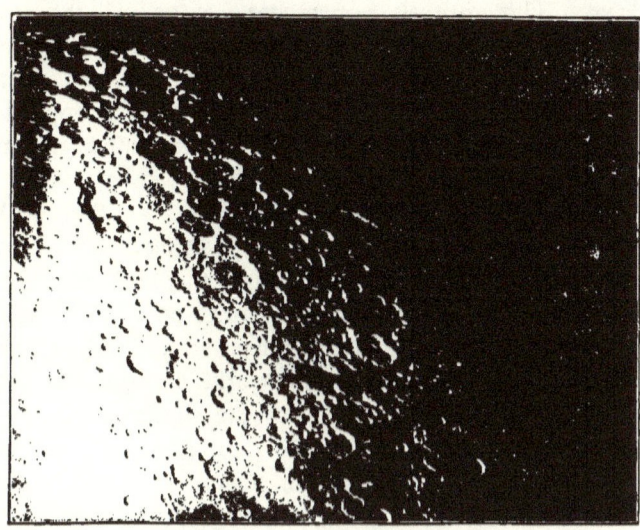

FIG. 105.—A RUGGED REGION NEAR TYCHO.

is not known accurately. For the "Nautical Almanac" gives the distance of the moon from certain bright stars at given Greenwich times, each day of the year. The mariner measures one or more of these distances with a sextant, and thus determines the true Greenwich time.

The moon is the chief agent in the production of the tides, which at their flood lift ships over harbor bars

The tides.

and bear them to the wharves. Without the tides the city of Liverpool would lose its commerce. Its harbor communicates with the ocean by a narrow neck, through which 600 million tons of water rush out every six hours during the ebb of the tide, scouring the channel, and carrying off the silt and débris which would otherwise choke it.

Chronology.

Eclipses either of the sun or the moon, which occurred at the times of notable events, have given much assistance to historians in threading the mazes of ancient chronology. The lunar eclipse of March 13 in the year 3 B. C. took place at the death of Herod, and thus serves to determine the date of the birth of Christ. Another eclipse has been employed to rectify the first year of the reign of Cyrus of Babylon.

The ruse of Columbus.

Columbus made use of the lunar eclipse of March 1, 1504, to obtain much-needed supplies for his men. The inhabitants of Jamaica refused to give them to him, and he threatened to take away the moon's light should they persist in their determination. When the eclipse came on, the savages were struck with terror and hastened to supply his wants.

Superstitions.

There have been many superstitions connected with the moon, some of which flourish even to-day in rural communities. Their absurdity is their sufficient refutation.

It has been said that the moon produces blindness by shining upon a sleeper's eyes ; that it fixes the hour of death, which occurs at the change of tide ; that cucumbers, radishes, and turnips increase at full moon ; that onions thrive best after the moon has passed its full ; that herbs gathered before full moon are of greatest efficacy ; that vines trimmed at night when the moon is in the sign of the Lion are safe from field mice and other pests ; that potatoes are best planted at a certain time of the moon ; that shingles will curl up if not laid at the right phase of the moon, etc., etc.

Especially persistent are those ideas which connect the moon with the weather. A change of lunar phase is said to be connected with a change of weather ; since the moon changes its phase every week, every change of the weather must occur within four days of a change of phase. People who watch for such changes are willing to wait more than four days, if necessary, for the weather to accommodate itself to the moon. "Wet" and "dry" moons are carefully watched for by farmers throughout the country. When the crescent moon hangs low in the west soon after sunset, if a line joining the two cusps is nearly horizontal, so that the moon can apparently hold water, it is a "dry moon." If the line joining the cusps be tipped up at a very marked angle, so that the moon's crescent cannot hold water, the moon is called "wet." The position of the cusps of the moon can be predicted for thousands of years to come, but no one can foretell the weather a week ahead. The moon and the weather.

The full moon is said to clear away clouds ; it is hard to see how a body which sends us so minute a quantity of heat can have any appreciable effect upon the clouds. Perhaps by showing their thinness, and making plain the rifts which exist in them, the moon gets the credit of thinning them. Clouds cleared away.

That small variations in the position of the magnetic needle take place, as the moon approaches and recedes, in pursuing its elliptical orbit, is admitted. Magnetic effects.

ECLIPSES.

Eclipses of the moon occur when it plunges into the shadow of the earth. If the sun were of the same size The earth's shadow.

as the earth, the shadow of the latter would be a cylinder, about 8,000 miles in diameter, stretching out to an infinite distance. But as the sun is much larger than the earth, the shadow is tapering. Its length varies somewhat, since the earth is sometimes farther away from the sun than at others. Its average length is 857,000 miles, and its average thickness, at the point where the moon encounters it, is 5,700 miles. The moon often merely dips a little way into the shadow, and suffers only a partial eclipse. Being only 2,163 miles in diameter, it is readily totally eclipsed, and may remain immersed in the shadow for two hours.

A lunar eclipse. Since the moon moves eastward, its eastern edge, which is at the left hand as one faces it, strikes the shadow first; a circular notch then seems to be eaten out of the moon's edge, much as if it were an apple out of which a boy had taken a bite. The notch increases till the lunar disc is overspread with shadow, but the moon does not usually disappear. The solid body of the earth casts a shadow sufficiently dense to blot the moon out as completely as if it were annihilated, but the transparent coating of air which the earth carries assists the moon in its otherwise gloomy experience. Many rays of sunlight pierce this transparent medium, are bent by it out of their otherwise straight course, and fall upon the moon, illuminating it rather dimly because they have been enfeebled by passing through our atmosphere. They have also acquired the sunset tinge, and give the moon a coppery-red hue. If clouds stop these rays, the moon vanishes entirely; if, on the other hand, the portion of the atmosphere traversed by them is exceptionally free from moisture, the lunar disc is lighted up so strongly that persons unaware of the eclipse simply wonder why the moon is not as bright as usual. After a

Fig. 109.—Moon's Shadow on the Earth, as seen from the Moon.

while the eastern edge of the moon emerges into sunlight and the shadow is gradually left behind.

The moon's shadow. Since the moon's diameter is a little more than one fourth that of the earth, and their distances from the sun are nearly equal, the moon's shadow is somewhat more than one fourth as long as the earth's. Its length varies because of changes in the moon's distance from the sun, caused chiefly by the varying distances of the earth, which carries the moon along with it. When the moon is between the other two bodies, its shadow is at times too short to reach the earth; at other times it is long enough and makes a small dark spot on the earth's surface. Since the moon is continually in motion, the shadow travels eastward over the earth; the earth is turning in the same direction. If the shadow is now falling on the city of New York, there is a race between the city and the shadow; but the latter is the swifter and passes out upon the Atlantic. A shot from a rifled gun would keep it company for a brief space of time. It is not often more than 150 miles in diameter, and cuts a pretty small swath on the earth's surface.

A solar eclipse. Any one who establishes himself within the limits of the swath may see the sun totally eclipsed, if the sky be clear, during the time occupied by the shadow in passing over him. An observer near the path of the shadow may see the sun partially eclipsed. On rare occasions there is an interrupted view of the corona and prominences for six or eight minutes before the brilliant photosphere peeps out at one edge of the retreating moon, and floods the landscape with light. Ordinarily the sun is entirely covered for only two or three minutes.

A total solar eclipse is one of the most awe-inspiring phenomena of nature. The approach of the moon, which quietly eats its way into the solar disc, is not noticed by those who are uninformed. For the sunlight is so piercing that no special diminution of it is perceived until the eclipse is well advanced. At last the light begins to pale, as though a haze were forming over the sun. One who takes a quick upward glance, or employs a dark glass, sees that the sun is now a narrow crescent. The supreme moment is at hand; the landscape assumes an unearthly hue. The beholders are silent and stricken with awe. One stationed on a mountain may see the shadow advancing over the plain below with appalling speed. In but a moment it has come; the moon hangs in mid-heaven, a ball of inky blackness, fringed with blazing prominences, and enveloped by the silvery corona. The moments are counted by heart-beats. The planets and brighter stars bedeck the sky; perchance a stray comet peers forth in the sun's vicinity. The upturned faces of the onlookers are ghastly. A piercing ray of light springs from the edge of the moon; the prominences are gone. The corona fades away; the stars return. The landscape glows with the returning light. The sublime spectacle is over.

A total solar eclipse.

It has not been without curious effects upon the lower orders of creation. The convolvulus closes its leaves, birds cease flying, chickens go to roost, beasts leave their food, bees return to the hives, caged birds die of fright or thrust their heads under their wings, crickets sound their nocturnal notes, bats fly about; some horses seem to be overcome with fright and sink down in the street; others are blind to the changes about them, and go on without even pricking up their ears. Oxen have been known to arrange themselves in a circle, heads outward, as if fearing attack.

Effects on plants and animals.

Among semi-civilized or savage nations a solar eclipse inspires great terror. Hindus believe that a great

Superstitious terror.

dragon is striving to devour the sun. They fill the air with unearthly screams and shouts, and beat their gongs fiercely; the monster must be frightened away. Great is their joy when the voracious jaws eject the scorching morsel.

Work during an eclipse. We have gone far afield, and must return to summarize briefly some of the work which modern astronomers attempt during the fleeting moments of a total solar eclipse.

I. The prominences and corona are observed telescopically.

II. Spectroscopic observations are made of the corona, the protuberances, and the chromosphere.

III. The light of the corona is studied with the polariscope; the purpose is to determine the relation between the light which the coronal particles reflect and that which they emit because of their incandescence.

Small planets. IV. A search for possible small planets revolving in the neighborhood of the sun, and usually hidden by its glare, is prosecuted. Reports of the discovery of such bodies have been the subject of rather acrimonious discussion. Professors Watson and Swift announced such discoveries during the eclipse of July 29, 1878, but no similar observations have been made at any succeeding eclipse.

V. Photographs of the corona and of the prominences, being more trustworthy than hurried drawings, are much in vogue.

CHAPTER XIII.

MERCURY AND VENUS.

'Lo ! in the painted oriel of the West,
Whose panes the sunken sun incarnadines,
Like a fair lady at her casement, shines ·
The evening star, the star of love and rest."
—*Longfellow.*

MERCURY and Venus are denominated *inferior planets* because their distances from the sun are less than that of the earth. *Inferior planets.*

They are in *conjunction* when they appear to us to be nearly in line with the sun ; the word conjunction suggests this. An *inferior conjunction* of Mercury or Venus occurs when the planet is between the sun and the earth ; a *superior conjunction* takes place when the planet is beyond the sun. When at inferior conjunction a planet may come so near a line joining the centers of the earth and sun that it is seen against the background of the solar disc as a small black circle moving across its face. It is then in *transit*. After an inferior planet passes inferior conjunction it moves out toward the right as we stand facing the sun ; it is then west of the sun, rising and setting before the sun does each day. In Fig. 107 S is the sun and E the earth, while the circle represents the orbit of Venus. When Venus is at C it is in inferior conjunction. It then moves toward V, getting further and further to the right of the sun each week. When at V it has attained its greatest apparent distance west of the sun, and is at its *greatest western* *Conjunction.*

Elongation.

elongation. When moving from V toward C' it apparently approaches the sun. C' is the point of superior conjunction. After passing C' Venus is at the left of the sun, rising and setting after the sun does. V' is the point of *greatest eastern elongation.* After passing V' the planet swings back toward the sun.

In this explanation we have tacitly assumed that the earth is at rest; in reality it is moving in the same direction as Venus, but more slowly. This simply lengthens the time which elapses between inferior conjunction and greatest western elongation, or between any two of the positions which we have just defined.

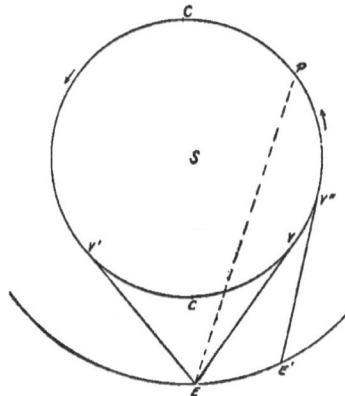

FIG. 107.—CONJUNCTION AND ELONGATION.

Greatest western elongation really comes when Venus has arrived at V''', the earth meanwhile having moved on to E'. When an inferior planet is west of the sun it is a morning star; when east of the sun it is an evening star and is to be looked for in the west.

Morning and evening star.

Phases.

Since Mercury and Venus shine by reflecting the sunlight, and have no intrinsic radiance, they exhibit phases similar to those of the moon. At inferior conjunction the dark side of the planet is toward us; as the planet moves out toward western elongation its phase is a crescent like that of the young moon.

At greatest elongation the phase is a semicircle, like the moon at one of its quarters. When the planet is at superior conjunction we look full in its illuminated face, which is a complete circle. Afterward it descends through the gibbous phase, to a semicircle, and thence to a narrow crescent again, as it approaches inferior conjunction.

Of Mercury little is known, for it is coy and keeps close to the sun. The most favorable times for seeing it in the evening are those when it reaches its greatest eastern elongation in March or April. For it is then nearly above the sun at sunset ; at such a time it may be seen every night for two successive weeks, one of which immediately precedes the time of elongation. It is then very plain, even in strong twilight, and is not likely to be confounded with any fixed star. *[Mercury.]*

Its mean distance from the sun is 36,000,000 miles. Its orbit is more eccentric than that of any other of the large planets, so that its actual distance from the sun ranges from 28,500,000 to 43,500,000 miles. *[Its distance.]*

Sunlight upon Mercury is more than twice as intense when it is nearest the sun as when it is farthest away. The average intensity is seven times that which we experience. The diameter of the planet is 3,000 miles, and eighty-eight days are consumed in making a revolution about the sun. *[Intensity of sunlight.]*

It is very difficult to make out any markings on Mercury's disc. The Italian astronomer, Schiaparelli,* whose observations of the canals of Mars have proven that he is exceptionally keen of sight, has observed certain dim and ill-defined spots whose motion renders it probable that Mercury rotates on its axis in eighty-eight days, and thus presents the same face continually to the sun. *[Rotation.]*

There is great uncertainty about the presence of air or water ; certain spectroscopic observations indicate that *[Air, water, and mountains.]*

---

* Astronomer at Milan, Italy.

there may be a thin atmosphere, in which water vapor is present. If these be accepted as correct, the dim shadings described by Schiaparelli may be the outlines of seas or continents.

One imaginative astronomer discovered mountains on the planet about a century ago. Though his telescope was a pigmy compared with those of to-day, modern observers have not verified the existence of the mountains.

VENUS.

Venus. Venus is a more interesting object than Mercury because it comes nearer to us and is larger and brighter, giving more light than any other planet. Its distance from the sun is 67,000,000 miles, and its orbit is nearly a circle. It is almost as large as the earth, having a diameter of 7,700 miles.

Revolution and rotation. Two hundred and twenty-five days are consumed in making a revolution about the sun. The time of rotation is generally given as about twenty-four hours, this period having been derived from old observations, which have received some confirmation in recent times. Schiaparelli's investigations cast discredit upon this value, and tend to show that Venus, like Mercury, keeps the same face toward the sun.

Shadings. Many astronomers have seen shadings upon the planet's surface, but they are so ill defined that their cause is unknown. When the planet is a crescent, the horns are brighter than the rest of the surface. Possi-

Ice and snow. bly ice and snow at the planet's poles cause this appearance. On the whole, it may be said that telescopic scrutiny of Venus has decided nothing as to the configuration of its surface.

It seems to be covered with a dense atmosphere, which is an effectual bar to our curiosity. The existence of the atmosphere is shown at the times of its transits. When Venus is just about to enter upon the sun's disc, or has just passed off, it is surrounded by a tiny rim of light. The sunlight has pierced through the planet's atmosphere and come on to our eyes. It is probable that the atmosphere is denser than our own, but not more than twice as dense. The spectrum contains lines which indicate the presence of water vapor. It is a reasonable inference that Venus is a planet whose sky is almost totally cloudy, and whose atmosphere is continually laden with moisture. On a day when the entire earth is enveloped in a cloud-shell, to an inhabitant of the moon it would present, on a huge scale, the appearance of Venus.

Atmosphere.

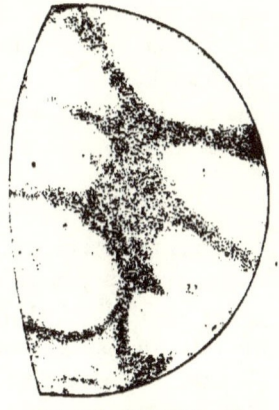

FIG. 108.—MARKINGS ON VENUS.

CHAPTER XIV.

MARS AND THE ASTEROIDS.

" And earnest thoughts within me rise,
When I behold afar,
Suspended in the evening skies,
The shield of that red star."
—*Longfellow*.

Mars.
MARS is perhaps the most interesting planet, because of the tantalizing chase on which he has led observers. He is at times almost as near as Venus when the latter is in inferior conjunction ; yet he is even then so far away that the more delicate features of his surface, like the canals, are seen with great difficulty, and are the source of much perplexity. Even the marked features which have for generations passed unchallenged under the names of continents and seas are now subjected to rigid scrutiny, and in some quarters are denied their time-honored appellations. While there is a fair consensus of opinion as to the majority of appearances seen upon the planet, there is considerable diver-

FIG. 109.—MARS.

Perplexities.

sity in the interpretations which are put upon them.

In considering such a subject one must maintain a judicial frame of mind, realizing that while conservatism is generally to be preferred to rashness, yet the age of a theory should not shield it from searching examination, as the novelty of a result should not debar it from the most candid treatment. *A judicial mind.*

The mean distance of Mars from the sun is 141,500,000 miles. His orbit departs farther from the circular form than that of any other planet save Mercury. The difference between his greatest and least distances from the sun is 26,000,000 miles. He is best seen when the earth lies between him and the sun; we are then nearer to him than at other times, and he appears bigger and brighter. *The orbit.*

At such a time if he happens to be near *perihelion*, which is the point of closest approach to the sun, and the earth is near its *aphelion*, which is the point of furthest recession from the sun, the distance between the two bodies is but 36,000,000 miles. This close approach occurs every fifteen years, and took place in August, 1892, for the last time during the nineteenth century. *Perihelion and aphelion.*

All those planets whose orbits are larger than that of the earth are called *superior* planets. When the earth is nearly in a line between a superior planet and the sun, so that the former appears to be on the opposite side of the celestial sphere from the sun, it is said to be at *opposition*. When the planet is beyond the sun and nearly in line with it, it is in *conjunction*. When Mars is at a favorable opposition it is more than fifty times as bright as at conjunction, and rivals Jupiter in splendor. When far from opposition it might readily be mistaken for a red fixed star, did not its motion betray its true character. *Superior planets.* *Conjunction and opposition.*

Diameter, revolution, and rotation.

The diameter of Mars is 4,200 miles. It consumes 687 days, or nearly twenty-three months, in making one revolution about the sun. Some of the markings on its surface are so well defined and stable that the time of rotation has been found very accurately by comparing drawings made in the seventeenth century with modern ones. The received value is $24^{hr.}\ 37^{min.}\ 22.67^{sec.}$ The rotation axis of the planet is not perpendicular to the plane of its orbit, but deviates 27° from that position. Therefore there must be seasonal changes on Mars just as on the earth.

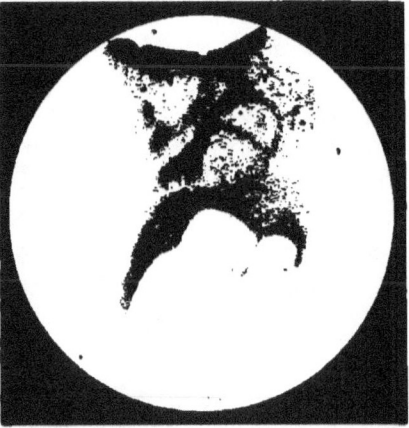

FIG. 110.—PROJECTIONS ON THE POLAR CAP.

The moons.

Two tiny moons attend the planet; they were discovered at the favorable opposition of 1877 by Professor Asaph Hall.* Their names, Deimos and Phobos, are translations of Greek words used by Homer as designations of the fiery steeds which drew the chariot of the god of war. They are the smallest known bodies in the solar system, with the exception of meteors. Deimos occupies $30^{hrs.}\ 18^{min.}$ in making one revolution, and is 12,500 miles from the planet's surface. From measures of its brightness its diameter has been estimated at five or six miles. Phobos, the inner moon, is only 3,700 miles from the surface of Mars; it accomplishes a revo-

---

* Then an astronomer at the United States Naval Observatory at Washington; now on the retired list.

lution in 7$^{hr.}$ 39$^{min.}$ and is the only known moon which makes the trip around its primary in less time than the primary takes to turn once on its axis. In consequence of this unusual speed it rises in the west and sets in the east. A man living near one of the poles of Mars would never see Phobos, because it revolves in the plane of the Martian equator, and keeps close to the planet. To us they seem to fill the office of nocturnal luminaries very imperfectly, the light given by Phobos to possible Martians being but one sixtieth of our moonlight. Deimos sheds upon Mars only one twentieth as much light as Phobos. They go through the same phases as our own moon.*

A quick trip.

The planet itself is subject to changes of phase. At opposition, when the earth is between the sun and Mars, the latter exhibits a full, round disc, as we

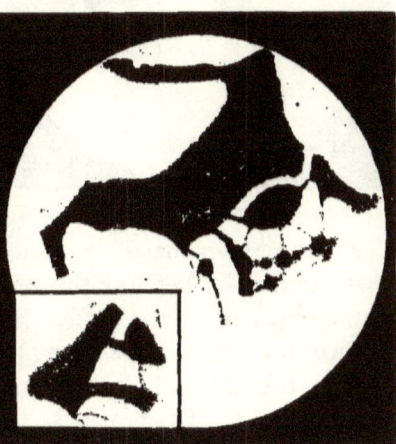

FIG. III.—THE LAKE OF THE SUN.

are directly in front of its illuminated hemisphere; at conjunction it has the same phase, but at intermediate times we cannot see all of the bright hemisphere.

Phases of the planet.

---

* The discovery of these satellites was curiously anticipated by Kepler, Dean Swift, and Voltaire. One of Kepler's strange speculations, which he mentioned in a letter to Galileo, was that Mars had two moons, Saturn six or eight, while Mercury and Venus were possibly blessed by a single attendant each. Dean Swift represents in "Gulliver's Travels" that the scientific Lilliputians had telescopes of great power, with which they had discovered "two lesser stars or satellites which revolve about Mars." Voltaire makes a hypothetical inhabitant of Sirius take a celestial voyage, in the course of which he visits Mars and sees two moons which are intended to make up for the comparative feebleness of the sunlight.

The most conspicuous appearances on the face of
The polar caps. Mars are roundish white masses at the poles. They were plainly seen soon after the invention of the telescope, and have been observed ever since. Neither one of them maintains a uniform size. When summer reigns in the northern hemisphere of the planet the white area around the north pole diminishes and almost vanishes; when summer yields to winter the white spot grows again. In October, 1894, the south polar spot became so small that many astronomers believed that it had vanished. But the Lick telescope, under the manipulation of Professor E. E. Barnard, still showed it, though with great difficulty; it was very small, and seemed to be partially obscured by an overhanging veil. The polar caps are supposed to be composed of snow and ice.

Most of the planet's surface is of a yellowish-red
The general surface. color; the remainder is usually of a dark gray tint. Many maps have been made, which agree quite satisfactorily in their main details. The yellowish-red regions are thought to be dry land; the dark gray regions bodies of water.

The canals. Fig. 112 exhibits several of the canals. Schiaparelli was not the first astronomer to notice them: some were observed by several distinguished astronomers before his day. But he has found so many that they are by common consent called "Schiaparelli's canals." No other observer, however large his instrument, has completely verified the mysterious network with which Schiaparelli's map is covered.* The majority of the canals are several hundred miles long. A canal occasionally appears to be doubled; that is, a new canal

---

* However, Mr. Percival Lowell, and the observers associated with him, at Flagstaff, Arizona, have mapped a large number of canals not detected by Schiaparelli. An account of these is given in Mr. Lowell's book entitled "Mars."

appears running by the side of the old one. Schiaparelli states that this duplication is probably periodical, and has some connection with the changes of the seasons. Several canals often meet at a point, as though they were spokes radiating from a hub. They are the most mysterious objects on Mars, and a host of theories have been broached about them. Schiaparelli has suggested that they may be natural water-ways

Doubling of canals.

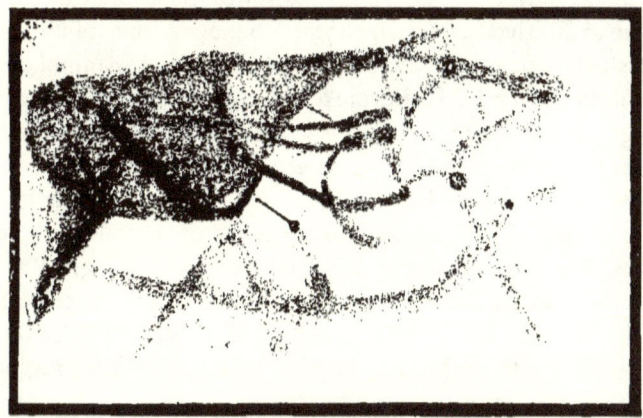

FIG. 112.—CANALS.

through which the waters caused by the melting of the polar snows flow toward the equator.

There are other more transient appearances. Sometimes there are small spots of tolerably definite outline which are visible for a time and then vanish. At other times there are large diffuse patches, which seem to obscure the familiar outlines shown on the map. Both of these appearances may be ascribed to clouds. Large reddish areas now and then have a whitish aspect, as though snow had fallen upon them. One small orange spot has often appeared white: perhaps it is a moun-

Clouds and snow.

242   *A Study of the Sky.*

tain or high table-land, where snow falls readily. Projections like saw-teeth are seen on the edge of the disc. Some of these may be large clouds floating high in the atmosphere of Mars; others may be due to mountains.

Inundations.

Large dark regions extend their boundaries, and seem to obliterate adjoining yellowish ones. After several weeks or months they resume their usual form.

FIG. 113.—PROJECTIONS ON THE EDGE OF THE DISC.

If lowlands adjoin a sea, their inundation would cause such changes of appearance.

Melting of a cap.

When a polar cap is diminishing, a dark rim has been seen about it, as if it were bordered by the water coming from the melting cap. In 1892 the south polar cap dwindled very rapidly, and there were very interesting changes in its vicinity. It lost 1,500,000 square miles of its area in a month. At first a dark spot

Mars and the Asteroids.

appeared in the midst of the cap; it gradually enlarged and cleft the cap in twain. A part of the region between the diminished cap and one of the well-known dark portions of the disc became dark, and then the dark region just mentioned was enlarged, intrenching upon the adjacent lighter regions. All of this is readily explained on the assumption that the first dark spot within the polar cap was water, which had been produced by the melting of the snow and ice. If this snow-water found its way across lowlands to an adjacent sea, and caused the latter to overflow its boundaries, the phenomena which followed the melting of the polar cap in 1892 are explained. *An overflow.*

There is one dark spot called Lacus Solis, the Lake of the Sun, which is plain at every opposition. It is surrounded by a bright ring, which, according to our previous theorizing, is dry land. Sometimes the ring is wide and conspicuous; at others it is narrow and not easily seen. A large dark spot, thought to be an ocean, is near at hand; at times canals connect the lake with the ocean, traversing a portion of the bright ring; at other times there is a break in the bright ring, which then looks like a horse-shoe, the vanished portion of the original bright ring being dark; the lake and the sea are ap- *Lacus Solis.* *A horse-shoe.*

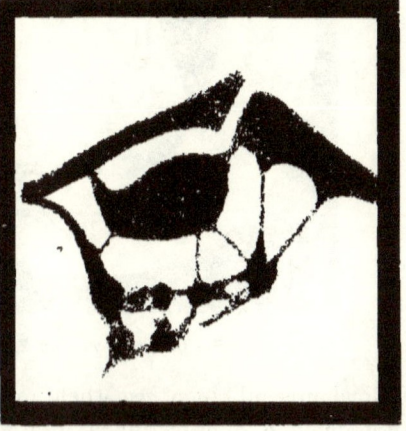

FIG. 114.—CANALS CONNECTED WITH LACUS SOLIS.

The canals fill. parently joined. If the land separating the lake from the sea is low, and slight changes in the water level are admitted, the preceding changes in appearance may be explained. When the water is low the bright ring is complete; when it is a little higher it fills the canals; when it is still higher it inundates the portion of the bright ring lying between the two bodies of water.

FIG. 115.—THE POLAR CAP IN JULY AND AUGUST, 1892.

Various theories. Plausible as all the theories about snow, seas, dry land, clouds, and inundations, which have been advanced, may appear, we must not forget that they are all subject to revision when new light is obtained. The most variant theories have already been proposed. It has been suggested that the polar caps are simply masses of cloud; that the bright portions of the planet's surface may be water, while the dark ones are land; that the doubling of the canals is an illusion; that the canals are not to be considered as water-ways, but as streaks of vegetation bordering upon streams which are themselves too narrow to be seen. One writer says that the canals are so straight and so well distributed over the planet's surface that they may be considered as the work of intelligent beings, who use them for *Irrigation.* purposes of irrigation. Another remarks that they are indefinite shadings, vague in outline, and often discontinuous.

The popular interest in Mars has arisen largely from

the possibility that it is habitable by human beings. Practical astronomers generally look upon such speculations with ill-disguised disdain; let us examine into the matter for a moment. If there be land and water, and freedom from disastrous inundations, in certain regions, a man would simply need an atmosphere like our own, and a suitable supply of warmth, together with a fertile soil. Habitability.

What has been determined concerning the atmosphere? If it were as dense as our own, and of similar composition, we could not see the polar caps and other prominent features so distinctly. The color of the caps would be altered from white to a reddish tint, since we always see them obliquely through quite a thickness of atmosphere. Furthermore the spectrum of Mars should contain strong absorption bands if the atmosphere were dense. More than one European astronomer, using a comparatively small instrument, has found spectroscopic evidence of the existence of water vapor in the planet's The atmosphere.

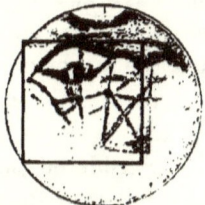

FIG. 116.—CANALS IN AUGUST, 1892.

atmosphere. But Professor Campbell,* with a large spectroscope attached to the great Lick telescope, found no evidence of water vapor, and sees no absorption bands whatever. In his opinion such bands would have been evident if the atmosphere of Mars were one fourth as dense as our own. A man therefore would gasp and A man would gasp and die.

---

* Of the Lick Observatory.

die, if Professor Campbell's conclusions are to be accepted.

<small>A warm climate.</small>
The climate of the planet seems to be mild; else why should the polar snows melt so rapidly and cause freshets? The sunlight which reaches Mars is less than half as intense as ours.

<small>Composition of the atmosphere.</small>
If its atmosphere be rare, why has it such a power of imprisoning the sunbeams and keeping the planet warm? Are we not led by this course of reasoning to suspect

FIG. 117.—THE CAP DIMINISHING, AUGUST 24-29, 1892.

that the composition of the Martian atmosphere is widely different from that of our air? Would not a human being fare ill on Mars?

<small>Caution.</small>
While the basis of our argument is confessedly slender, and the conclusions may be wide of the facts, does not the best light available indicate that Mars is probably not a suitable place for human habitation? We cannot deny that our neighbor may be inhabited; its inhabitants may be far superior to mankind, in both physical and mental endowments. But such speculations are no part of the science of astronomy.

THE ASTEROIDS.

<small>An arithmetical scheme.</small>
In the year 1772 Professor Johann Titius, of Wittenberg, devised an arithmetical scheme for representing the relative distances of the planets from the sun. By adding four to each of the numbers 0, 3, 6, 12, 24, 48,

and 96, he obtained a series which approximately represented the data. If we represent the earth's distance by 10, the correspondence between theory and fact is shown below :

	Theory.	Fact.
Mercury	4	3.9
Venus	7	7.2
Earth	10	10.0
Mars	16	15.2
	28	
Jupiter	52	52.0
Saturn	100	95.4

The gap between Mars and Jupiter made a profound impression upon Bode, a Berlin astronomer, and he boldly predicted that a planet would some day be found which would fill out the series. The discovery of Uranus in 1781 at a distance agreeing fairly with the next term of the series gave a powerful impetus to the idea that there must be a planet between Mars and Jupiter. *(The gap.)*

Half a dozen German astronomers formed an association of celestial police to search for the truant planet. Before these officers had gotten their belts fairly tightened up, a Sicilian astronomer, Piazzi by name, caught sight of the missing body. *(Celestial police.)*

He was engaged in the somewhat prosaic work of making a star catalogue, and had observed the right ascensions and declinations of a large number of stars. On January 1, 1801, the first evening of the century, he observed the position of a star of the eighth magnitude ; on the next night he observed it again. The two observations did not agree. The third night he tried it, and encountered another disagreement. He was satisfied that it was in motion, and observed it for six weeks, until a serious illness seized him. *(The discovery.)*

Meanwhile he had written letters to Bode and another

astronomer, telling of his good fortune; but there were no express trains in those days, and the letters tumbled about for a couple of months before they reached their destinations. It was then too late to look for the new body, for the sun had gotten around into that part of the sky. The celestial police took extra hitches in their belts and ruminated, but their ruminations were of no avail; not one of them could find out where to look for the fugitive, after the sun had passed by.

Delayed letters.

A rising young mathematician, Gauss by name, who afterward became one of the foremost of astronomers, set himself at work on the problem and unraveled the hard knots in it. By November he was able to tell the celestial police (as they called themselves) where to hunt. The clouds and storms of winter now baffled the searchers. But on the last day of the year the fugitive was caught. At Piazzi's request it was named after one of the lesser divinities, Ceres, the tutelary goddess of Sicily.

Gauss.

Three months afterward Olbers, of Bremen, chanced upon a similar object, which proved to be another small planet, revolving in an orbit of nearly the same size as that of Ceres. To it the name Pallas was given. Within half a dozen years two more, Juno and Vesta, were captured. The progress of discovery was slow up to 1850, when about thirteen were known.

Other asteroids.

The method of search was laborious, but easily understood. Star charts were constructed, showing all stars (except the very minutest) visible in certain regions of the sky. Night after night the charts were compared with the heavens to see if any object not on the chart was in evidence. Whenever a faint star-like object was found to be in motion, it was hailed as a new minor planet, observed with diligence, enchained by the toils

The old method of search.

of mathematics, and finally imprisoned in an astronomical almanac.

Nowadays astronomers hunt this sort of game with a camera, which is attached to a telescope of short focal length, having a large field of view. The image of each star photographed is a tiny point on the sensitive plate. The photographic signature of an asteroid differs from *The new method.*

FIG. 118.—ASTEROID TRAIL ON A PHOTOGRAPH OF THE PLEIADES.

that of a star; since it is in motion with reference to the surrounding stars, its image on the plate moves, producing a short streak. When the plate is developed the astronomer soon discovers this anomalous mark among the other little dots, and knows that he has photographed an asteroid, new or old.

A "Rechen Institut" in Berlin, composed of astronomical computers, takes care of these members of the *Who takes care of them?*

sun's family, sifts out the new ones from those previously known, computes their orbits, predicts their places from year to year, and calls attention to those whose orbits are not yet securely determined, so that they may be observed afresh before they are lost. They now (1896) number over 400, and are being discovered too rapidly for the comfort of the computers who have them in charge. By the end of the nineteenth century five or six hundred of them will probably be known unless the zeal of certain astronomical photographers is checked.

Their orbits. The mean distances of the known asteroids range from 200,000,000 to 400,000,000 miles, and their periods of revolution from three to nine years. A few of them approach so near Jupiter as to suffer considerable perturbations by their giant brother. One of them is sometimes nearer the sun than is Mars. Despite the great entanglement of the various orbits, there is no special danger of collision, except on the part of Fides and Maia, which may become united into one body or become a system like the earth and moon.

Their sizes. Vesta is the brightest and is occasionally visible to the naked eye. The diameters of four of them have been measured by Professor Barnard with the Lick telescope with the following results :

Ceres	485 miles.
Pallas	304 miles.
Juno	118 miles.
Vesta	243 miles.

Their faintness indicates that most of them do not exceed fifty miles in diameter. Those which are discovered by photography are, as a rule, decidedly insignificant, many of them having probably as small a diameter as ten miles. Five hundred of them together would be only a millionth as large as the earth.

A man would be much interested in paying a visit to one of these tiny worlds, if he could get along without his usual supply of air, and endure the rigors of cold which obtain there. If the asteroid were composed of as dense materials as the earth, and were only eight miles in diameter, the force of gravity at its surface would be one thousandth as great as on the earth. A baby who tosses a ball to a height of five feet could there toss the same ball a mile. The man could throw a baseball clear off the planet. Should he essay to walk, the first spring of his ankle would project him upward off the ground. An attempt at running would be a ludicrous series of one-legged leaps. Should he leap off a cliff 1,000 feet high, he would reach the bottom in a little over four minutes, and would experience no more severe a shock than if he had jumped down a space of one foot on the earth. If he tried to sit down, his feet would be lifted off the ground, and he would gently fall into his seat. If he lifted up a basket of eggs with no more care than he would take on the earth, the eggs would leave the basket, rise about 140 feet, and return in three minutes and a fraction.*

A visit to an asteroid.

At first it was supposed that the asteroids were fragments of a larger planet, which had been shattered by an explosion. If this were the case, the orbits of all the fragments would at first intersect at the point where the explosion occurred. The disturbances caused by the attractions of the other planets would so alter the different orbits that after a few thousand years they would be very far from meeting at any given point. The changes which a few of the orbits have undergone in the past have been approximately ascertained, and no clue to a common point of intersection has been found. The

Origin of the asteroids.

---
* These calculations are based on an initial velocity of three feet a second.

hypothetical explosion must have occurred hundreds of thousands or millions of years ago, if ever.

<small>A ring of matter.</small> According to the nebular hypothesis (to be set forth hereafter), the asteroids may have arisen from the condensation of a ring of nebulous matter, which was left behind, as the original solar nebula contracted. This is the commonly received explanation of their origin.

CHAPTER XV.

JUPITER, SATURN, URANUS, AND NEPTUNE.

" Some displaying
Enormous liquid plains, and some begirt
With luminous belts, and floating moons, which took,
Like them, the features of fair earth."
—*Byron.*

JUPITER is the giant of the sun's family of planets. The distance from pole to pole is over 84,000 miles. At the equator his diameter is nearly 90,000 miles. He is therefore decidedly out of round. The elliptical shape of his disc is readily perceived with a telescope, or in any good picture of him. So marked an equatorial bulge may be due to one or both of two causes. He may rotate with extreme rapidity, so that the "centrifugal force" at the equator is large, or he may be so plastic that even a low velocity of rotation would cause the bulging observed. As we shall see presently, there is good reason to believe that both of these causes operate. *Jupiter's dimensions and shape.*

His bulk is 1,300 times that of the earth; all the other planets compacted together into one would not equal him in volume. His mean distance from the sun is 483,000,000 miles, which is more than five times the earth's; 11.86 years are occupied in one revolution about the sun. *Size, distance, and time of revolution.*

Like all other superior planets he is brightest at opposition, attaining then a luster which exceeds that of any other planet except Venus; at such a time he casts *His appearance.*

Rotation.

perceptible shadows of terrestrial objects. Many spots can be seen on his surface, even with a telescope of moderate power; by watching their motion the time of rotation has been determined; it is about $9^{hrs.}$ $55^{min.}$

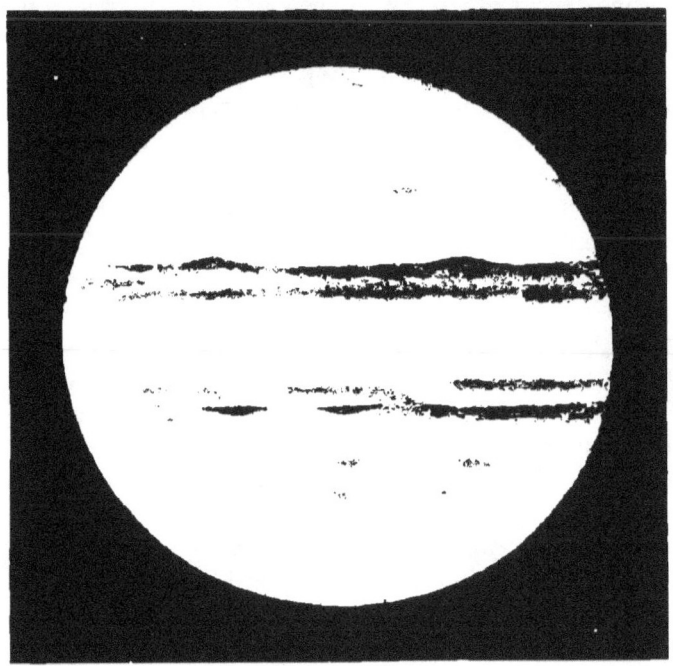

FIG. 119.—JUPITER.

The swiftness of rotation makes the delineations of its surface markings difficult.

The belts.

In a small telescope dark belts parallel to the planet's equator are plainly contrasted with the general yellowish-white background. A large telescope reveals a wealth of detail and a richness of coloring, which call forth the admiration of the beholder. The principal belts near the equator have a reddish cast; the hue is modified from time to time, being sometimes salmon-colored and at others a rich rose pink. There are many subsidiary stripes of smaller size and less pronounced color.

The whitish portions of the planet's disc are by no means devoid of interest. They look like aggregations of cumulus clouds, such as deck the summer sky. One who looks down from the top of a mountain upon a layer of clouds below may see the general aspect of the Jovian clouds. Small white, dark, and red spots are strewn here and there over the surface. *White clouds.*

In 1878 there suddenly appeared a pink spot of unprecedented dimensions; the length is given as 30,000 miles, the breadth as 7,000. In another year its hue was a full Indian red. So completely did it dwarf all other recorded spots that it was henceforth known as the "great red spot." It faded away, and was almost invisible in 1883 and 1884. Since then it has had irregular spells of brightening, but has never recovered its pristine beauty. The time of rotation of the red spot is not the same as that of the adjacent cloud-forms. In 1890 a large spot was moving directly toward the red spot; but it was diverted from its course, and passed by at one side of the spot. After it passed by it did not return to its original course, but remained at the higher latitude into which it had been shunted; it passed the red spot at the rate of twenty miles an hour. Professor Keeler* has likened the great red spot to a sand bank in a river, past which the flecks of foam go scurrying. *The great red spot.*

The red belts are thought to be cloudless regions; the sunlight striking against the whitish cloud-masses is reflected back in large measure; but that which falls upon the red rifts between the clouds is not so well re- *The red belts.*

---
* Prof. James E. Keeler, of the Allegheny Observatory.

256   *A Study of the Sky.*

A red atmosphere.
flected. If Jupiter's atmosphere is red and the white masses are clouds floating in it at various heights, the general appearances are explained. What we have called the atmosphere may be a liquid having a reddish color.

Not only do the different parts of Jupiter's cloud mantle rotate with different velocities, but even the

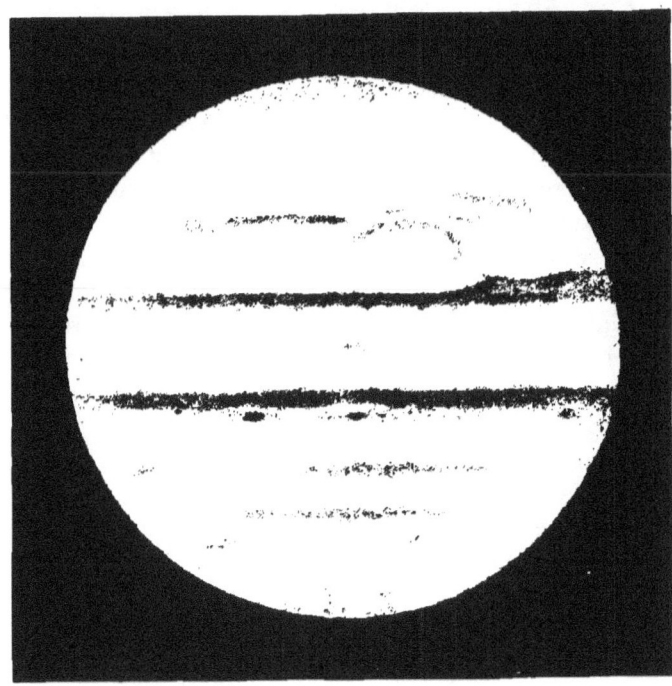

FIG. 120.—THE GREAT RED SPOT.

Variable rotation.
great red spot has not kept a constant period of rotation. At first the whirling of the planet on its axis brought it around in $9^{hrs.}$ $55^{min.}$ $34^{sec.}$ In seven years the period had lengthened seven seconds. If it had kept the new rate and Jupiter itself had been a solid rotating at the old rate, it would have gone clear around

the planet in less than six years. If Australia were cut loose from its moorings and drifted toward Africa, we should have a parallel to the drift of the red spot. During the past ten years (1886–96) the spot has apparently been at anchor.

Though changes on Jupiter's face are not very rapid, no feature is permanent either in form or position. It is then a reasonable hypothesis that Jupiter has no solid crust. To this conclusion some other facts point. Though Jupiter is 1,300 times as large as the earth, it is only 316 times as heavy; it is therefore only one fourth as dense and may plausibly be regarded as a fluid mass enveloped in a deep shell of cloud-laden vapor.   No permanent forms.

But what is the cause of the abundant supply of clouds? Why is not Jupiter's atmosphere clear like that of Mars? Clouds cannot be formed unless there is heat to produce the vapors to which they owe their origin. As the sunlight is only one twenty-seventh as intense as ours, the necessary heat can hardly come from that source, and we are forced to conclude that Jupiter is itself a warm body. This conclusion is directly in line with the nebular theory, according to which all the planets were once heated bodies. Jupiter, being much larger than the other planets, would cool off more slowly and require a longer time to solidify. But if Jupiter be a hot body, why does it not shine with some such vividness as a fixed star manifests? A body may be hot without being luminous; a kettle of boiling water would hardly fill the office of a student lamp. Jupiter may well be regarded as a semi-sun. Its interior may be a pasty mass of sufficient consistency to give considerable permanence of location to such an object as the great red spot, which probably owes its origin to a disturbance in the depths of the planet.   Internal heat.
A semi-sun.

The moons. Jupiter is accompanied by a goodly retinue of attendants, five in number. Galileo discovered four of them, the smallest being of the size of our moon, while the largest is comparable with Mars. They are designated by Roman numerals, I being nearest to its primary and IV farthest away. As they circle round the planet, they are in occultation when hiding behind him, in eclipse when immersed in his shadow, and in transit when crossing his disk. The times of all these phenomena are given in the "Nautical Almanac."

Discovery of the velocity of light. Observations of them in the seventeenth century led to the discovery that light takes an appreciable time to fly from one world to another. How this came to pass is not difficult to understand. Let an astronomer observe the times of a number of eclipses of satellite I when Jupiter is in opposition, the earth at that time being at nearly the same distance from him for several weeks. Since eclipses occur at pretty regular intervals it will not be difficult for him to predict from his observations the times at which fresh eclipses will occur several weeks afterward. Meanwhile the earth and Jupiter are getting farther apart and the predicted eclipses come later than expected. The reason is that the light which brings from Jupiter the message that the eclipse has begun now takes longer to perform its journey than it did when the earth and Jupiter were nearer together.

Rotation of the satellites. Spots have been seen on Jupiter's satellites at times; attempts have been made to find their times of rotation by observing these. The moons have also appeared elongated. If one looks at an egg one hundred feet away, while it is held with its end toward him the egg appears round; when it is held sidewise it looks oval. So the satellites, if really oval, will appear to be out of round at times. The high tides raised upon them by

Jupiter may have elongated them. There is evidence that some of them, at least, keep the same face toward the planet.

The fifth satellite, which was discovered by Barnard with the Lick telescope on September 9, 1892, is much smaller than the others, its diameter being estimated at one hundred miles. It is less than 70,000 miles from Jupiter's surface and occupies nearly twelve hours in making one revolution. Only the largest telescopes can deal successfully with it; the other moons can be seen with a good opera-glass. People of extremely acute vision can see with the naked eye satellite III, which is 660,000 miles from Jupiter's center, or IV, which is 1,160,000 miles away, under favorable conditions.

The fifth satellite.

SATURN.

The ancients regarded Saturn as the most distant of the planets because of his dimness and the slowness of his motion. Little did they imagine that this dull-looking object would one day be transformed into a marvel which would ever after challenge the admiration and awaken the enthusiasm of mankind. Galileo was the first to perceive that it was no ordinary planet. So many imitators had followed in his footsteps, laying claim to greater discoveries than he had made, that he had grown wary. These men had seen twice as many moons circling around Jupiter as Galileo had announced. To baffle them he set forth his discovery about Saturn in the form of an anagram. This procedure had the desired effect, and the pseudo-scientists were put to flight by its uncanny array of disjointed Latin. The emperor Rudolph finally prevailed upon Galileo to arrange the letters of the anagram in their proper order; it then became: "Altissimum planetam tergeminum obser-

The ancients and Galileo.

260   *A Study of the Sky.*

<small>The triple planet.</small>

vavi" (The most distant planet three-fold I have observed).

Galileo's imperfect telescope had shown Saturn as a large ball, flanked by two smaller ones. But in less than two years a change took place which was a sore trial to him. He says :

<small>The mockery.</small>

Looking at Saturn within a few days I found it solitary, without the aid of its customary stars, and, in short, exactly round and well defined like Jupiter, and thus it still remains. Now what can be said of so strange a change? Have the two lesser stars been consumed like spots on the sun? Have they suddenly vanished and fled away? Or has Saturn eaten up his children? Or was the appearance a delusion and a snare, with which the glass has deceived me and many others who have often observed with me?

He never divined the cause of their disappearance. In his old age a veil was drawn over his eyes, which had done so much in unveiling the mysteries of the skies, and he wrote pathetically :

<small>Galileo's affliction.</small>

Alas! your dear friend and servant is entirely blind. Henceforth this universe, which I have enlarged a thousand times beyond the ideas of former ages, has shrunken for me into the narrow space which I myself fill in it. So it pleases God ; it shall therefore please me also.

<small>Huyghens.</small>

In less than fifty years after Galileo's anagram was given to the world, a Dutch astronomer, Huyghens by name, set another one afloat in the sea of scientific thought. His alphabetical agglomeration, when marshalled in correct array, took the following form :
"Annulo cingitur, tenui, plano, nusquam cohærente, ad eclipticam inclinato" (It is girdled by a thin, flat ring, nowhere touching, inclined to the ecliptic).

<small>The ball and ring.</small>

This admirably correct statement renders possible an explanation of the change which perplexed Galileo. To build up a mental picture of Saturn we must imagine

a rotating ball the polar axis of which is 70,000 miles long, while its equatorial diameter is 76,000 miles. Encircling this ball and lying in the plane of its equator is a thin flat ring, the outer diameter of which is 173,000 miles, the inner diameter being 110,000 miles; its thickness probably does not exceed 100 miles.

<small>Phases of the rings.</small>

As Saturn wheels about the sun in his appointed path we see the ring in different positions. Now it is turned edgewise to us, and is invisible because of its thinness. Again it is turned at such an angle that an imperfect telescope shows it as two projections, one on each side of the central ball. The greatest angle at which it is inclined to our line of vision is 28°. Saturn takes twenty-nine and one half years to perform one revolution about the sun, and the rings are edgewise to the sun twice during a revolution. Midway between these two times they are in the best position for observation. Two favorable years are 1899 and 1914. The best views of Saturn in any particular year are obtainable when it is at opposition. Its mean distance from the sun being 886,000,000 miles, it is then about 800,000,000 miles from us.

<small>Divisions of the ring.</small>

Hitherto we have spoken of "the ring." It is really composed of three concentric rings lying in the same plane. The outermost ring is 10,000 miles in width, and is separated from the middle ring by a space 2,200 miles wide, which is called "Cassini's division." Other fainter divisions have been glimpsed. The middle ring is 17,500 miles wide. These two rings are of the same yellow hue as the ball; the innermost ring is very dark, and is known as the *crêpe* ring, or gauze ring. It is 9,500 miles wide and there is no division between it and the ring outside of it; between its inner edge and the ball is a space of 7,000 miles.

As to the structure of the rings there has been much discussion; they look solid, but mathematicians are not satisfied with appearances. The hypotheses of solidity and fluidity have both been rejected, because the rings would not be stable, but would be destroyed by precipitation upon the ball. Clerk Maxwell, the famous English man of science, has shown that if the rings are composed of myriads of little bodies too small to be separately visible to us, the system is stable. So elegant and complete were Maxwell's researches, and so cogent was his train of reasoning, that the Cambridge students averred that he paid a visit to Saturn one evening, and cleared up the mystery with his own eyes. *Structure of the rings.*

The largest telescopes have given no ocular proof of the correctness of Maxwell's theory; that honor has been reserved for the spectroscope, which, in the hands of Keeler, first gave a satisfactory demonstration. The work has since been confirmed by others. One of the offices of the spectroscope is to determine whether a body is approaching us or receding; it is now possible to measure with a reasonable degree of accuracy the velocity of approach or recession. If Saturn's ring-system rotated as a solid mass the outer edge would move more swiftly than the inner one. If, on the other hand, the rings are composed of separate small bodies, those bodies which are near the inner edge must travel more rapidly than those near the outer edge, because they are more strongly attracted by the ball. Dr. Keeler's beautiful photographs of the spectrum of the ring-system show not only that the outer edge moves more slowly than the inner one, but that the intermediate portions move with intermediate velocities; these velocities agree with what would be expected of bodies moving in conformity with Kepler's laws. *Keeler's spectroscopic observations.*

Thus another instance is added to the list of cases where mathematicians, emboldened by confidence in the unerring symbols and apparently immutable laws with which they deal, have described processes going on in distant worlds, which observers have afterward verified.

Is the system of rings really stable? What must be continually happening in a dense swarm of bodies moving with various velocities? Are not collisions frequent? When two of them collide, the swifter is checked, and the slower accelerated. If the earth's motion about the sun were suddenly checked, it would seek a new path of smaller diameter. If its velocity were increased by a blow from some body which was chasing it, the earth would swing out into a larger orbit. Collisions in Saturn's ring must therefore cause a broadening of the ring, since some of the bodies are getting larger velocities and others smaller ones.

Are the rings stable?

The earliest drawings show a much wider space between the ball and the ring than now exists, and thus bolster up the theory, but, on the other hand, careful measures of the dimensions of the ring system, made during the past fifty years, afford no evidence of enlargement.

The gauze ring.

The dark inner ring is called the gauze ring, because it is not opaque; through its edge one can sometimes see the ball. Professor Barnard has made an interesting observation with reference to its transparency. One of Saturn's moons, which had been eclipsed in the shadow of the ball, emerged into the sunlight for a while, and then plunged into the shadow of the dark ring. It did not disappear at once, but grew fainter till it encountered the shadow of the inner bright ring, then it vanished. The gradual diminution of its brightness indicates that the dark ring is denser on its outer edge than on its inner. It is likely that the small bodies are more closely crowded together near one edge than at the other.

The ball, though large, is not heavy; its average density is only one eighth that of the earth, being considerably less than that of water. The equator is brighter than the regions on each side, and faint belts are sometimes seen well up toward the poles. There is but little change in appearance from year to year. In December, 1876, a small white spot suddenly burst forth near the equator, and was visible for a month; the planet's rotation carried the spot around in 10$^{hrs.}$ 14$^{min.}$ The placid cloud-mantle in which the ball is enveloped hides most of the commotion within; the interior does not seem to be in such a state of activity as Jupiter manifests. *The ball.*

Eight satellites accompany Saturn. Their names, from the outermost inward, are: Iapetus, Hyperion, Titan, Rhea, Dione, Tethys, Enceladus, and Mimas. Titan, the largest, is four times as big as our moon, and occupies nearly sixteen days in a revolution. The existence of Cassini's division in the rings has been attributed to Titan's pull, which so disturbed the moonlets which once were there that they forsook their paths. Iapetus is 2,225,000 miles from the planet's center, and looks twice as bright when it is on one side of it as when on the other side. This is explained by the hypothesis that a large part of the surface is much darker than the rest, and that, like our moon, it keeps the same face toward its primary. *The moons.*

URANUS.

Uranus was discovered by Sir William Herschel. This remarkable man, to whom astronomy owes so much, was a native of Hanover. His father was a musician, *Sir William Herschel.*

and the son was diligently instructed in that art. At the age of seventeen he was oboist in a regiment of Hanoverian guards ; but two years afterward he deserted, and employed his musical talents in other directions. He speedily rose to prominence, and in a few years became organist of the Octagon Chapel at Bath. The society to which he was thus introduced was brilliant and fashionable, and his talents brought him prominence and prosperity. But despite manifold professional engagements, which would have entirely absorbed the energies of an ordinary man, his restless mind reached out into other fields. Studies in Italian, Greek, pure mathematics, optics, and astronomy failed to satiate his thirst for knowledge.

A musician.

FIG. 122.—SIR WILLIAM HERSCHEL.

When thirty-five years of age he obtained the use of a small telescope. Its revelations fired him with a purpose to obtain a knowledge of the construction of the heavens. He set himself resolutely at the task of making a larger telescope. His pertinacity knew no limit. Mirror after mirror was ground and polished. His sister Caroline, who was his constant attendant, writes : "My time was taken up with copying music and practicing, besides attendance upon my brother when polishing, since by way of keep-

He grinds mirrors.

ing him alive I was constantly obliged to feed him by putting the victuals by bits into his mouth." By day he ground mirrors and gave music lessons; in the evenings he conducted concerts and oratorios, running out at intervals to look through a telescope; at night he scanned the sky.

After seven years spent in this way Uranus swam into his ken on March 13, 1781. He tells of the discovery thus: "On this night, in examining the small stars near Eta Geminorum I perceived one visibly larger than the rest. Struck with its uncommon appearance I compared it with Eta Geminorum and another star, and finding it so much larger than either, I suspected it to be a comet." Professional astronomers began to observe the new body, and later computations showed that its orbit was nearly a circle; it was therefore no comet, but a new planet. *Uranus swims into his ken.*

The discovery aroused great enthusiasm, since all the other planets had been known from the earliest antiquity. Herschel was at once brought into royal favor, received a pension, and was given all needed funds for constructing a twenty-foot reflecting telescope, which was much larger than any hitherto made. With this instrument and a forty-foot, built afterward, Herschel carried forward the wonderful series of observations which made him supreme among astronomical observers of all ages. His faithful sister Caroline was his indefatigable assistant, recording his observations at night, as he dictated them to her, and making tedious calculations by day. Herschel and Uranus were discovered simultaneously; the importance of the discovery of the man is a sufficient excuse for devoting so much attention to him. *Herschel's prosperity.*

Of Uranus little is known which cannot be expressed

268   *A Study of the Sky.*

Details about Uranus. in cold figures. Its distance from the sun is 1,780,000,-000 miles, and its diameter is 32,000 miles. Its time of revolution is eighty-four years. It is visible to the naked eye, and even the most powerful telescopes show simply a greenish disc on which there are faint belts. A dense atmosphere produces marked absorption bands in its spectrum. What is beneath the atmosphere no one can tell. Four satellites attend it; strange to say, the plane in which their orbits lie is so tipped up as to be nearly perpendicular to the plane of the planet's orbit. The moons also revolve from east to west, while all other satellites heretofore considered go from west to east.

NEPTUNE.

Short and simple annals. More than 1,000,000,000 miles beyond Uranus plods slow-footed Neptune, the outpost of the solar system. Its mean distance from the sun is 2,792,000,000 miles, and its diameter is 35,000 miles. An opera-glass will render it visible; it exhibits in a large instrument a small greenish disc on which no details can be seen. Like Uranus it is enveloped in a dense atmosphere, through which struggles sunlight only $\frac{1}{900}$ as intense as ours. Its one moon is a tiny speck of light, and is supposed to be about as big as ours. Like the moons of Uranus it revolves backward in its orbit. Neptune requires 165 years to complete a journey around the sun.

Its discovery. The circumstances of its discovery are of high interest and involve one of the greatest triumphs of mathematicians. The discovery arose from the strange behavior of Uranus, which refused to follow the path which had been laid down for it by the mathematicians. After they had thought that it was securely ensnared it persisted in breaking the chains of their analysis, wandering into by and forbidden paths. Sixty years after its discovery it had gone so far astray that no one could doubt that something was wrong ; to be sure, the theoretical and the actual planet were so close together that the unaided eye would see them as one body, but the discrepancy was intolerable to a mathematical mind. *An intolerable discrepancy.*

So firmly convinced were astronomers of the accuracy and universality of Newton's law of gravitation that they became convinced that the observed irregularities must be due to the attraction of some other body, which pulled Uranus away from its proper path. It is a problem of no mean difficulty to compute the effect of one planet's pull on another, when the masses and relative positions of the bodies are known. How much greater the difficulty of discovering the mass and successive positions during a series of years of an unknown body, which, as the upshot showed, was more than 1,000,000,000 miles away from Uranus. Several eager minds attacked the problem, but found it too difficult for their powers. *A difficult problem.*

Mr. J. C. Adams, a student of the University of Cambridge, resolved to look into the matter as soon as his final examinations were over. In January, 1843, having graduated as senior wrangler, he set to work. In October, 1845, he communicated his results to the astronomer royal, who naturally thought it very improbable that a young and unknown student should have solved so profound a problem. He looked over the papers, and seeing that they gave evidence of careful research, wrote to their author concerning an obscure point in the investigation. Unfortunately Mr. Adams did not reply at once, and his communication was pigeon-holed. *Adams.*

Meanwhile a young Frenchman, Leverrier, had concentrated his marvelous powers upon the problem. In *Leverrier calculates.*

November, 1845, he sent a paper to the French Academy, in which he showed that no known causes of error would account for the wanderings of Uranus. A second paper in June of the next year assigned to the disturbing body a definite place in the zodiac. When this news reached England the astronomer royal was astonished to find that Adams and Leverrier were in substantial agreement.

Challis hunts. He at once wrote to Professor Challis of Cambridge, asking him to search for the suspected planet. Professor Challis was not very enthusiastic, but set about the work with due regard to thoroughness and to leisurely dignity. He began to take the positions of all visible stars in the suspected region, going over the same locality three times. It was his intention at some convenient season to prepare a map from each night's work, and by comparing them to find out if any one of the objects noted had moved.

Galle finds it. While he was engaged in manipulating his astronomical drag-net, Leverrier, who knew nothing of the work of the Englishmen, completed his investigations and requested Galle, director of the observatory at Berlin, who was already in possesssion of an excellent star chart, to look in a certain place ; there he would find the planet. The letter was received on September 23, and on the same night Galle came upon the planet within a degree of the predicted place. When the news reached England Professor Challis bestirred himself, looked over his note-books, and found that he had observed the planet on August 4 and August 12. Had he been prompt in comparing his results, he would have detected the new body before Galle looked for it ; but his burst of speed came after the race was over. Thus did confidence and energy win the victory over doubt and delay.

CHAPTER XVI.

COMETS AND METEORS.

"Stranger of Heaven, I bid thee hail!
Shred from the pall of glory riven,
That flashest in celestial gale—
Broad pennon of the King of Heaven."
—*Hogg.*

"And certain stars shot madly from their spheres,
To hear the sea-maid's music."
—*Shakespeare.*

FEW astronomers devote themselves to searching for comets; such work requires extreme patience, involves irregular hours of work, requires very little mathematical training, and is quite monotonous except at the supreme moment of discovery. If the moon is bright in the early evening the comet hunter waits till it has set. Night after night he shifts the pointer on his alarm clock and alters his hours for sleep. When once at his telescope he sweeps over a certain part of the sky, keeping his eye closely confined at the eyepiece, that nothing may escape. If a faint wisp of nebulous light comes into view he inspects it with care; if he does not recognize it he looks in his catalogue of nebulæ to see if it is described there. If not, he concludes that it is new, and watches it for an hour or so to see whether it appears to move among the surrounding stars. Any motion betrays its cometary nature; if it remains at rest it is a nebula. A comet may also be discovered by an astronomical photographer, who finds its image impressed upon one of his plates.

Comet hunting.

The comet ensnared.

The new comet is promptly announced, so that observations of it may begin at once. Its right ascension and declination are measured by comparing it with known stars which lie along its path. The star catalogues contain the places of several hundred thousand stars, so that a known one can always be found in the vicinity of the comet. With his micrometer, which has been previously described, the astronomer measures the position of the comet with reference to the star. He may find, for instance, that the comet's right ascension is 29.42$^{sec.}$ greater than that of the star, and the declination is 4' 13".2 less. Applying these quantities to the

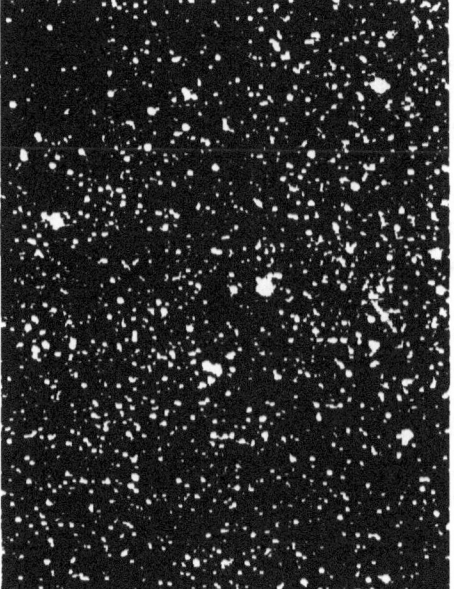

FIG. 123.—DISCOVERY OF A COMET BY PHOTOGRAPHY.

known right ascension and declination of the star he obtains the comet's place. After a comet's place has been measured three times, a preliminary orbit of it is computed and its location is predicted for a month or so in advance, so that observers may more readily keep on its track. When a large number of observations have been made, a more accurate computation of its path is executed.

Three observations.

Its orbit must be a parabola, or an ellipse, or an hyperbola; so Newton's law demands. Most comets move in orbits so nearly parabolic that it is customary to compute the first orbit on the assumption that it is a parabola. If the comet refuses to follow this curve, it is generally found to move in an ellipse. Hyperbolic paths are rare. While an ellipse is a closed curve, a parabola or an hyperbola is not.

The shape of the orbit.

Some elementary notions about celestial mechanics assist one in understanding the history of these wanderers, prior to their introduction to us. If one of them is moving slowly along in space, millions of millions of miles from the sun, the attraction of the latter compels it to fall toward him. Were the sun and comet originally at rest, the comet would make straight for the sun; but as both are moving, the comet comes down in a parabolic curve, whisks around the sun, and is off again, never to return.

Elementary mechanical notions.

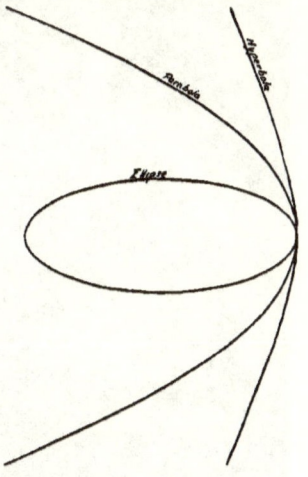

FIG. 124.—PATHS OF COMETS.

If the comet, while passing through the solar system, happens to come near one of the larger planets, its path may be seriously altered. If Jupiter, for example, is so situated with reference to the comet that its attraction increases the latter's velocity, the orbit will become an hyperbola. But if Jupiter diminishes the stranger's velocity, the orbit changes to an ellipse, and the comet is compelled to become an *attaché* of the sun. Jupiter's brigandage has led to the capture of several small com-

A planet's attraction.

ets, which are denominated his family. Saturn, Uranus, and Neptune have also indulged, to a lesser extent, in this piratical business.

Groups of comets.

There are a few instances of groups of comets which have nearly the same paths during their visibility, but revolve in different times. The comets of 1668, 1843, 1880, 1882, and 1887 form such a group. Each of them passes close to the sun's surface, and is therefore exposed to a tremendous heat, and also subjected to a powerful tidal strain. A modern French mathematician has proved that if a comet be disrupted in this manner, its fragments will afterward pursue similar paths.

The make-up of a comet.

Comets are erratic, not only in their motions, but also in their appearances; they are continually doing something *outré*. The peculiarities of their behavior must be attributed largely to their make-up. They are not compact masses of matter like the earth or the moon, but rather loose aggregations of small bodies, which fly along together like so many grape-shot. These bodies must sometimes be reduced to liquids, when exposed to intense solar heat, and carry with them a certain amount of gaseous matter. Of their sizes no certain estimate can be made, but they probably vary from the merest particles, like grains of sand, to more substantial masses as big as a house, or even larger. The connection between certain comets and meteoric swarms renders it almost certain that comets are largely bunches of small bodies.

Light and airy.

Large as comets are, they are comparatively insignificant in mass and density. As they dash along over the face of the sky they scarcely obscure even the faintest of the stars which lie behind them. Though their texture is so diaphanous, yet the gases which accompany the more solid portions are sometimes of sufficient refractive power to bend by a minute amount the rays of light coming through them from the stars beyond. Were comets as dense as planets, some of them would derange the orbits of the planets seriously by their attraction. It has been estimated that 100,000 of the largest comets put together would not weigh as much as the earth.

Having premised these facts we are better able to understand the changes which take place in a comet's appearance as it approaches the sun and recedes from him again. As it draws near, the increasing heat and the electrical influences which the sun probably exercises cause it to brighten. The densest portion of the cometary mass, which is called the nucleus, comes into prominence as a hazy mass, more compact and brilliant than the surrounding nebulosity. *Changes of appearance.*

The tail forms gradually, and prudently keeps on the side away from the sun. The nucleus seems to be the seat of the greatest activity; it spurts out jets toward the sun, or throws off masses of vapor, which are driven back into the tail. The entire body of the comet is affected to an extent which would be impossible were it a single compact mass. After the comet has passed perihelion the disturbances die away; the nucleus grows fainter and more sluggish in its actions; the tail shortens up and disappears. After a few weeks or months only a pale nebular gleam remains, which soon vanishes. Such is a crude outline of the general behavior of a comet of moderate size and average friskiness. *The tail forms.*

We proceed to consider various details. First as to the *jets* and *envelopes*. These are rarely seen in faint comets, but are conspicuous in bright ones. The sunward side of the nucleus is the seat of forces which project bright jets; as the jets rise higher and higher they spread out and become lost in the general nebu- *Jets and envelopes.*

losity of the comet's head. The formation of envelopes is a less violent and more orderly procedure. These umbrella-shaped forms rise toward the sun one after another at intervals of some hours, as if the comet were endeavoring to protect itself from the solar radiation. As they ascend they expand and grow fainter till their distinctive appearance is lost, like that of the jets.

The magnificent trains which accompany bright

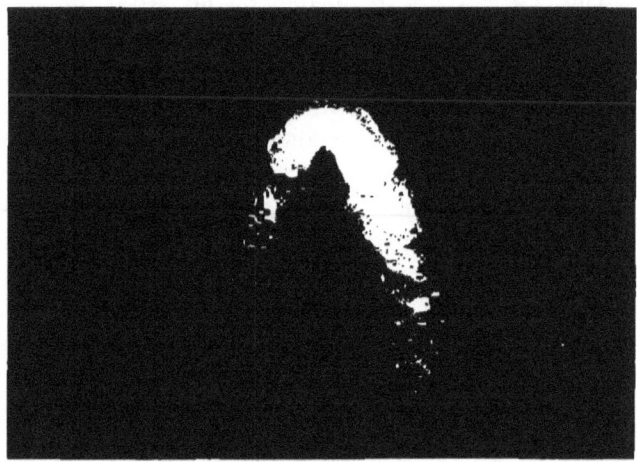

FIG. 125.—JETS AND ENVELOPES.

comets are their most characteristic features. Often they are tens or even hundreds of millions of miles in length. Occasionally they are nearly straight, but usually they have the graceful contour of the plume on a knight's crest. The material projected toward the sun by the jets and envelopes encounters a resistance which destroys its original motion, and drives it backward past the nucleus into the tail. If a locomotive puffed its smoke forward instead of upward, it would be swept backward in much the same fashion.

The repellent force, which triumphs so signally over the pull of the sun on these little solid, liquid, and gaseous emanations, is supposed to be electrical. In any physical laboratory may be seen pith-balls and light strips of paper, which are lifted by electrical forces in opposition to the force of gravity. In a similar way the lightest portions of a comet may be driven off by an electrical repulsion originating in the sun, while the heavier portions are dominated by his attraction. *Electrical forces.*

The spectroscope certifies to the presence of a few known elements in comets. The predominant gases seem to be hydro-carbons, which are compounds of hydrogen and carbon. Sodium and iron have been certainly identified, and magnesium and calcium are thought to be present. What happens to these different materials as they are being driven off by the electrical repulsion? Manifestly the lightest elements attain the greatest velocity; moderately heavy ones move with less velocity, and the heaviest with still less. These motions, combined with the orbital motions of comets, cause various degrees of curvature in their tails. *Different materials.*

There are three special types of tails. Tails of the first type are nearly straight and point almost directly away from the sun. They are believed to be composed largely of hydrogen. The majority of the trains belong to the second type, and are gracefully curved; here the repulsive force has less effect than before, as the particles on which it acts are heavier. Tails of this type are composed of hydro-carbons. The third type of tail is uncommon; it, too, is plume-like, but it curves very sharply at the comet's head, and trails behind the nucleus as the latter moves swiftly in its appointed path. Iron vapor is thought to be present in such tails. *Types of tails.*

The appearances of the three types are aptly represented by the smoke which issues from a freight engine moving in a quiet atmosphere at a moderate speed. If the steam pressure is very high, the puffs of smoke go nearly straight up ; if the pressure is only moderate, the stream of smoke forms a curving plume; when the steam is nearly shut off the smoke trails lazily behind the smoke-stack.

The smoke of a locomotive.

Some comets exhibit more than one type of tail ; even so strange a phenomenon as a tail pointing directly toward the sun has been observed. Wonderful changes have been noticed, as in the case of Swift's bright comet of 1892. On April 4 its tail was straight and twenty degrees in length, but consisted of two distinct branches lying close together. On the next night a third tail was seen between the other two ; each of the three appeared to be composed of several, so that the whole looked like a fan partially opened. Within twenty-four hours more one tail vanished, and the other two joined their boundaries. One of these then grew bright at the expense of the other, and finally split up into half a dozen branches. These are the most noteworthy of the changes which took place in five days.

Anomalous tails.

The particles which are driven off into the tails are lost. A *periodic* comet, *i. e.*, one which moves in an ellipse and returns at stated intervals, loses some of its substance at each perihelion passage, and must be wasted away in time.

Fate of comets.

Comets are sometimes accompanied by smaller companions. In 1889 one was seen which had no less than four of these attendants ; two of them were very faint, and did not last long ; for a while the other two were veritable twins, and bore a striking resemblance to the main comet. Like foolish children they cut the maternal apron strings and began to move away ; this move sealed

Companions.

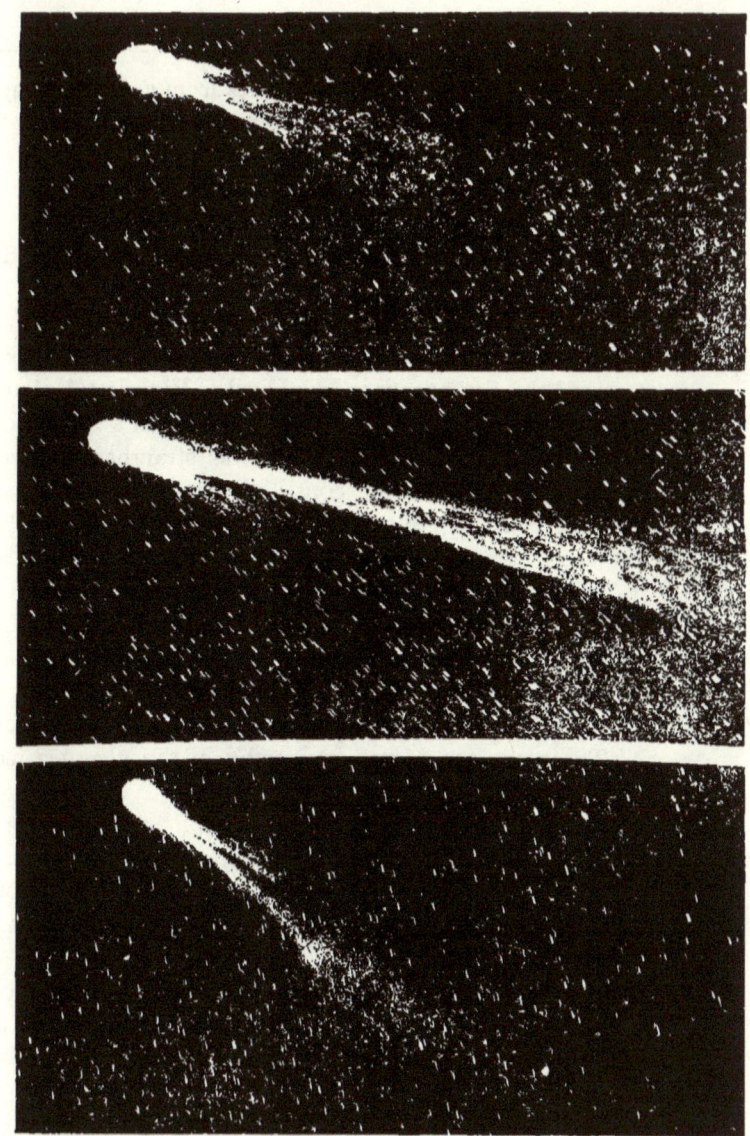

Fig. 126.—Photographs of Swift's Bright Comet of 1892.

the fate of one of them, which soon faded into invisibility. The other made a brave show for a time, but came back in a few weeks with a swelled head and no tail. The moral is obvious.

<small>Changes of brightness.</small> Though the brightness of a comet generally changes with considerable regularity as its distances from the sun and earth vary, there are often anomalous variations, which are best explained by electrical discharges between the small masses of which it is made up. The existence of such discharges is not merely conjectured. During the past few years spectroscopic observations of comets have gone hand in hand with laboratory experiments upon gases confined in Geissler tubes, and lit up by electric discharges. A mass of evidence has thus been accumulated which cannot be set aside; unfortunately it is too technical to be reproduced here.* Suffice it to say that the coincidences between electrical appearances produced in the laboratory and those observed in the spectra of comets are very complete.

<small>Superstitious terror.</small> It is well known that in past centuries comets were objects of superstitious terror, not only to the ignorant, but even to the higher classes of society. The comet of 1528 is thus described by Ambrose Paré:

This comet was so horrible, so frightful, and it produced such great terror in the vulgar that some died of fear and others fell sick. It appeared to be of excessive length, and was of the color of blood. At the summit of it was seen the figure of a bent arm, holding in its hand a great sword, as if about to strike. At the end of the point there were three stars. On both sides of the rays of this comet were seen a great number of axes, knives, blood-colored swords, among which were a great number of hideous human faces, with beards and bristling hair.

<small>Collisions.</small> Though some unaccountable superstitions still survive

---

* See Scheiner's " Astronomical Spectroscopy," pages 207-22.

among fairly educated members of enlightened communities, very few of them are connected with comets. But there is apprehension in many quarters concerning the results of a collision between a comet and the earth. The fear is that the great heat generated by the impact would blast the earth's surface as effectually as if it were tossed into a gigantic furnace, and would dissolve all its inhabitants in the twinkling of an eye. It appears from what we have learned of the constitution of comets that nothing of the sort is to be feared. Astronomers would be delighted if any ordinary comet should run into the earth, for there would be a shower of falling stars most beautiful to behold. A very large comet might make more trouble; for such an one probably contains a good supply of metallic masses, which would come through the air without being consumed. Fortunately they would not be close together, for stars have been seen shining with undiminished splendor through the nuclei of large comets; a city as large as Chicago might catch only a few of the celestial missiles. Some of them might be as large as houses and cause decided havoc where they struck. The celestial spaces are so vast in comparison with the bodies which traverse them that there is little danger to be apprehended from comets. *No great danger.*

In November, 1892, there was a comet scare, caused by the apprehension that Biela's comet* was about to dash against our planet. The fright inspired in certain localities is evidenced by the following press-dispatch from Atlanta, Georgia: *A comet scare.*

> The fear which took possession of many citizens has not yet abated. The general expectation hereabouts was that the comet would be heard from on Saturday night. As one result the confessionals of the two Catholic churches were crowded

---

* Holmes's faint comet was erroneously thought to be a return of Biela's.

The stifling air. yesterday evening. As the night advanced there were many who insisted that they could detect a change in the atmosphere. The air, they said, was stifling. It was wonderful to see how many persons gathered from different sections of the city around the newspaper offices, with substantially the same statement. As a consequence many families of the better class kept watch all night, in order that if the worst came they might be awake to meet it. The orgies around the colored churches would be laughable, were it not for the seriousness with which the worshipers take the matter. To-night (Saturday) they are all full, and sermons suited to the terrible occasion are being delivered.

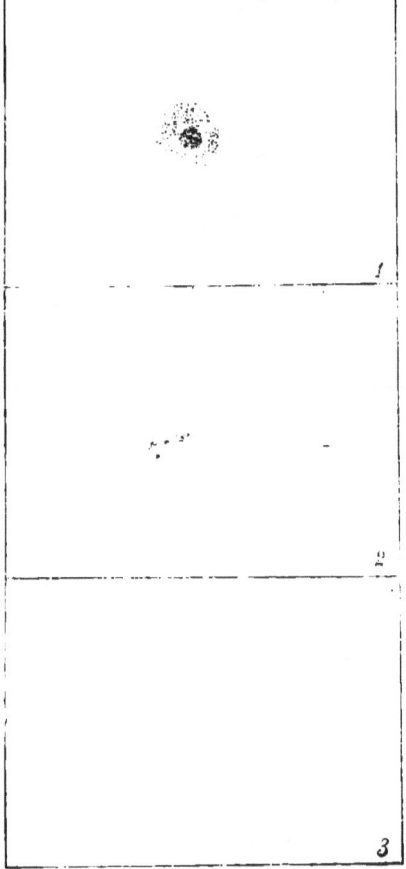

FIG. 127.—HOLMES'S COMET.

Fine comets. So great is the number of splendid comets the histories of which are written in astronomical annals, that it would be a hopeless task to enumerate the thousands of interesting details about them. We pay brief attention to a few.

The great comet which appeared in September, 1882,

was the most magnificent one of recent years. It was bright enough to be visible in full daylight, close to the sun. On September 17 it passed across the sun, coming within 300,000 miles of the photosphere. Though it thus dashed directly through the corona, and may indeed have encountered some of the solar prominences, its speed was unabated. But the intense heat to which it was exposed, together with the strain caused by the tidal action of the sun, apparently disrupted the nucleus. In less than a month it exhibited two centers of condensation. As the days rolled by still further changes took place, until the nucleus had become 50,000 miles long, and was ornamented by a number of centers of condensation, the largest of which was 5,000 miles in diameter. *The comet of 1882.*

The tail, at its best, was 100,000,000 miles in length, and stretched across the sky as a splendid golden bar. Along its track were scattered filmy débris, in the form of companion comets six or more in number. For nearly two months there projected in front of its head a luminous sheath, as though the comet were a sword which was being thrust into its scabbard. *Filmy débris.*

The spectrum was very bright, and indicated the presence of hydro-carbons, sodium, and iron; calcium and manganese were also suspected. The comet was not lost to view till it had reached a distance of nearly 500,000,000 miles from the sun. Its orbit is a very elongated ellipse, and it is expected to return in the middle of the twenty-seventh century.

Encke's comet was discovered in 1786, and was found to be making its round trip in only three years and a quarter, the shortest known cometic period of revolution. It is insignificant in appearance, but made trouble for astronomers as soon as they had obtained a fair grip *Encke's comet.*

on it. No matter how carefully they predicted its successive returns, it always outran the figures, and arrived at perihelion ahead of time. Such an effect would be produced by encounter with meteoric bodies, which offered a resistance to its motion. For a body which is retarded loses "centrifugal force," and is consequently pulled nearer to the sun, and compelled to describe a smaller orbit, in which it goes more rapidly than before. Should the resistance continue, Encke's comet must inevitably be drawn into the fiery embrace of the sun.

Biela's comet. Biela's comet was discovered in 1826, and was soon proven to be one of short period; it should come around once in six and three fourths years. In 1832 this harmless object gave rise to a comet-scare; for the fact became noised abroad that it crossed the path of the earth, and people jumped to the conclusion that there would be a collision. But when the comet crossed the earth's orbit our planet was many millions of miles away.

Twins. Thirteen years afterward the comet split in twain, under the very eyes of the watchers. The operation occupied several days, and after the parts had separated to a distance of nearly 150,000 miles, tails were shot out, and nuclei blazed up in rivalry. The original comet had possessed neither of these marks of cometic blue blood. They interchanged cometary compliments by alternately brightening and fading out. In 1852 they were seen again, the distance between them being then ten times as great as before. They were still exchanging compliments, and thus politely bowed themselves out; for they have never been seen since.

A meteoric shower. On November 27, 1872, the earth, when crossing the orbit of the missing comet, encountered a fine meteoric shower. The comet should have been millions of miles

FIG. 128.—PHOTOGRAPH OF RORDAME'S COMET, SHOWING MASSES OF MATTER DRIVEN OFF INTO THE TAIL.
The motion of the comet causes the stars to appear as streaks on the negative.

beyond on that date. Perhaps the earth did not dash into the comet, but into a mass of meteoric matter which was following in its wake. In 1885 there was another shower, and again in 1892 ; these were probably due to the same group of bodies. Either the comet has become invisible, or has met with some accident, which has disintegrated it.

Lexell's comet. Lexell's comet is perhaps the most tantalizing one with which astronomers have had to deal. It was first seen in 1770, and Lexell found that it was moving in an elliptical orbit, with a period of five and one half years. It did not reappear in 1776, but the earth was not then in a favorable position with reference to it and the sun. In 1781 circumstances were favorable, but the comet was a truant. Lexell and Laplace investigated the matter, and detected Jupiter in the rôle of mischief-maker. Before 1767 the comet had come so near this planet that its previous orbit had been transformed in the five and a half years ellipse. In 1779 it came altogether too near to Jupiter, and was tangled up among his moons ; the moons moved on with their accustomed serenity, but the comet's orbit was so altered that it was given up for lost. But in 1843 a comet appeared whose orbit was somewhat similar to that of the long-lost Lexell. Leverrier went to the bottom of the question, and decided against their identity.

Supposed returns. In 1889 Mr. W. R. Brooks[*] found a comet which has already been mentioned as accompanied by four companions. It too had been troubled by Jupiter, and had skirmished with his moons. Surely this was the returned prodigal ; but months of tedious calculation rendered its identity with Lexell's doubtful. Six more

---
[*] Of Geneva, N. Y. ; director of the Smith Observatory.

years rolled by, and in August, 1895, Dr. Swift* picked up a comet which proved to be a claimant for Lexell's vacant chair. A European astronomer has made what he considers to be a crucial test of the matter, and announces that Lexell is found at last.

A crucial test.

FIG. 129.—COMET C, 1893 (BROOKS).

The designation of this comet indicates that it was the third one discovered in 1893. The first one discovered in a given year is called comet a, the second comet b, etc. When this comet was first seen it had two tails. The main tail was beautifully symmetrical. Four years

Comet c, 1893 (Brooks).

---
* Director of the Lowe Observatory, Echo Mountain, Cal.

afterward its beauty was gone. It was bent and shattered. The subsidiary tail was no more, and the principal tail was full of knotty masses of nebulosity. The appearance suggested that the comet had encountered some resisting medium, which had struck its tail near the middle, and bent it. The comet itself was considerably brighter. The strange appearance of the tail may have been due to some other cause, for comets are noted for trickiness.

SHOOTING STARS.

Space not empty.

We are accustomed to think of space as empty, except where here and there a massive sun, or an obedient planet, or perchance an erratic comet pursues its lonely way. But the case is far otherwise. Innumerable small bodies traverse that part of space in which the solar system is now, in every direction. They are dark and cold. Those in our neighborhood are revolving about the sun, which is as careful to enforce obedience upon these specks of matter as upon the planets themselves; each has its own curve, and obeys the law of gravitation.

The air is a target.

When one of them collides with the earth a shooting star is produced. The shooting star does not strike the earth's surface, but impinges upon its atmosphere. So swift is its motion that it flames into incandescence when it encounters the higher strata of the air, just as a cannon ball is heated when it strikes a target. If the shooting star is coming directly toward the observer, so that he looks endwise at its path, it is simply a bright spot which flashes out for an instant. The vast majority of meteors dart at one side of the observer, and traverse long paths across the heavens. One can hardly look at the sky for fifteen minutes, on a clear moonless night, without seeing at least one of these bodies.

If two men in neighboring towns watch meteors for an hour or two, and each marks on a star map the apparent path of every one which he sees, noting also the time at which he observes it, the height of any meteor which both have observed may be calculated. For the apparent path as seen by one man is slightly different from that seen by the other, and if the distance between the observers is known, the distances of the meteor from each of them at the instants of its appearance and disappearance can be found by a simple calculation. In this way the average height of a shooting star has been found to be seventy-five miles when it is first seen, and fifty miles when it disappears. Their visible paths are forty or fifty miles long; their average velocity is twenty-five miles per second. *Observations for distance.*

Estimates of their sizes and weights are obtained from the amount of light which they emit. One which rivals Venus at its best may weigh from fifty to one hundred grains. Faint ones weigh less than a grain; many of them may be likened to grains of sand or canary seeds. One observer sees only a very small fraction of the total number which bombard the earth daily; he can ordinarily see from four to eight an hour. If a sufficient number of observers were distributed uniformly over the entire earth they would see from one to two millions every two hours. *Sizes of meteors.*

When a great meteoric shower comes, the sky is veined with thousands of luminous paths; all of them prolonged backward meet in a certain place, which is called the radiant. It must not be supposed that the meteors emanate from this point, and diverge as they come on. The little bodies, which have joined in so bootless a fusillade against the earth, are really traveling *The radiant.*

in parallel paths, like the drops in a rain storm. One who looks out of the rear door of a passenger train notices that the rails appear to converge in the distance. In the same manner the parallel meteoric paths seem to converge to the distant radiant. If the radiant of a shower is in the constellation Andromeda, the meteors are called Andromedes ; if in Perseus, Perseids, etc.

Definite times for showers. One bright shower is expected within a day or two of November 13 each year. The reason for this will appear from a simple illustration. Suppose that a man walks round and round a circular grass plot upon which a spray of water is being thrown from without. Just as

FIG. 130.—A BESPRINKLING.

A meteoric river. often as he passes the spot where the stream of water plays he is besprinkled. Replace the man by the earth, and the stream of water by a mighty river of meteoric matter, which persistently flows by a certain spot in the earth's orbit. Whenever the earth passes by that spot, as it does at a given time every year, it is besprayed with meteors.

The meteoric river does not have a source and a mouth as terrestrial rivers have. Its source and mouth are united, the entire stream being a vast ellipse within which the sun lies. In some parts of the stream the meteors are more thickly crowded together than in *The August meteors.* others. Whenever the earth dashes into a dense portion, the shower is unusually magnificent. A stream is broader in some places than in others; when the earth plunges into a broad portion the shower may begin before its usual time. The meteors in some streams are mostly massed in a vast shoal, instead of being distributed around the orbit.

The August meteors are most numerous about the tenth of the month; but the meteoric river is so broad that the earth takes over a month to go through it. Night after night, from July 18 to August 22, some meteors belonging to this aggregation may be observed. Their radiant is in Perseus. There are occasional gaps in the stream, so that some years bring no August display worthy of the name of a shower. The elliptical orbit in which the meteors move extends beyond Neptune, and the stream requires over one hundred years for a single revolution.

The shower of November 13 emanates from the constellation Leo; the meteors are therefore known as Leonids. Generally the display is not at all brilliant; but once in thirty-three years it is of wonderful splendor. The first recorded appearance of this shower was in 902 A. D., which was long known as "the year of the stars." For during the night in which the ancient Sicilian city of Taormina was captured by the Saracens, men saw "as it were, lances, an infinite number of stars, which scattered themselves like rain to right and left." *The shower of November 13.*

An imaginative Portuguese chronicler relates that in the year 1366, "three months before the death of the king Dom Pedro, there was in the heavens a movement of stars such as man never before saw or heard of. At midnight and for some time after, all the stars moved from the east to the west, and after being collected together, they began to move, some in one direction and others in another. And afterward they fell from the *The shower of 1366.*

sky in such numbers, and so thickly together, that as they descended low in the air, they seemed large and fiery, and the sky and the air seemed to be in flames, and even the earth appeared as if ready to take fire."

On November 12, 1833, the falling stars were as thick as snowflakes; many were brighter than Venus. The negroes in the Southern States were struck with terror, believing that the end of the world was at hand. They groaned, wept, prayed, and rolled on the earth in ecstasies of terror.

The year 1866 brought another fine shower. The next date on the program is 1899. The length of the dense part of the meteoric stream is 2,000,000,000 miles, and it occupies nearly two years in passing any given point. The year 1898 may therefore furnish a fine shower. The periodic time of this shower is $33\frac{1}{4}$ years. The direction from which the meteors come is nearly opposite to that in which the earth moves: they travel at the rate of twenty-six miles a second, while the earth has a velocity of eighteen miles a second. The effect is the same as if the earth were at rest, and the meteors hurled themselves against it with a velocity of forty-four miles a second. Such missiles, if not checked by the air, would go from New York to Chicago in twenty seconds. It is not astonishing that the meteors are bright and leave vivid trails behind them.

In the latter part of November comes another shower, the radiant of which is in the constellation of Andromeda. The meteors pursue the earth and overtake it; because of this they do not rush into the air with the impetuosity which characterizes the Leonids. Their trains are short and of a reddish hue. In 1872 some of them looked as large as the moon; in 1885 and 1892 there were fine showers; another is expected in 1898 or 1899. This shower derives special interest from its supposed connection with Biela's comet. The meteors pursue the same orbit as the lost comet, and it is possible that they are the products of its disintegration. During

Connection with Biela's comet.

Fig. 131.—Photograph showing a Meteor's Path among the Stars.

the 1885 shower there fell at the town of Mazapil in Mexico a piece of meteoric iron, which may have been a piece of the comet. In 1892 the meteors came on November 23, instead of November 27, the date usually assigned; this was due to a disturbance of the meteoric orbit caused by the attraction of Jupiter.

The Mazapil meteorite.

A Study of the Sky.

<small>Relation between comets and meteors.</small>

There are other instances of a connection between a meteor-shower and a comet. The orbit of the August meteors is identical with that of the bright comet of 1862. The great thirty-three year shower of Leonids follows hotly on the trail of Tempel's comet.

The relation between comets and meteors is therefore intimate. A comet is a group of small bodies somewhat compacted; a meteoric shower is caused by a group of small bodies more widely separated. The change which took place in the nucleus of the great comet of 1882 is one of many instances of the disruptive power which the sun exercises upon comets; its tidal action upon them tends to scatter the bodies of which they are composed. These bodies when scattered cause a meteoric shower, if they collide with the earth.

<small>The zodiacal light.</small>

Akin to meteors and comets is the zodiacal light, which is a hazy white beam of light, best seen early on a spring evening. Resting on the western horizon it slants upward toward the south. In the tropics it is seen as a light girdle encircling the sky. It lies in the zodiac and is surmised to be an envelope of meteors surrounding the sun, after the fashion of a huge lens.

METEORITES.

<small>Appearance of a flying fire-ball.</small>

The term meteors includes both shooting stars, which we have already considered, and meteorites. .The latter are bodies of such size and toughness that they can pierce the earth's atmosphere and find a resting place upon its surface. The flight of a large meteorite is signalized by striking phenomena. If it come in the night time, it is a splendid fire-ball followed by a flaming train; there is a roar like that of the sea in a storm, accentuated by occasional detonations. In a few seconds there remains only a luminous streak of glowing material, which has been wiped off from the exterior of the meteorite, as it dashed through the aërial furnace.

The intensity of the heat which a meteorite experiences may be imagined from the appearance of a fire-ball which was seen in England in 1869. The fiery envelope which enswathed it was more than four miles in diameter, and the entire body was consumed in five seconds. A cloud of glowing vapor fifty miles long was visible for nearly an hour. *A tremendous fire-ball.*

Sometimes a meteorite traverses a course hundreds of miles in length before the steady pressure of the air triumphs and brings it to the earth. Usually it breaks into numerous fragments while flying, and descends as a shower of stony missiles.

The fragments do not penetrate the earth as deeply as would a projectile hot from the mouth of a rifled gun. Still their destructive powers are by no means to be despised, for they have been known to kill men and to destroy buildings. Very few such catastrophes have been recorded, because buildings and men cover a very small part of the earth, and meteorites are infrequent visitors. *Destructive powers.*

Meteorites have been known to come to earth so quickly that the heat to which they were exposed had not time to penetrate their interiors. A meteoritic fragment, which once embedded itself in a moist spot of ground in India, was found half an hour afterward coated with ice. *Coated with ice.*

The appearance of a fallen meteorite testifies loudly to the experience which it has passed through. Most of these objects are stones which have thin crusts produced by the fusion of their surfaces. In case a meteorite bursts just before it is brought to rest, the freshly cracked surfaces, having been exposed to very little heat, preserve their roughness, and may be fitted to- *Appearance of a fallen meteorite.*

gether again. Some parts of the stony masses are often softer than others, and are quickly fused and swept away into the meteoric train. The captured meteorite is then pock-marked with numerous pits.

Their composition. In all large collections of these bodies are a few composed of iron alloyed with nickel; some of them are very formidable projectiles weighing several tons. Stony meteorites often have bits of iron scattered through them; iron meteorites frequently have pockets laden with stone. These combinations are not limited to meteorites, but are also found in such basaltic rocks as those of the Giants' Causeway.

Chemical analyses of meteorites have brought to light no new element; twenty-five elements have been found, most of which are common on the earth; the precious metals have not been discovered. Meteoric stones are composed of minerals, which are abundant in terrestrial rocks of volcanic origin.

In 1891 some 300 fragments of meteoric iron were found in the Cañon Diablo in Arizona; minute diamonds were embedded in them.*

Old records. There are hundreds of accounts of falls of meteorites during the past 2,500 years. The Greeks and Romans considered them as celestial omens, and kept some of them in temples. One at Mecca is adored by the faithful. The emperor Jehangir is said to have had a sword forged from a meteorite, which fell in 1620 in the Punjab. An Ohio Indian mound has yielded up copper earrings plated with meteoric iron.

A rare tract. We subjoin four interesting accounts of meteorites. The first is taken from a rare tract preserved in the British Museum; its opening sentences are:

---

* The diamonds were used at Tiffany's pavilion in the World's Fair at Chicago for polishing other diamonds.

So Benummed we are in our Senses, that albeit God him- **Heedlessness.** selfe Holla in our Eares, wee by our Wills are loath to heere him. His dreadfull Pursiuants of Thunder and Lightning ter- rifie vs so long as they have vs in their fingers, but beeing off, we dance and sing in the midst of our Follies.*

After moralizing at some length the author narrates the event which has inspired his pen :

The name of the Towne is Hatford, some eight miles from Oxford. Upon Wensday, being the ninth of this instant Moneth of April 1628, about five of the clocke in the afternoone this miraculous prodigious and fearefull handy-worke of God was presented. . . . It beganne thus: First for an onset went off one great Cannon as it were of thunder alone, like a warning peece to the rest that were to follow. Then a little while after was heard a second : and so by degrees a third, on- till the number of 20 were discharged (or there-abouts) in very good order, though in very great terror. In some little dis- tance of time after this was audibly heard the sound of a Drum beating a Retreate. Amongst all these angry peales shot off from Heauen this began a wonderfull admiration, that at the end of the report of euery cracke, or Cannon-thundering, a hizzing Noyse made way through the ayre, not unlike the fly- **A "hizzing** ing of Bullets from the mouthes of great Ordnance : and by **Noyse."** the judgment of all the terror-stricken witnesses they were Thunderbolts. For one of them was seene by many people to fall at a place called Bawlkin Greene, being a mile and a half from Hatford : Which Thunderbolt was by one Mistris Greene caused to be digged out of the ground, she being an eye-wit- nesse amongst many others of the manner of the falling. The form of the Stone is three-square, and picked in the end. In colour outwardly blackish, somewhat like iron : crusted over with that blacknesse about the thicknesse of a shilling. Within it is a soft, of a grey colour, mixed with some kind of minerall, shining like small peeces of glasse.

A detonating fire-ball, no fragments of which came to **A detonating** the ground, was seen on December 21, 1876. From **fire-ball.** some point in Kansas it sped to Niagara Falls, travel-

---

* See Lockyer's " Meteoritic Hypothesis," pages 5-7.

FIG. 132.—A METEORITE SEEN JULY 27, 1894.

ing at the rate of ten miles or more a second. When passing over Illinois it exploded, and formed a cluster of fire-balls which occupied a space forty miles long and five miles broad. Several minutes after the inhabitants of Bloomington saw the stream of fire-balls coursing past overhead, they were startled by a thunder-peal, which fairly shook the town, and led some to believe that a miniature earthquake was in progress. Sound travels a mile in five seconds, and the explosion was heard in Bloomington fifteen minutes after the disruption of the meteor occurred. The sound of the explosion must have traveled 180 miles before it smote upon the ears of the people of Bloomington. Had the fiery visitor come within eighteen miles of Bloomington instead of 180, how appalling the thunderings, which would have been multiplied a hundred fold! Fortunately it was at an altitude of seventy-five miles when it was first seen, and kept at a great height, finally escaping from the air after it had passed Niagara Falls.

<small>A cluster of fire-balls.</small>

Brenham township, Kiowa County, Kansas, was visited by a shower of meteoric iron at some time before white men had established themselves there. From time to time the early settlers plowed up these curious pieces of iron. Though the people called the strange masses meteors, they did not realize their pecuniary value. A cowboy, however, attempted to carry some off, but his pony was unequal to the task. He therefore buried them, expecting to return at some future time; but death frustrated his plan. A good woman, who was unable to persuade her relatives of the value of these chunks of iron, finally took matters into her own hands, sent for a college professor, sold her meteors, and paid off the mortgage on the farm from the proceeds.

<small>An iron hail.</small>

The Madrid fire-ball.

On February 10, 1896, a fire-ball exploded over the city of Madrid, in the middle of the forenoon. The sun was shining brightly, so that the celestial visitor was seen only as a swiftly moving cloud. There was a loud report, which caused a panic in schools and factories, and thus led to the injury of several people. Many windows were shattered, and a partition wall in a building occupied by the United States legation collapsed. *

---

* So said the newspapers.

CHAPTER XVII.

THE FIXED STARS.

" Ye stars ! bright legions that, before all time,
Camped on yon plain of sapphire, who shall tell
Your burning myriads, but the eye of Him
Who bade through heaven your golden chariots wheel?"
—*Croly.*

THE number of stars visible to an average eye on a good night is not far from 2,000. Near the horizon faint stars are blotted out by atmospheric vapors. If we could see all the stars on the celestial sphere as well as we see those near the zenith, 6,000 would be visible without optical aid. A spy-glass brings out thousands otherwise unseen. By the largest telescopes millions are revealed; hundreds of millions are sufficiently bright to record themselves on photographic plates. Their number.

The Milky Way or Galaxy has been previously described as the beautiful river of light which flows across the sky, embracing a countless host of faint stars. One of the most interesting parts of it is in the south, when the summer twilight has faded. The Galaxy there divides for a portion of its length into two roughly parallel streams, and glows in places, as if illuminated by cosmical fires. The Galaxy.

A marvelous complexity of structure is brought out by photographic plates exposed for several hours. There are curious curved lines of stars, vast cloud-like forms, long narrow lanes, and dark spots of various shapes. Complexity of structure.

Tree-like forms, similar to those of some solar promi-

Tree-like forms. nences, are of not infrequent occurrence; some of them are dark, and some bright. They have been supposed to be analogous to solar prominences, not only in form, but also in origin. According to this view they are due to stupendous uprushes into a resisting medium. The dark forms may be caused by an absence of matter, or by the presence of vast masses of absorbing material, which obscure the stars lying beyond them.

Naked-eye stars are distributed over the entire celestial sphere with considerable uniformity, but those which are invisible without telescopic aid are arranged very differently. They

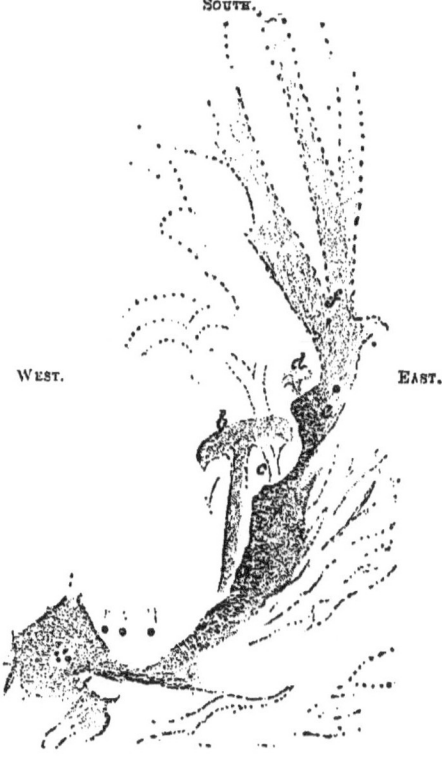

FIG. 133.—OUTLINES OF DARK STRUCTURES IN THE GALAXY.

Distribution in the sky. are most thickly crowded in the Milky Way. On either side of it the number in a given area is less. The further one goes away from the Galaxy, the fewer the telescopic stars are. If we call the Milky Way the galactic equator of the celestial sphere, a given area in it contains on the average thirty times as many stars as an equal area at either galactic pole.

We have already learned how the stars are divided into constellations, how they are named, how their brightness is estimated in magnitudes, and how catalogues of them are made. The greatest of all star catalogues is now being formed by the aid of photography. A number of observers scattered over the world have united to photograph the entire heavens, using instruments of the same size and construction, and after the photographs have been taken several years will be required to measure them and to prepare the results for publication. *A photographic catalogue.*

Astronomers are far from being content with making catalogues or maps of the stars. They wish to know how far they are away, what their dimensions are, of what substances they are composed, how they change appearance, how they move, what relation they bear to our sun, and what their origin and destiny may be. Let us take a glimpse of what has been done along these lines. *Questionings.*

In order to measure the distance of a star a base line of known length must be available. When an Atlantic liner passes by a lighthouse, a man at the prow sees the lighthouse in a direction different from that in which a man at the stern sees it. If they knew the length of the ship, and had suitable instruments for measuring angles, they could find the distance from the lighthouse to either one of them, at a given instant. *Measurements of distance.*

If two astronomers, one in northern Russia, the other at the Cape of Good Hope, should both look at the moon at the same instant, it would appear to them to lie in slightly different directions, and they could calculate its distance. But if they were to try the same plan with a fixed star they would be balked because no instruments are sufficiently delicate to measure the very slight difference between the directions in which the two men see the star. A longer base line must be used than the distance from St. Petersburg to the Cape of Good Hope.

A long base line.

If an astronomer measure the right ascension and declination of Sirius on January 1 and again on July 1, when the earth has gone half way around its orbit, to a

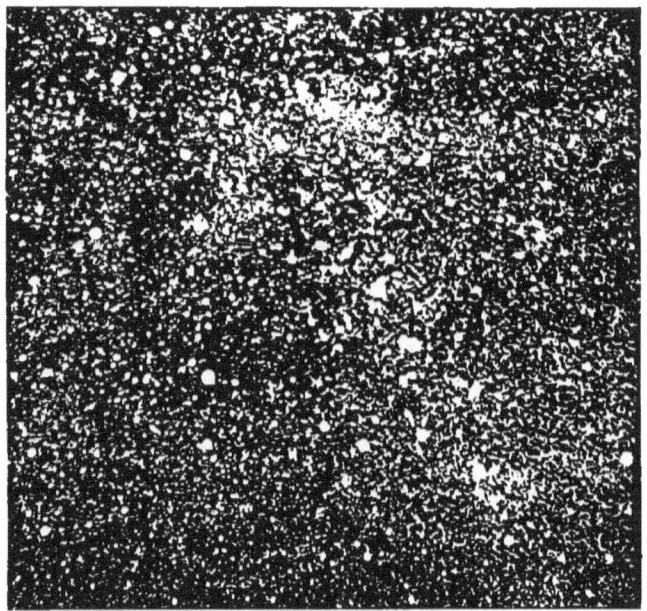

FIG. 134.—A PART OF THE MILKY WAY IN CYGNUS.

point 186,000,000 miles distant from its former position, he will find that Sirius has apparently changed its position slightly, on account of the observer's change of view-point. With the aid of a little mathematics the celestial surveyor computes the distance to Sirius.

The nearest star.

Most of the stars are at such inconceivable distances

that even the base line of 186,000,000 miles is insufficient. Our nearest neighbor, so far as present knowledge goes, is Alpha Centauri, which is 275,000 times as far away as the sun ; its distance is over 25,000,000,-000,000 miles. Sirius is twice as far away, and light takes eight years to come from it to us. The pole-star shines by light which left it fifty years ago.

No one has yet been able to measure directly the diameter of any star, on account of their amazing distances. Though the sun's diameter is 860,000 miles, it would look to an eye near Sirius as small as a marble 2,000 miles away. Yet we can get a rough estimate of the probable size of a star, the distance of which is known, by measuring the amount of light which it emits. Capella and Vega are thought to be much larger than the sun. Some are so bold as to estimate that Arcturus is 1,000,000 times as large as the sun ; but such an estimate must be considered very insecure. When two stars are close together and revolve about their common center of gravity, the swiftness of their motion combined with their distances from us and each other gives a clue to their masses. Periodic shiftings of the lines in a star's spectrum also furnish evidence, which we cannot here detail.

The sizes of stars.

Mizar at the bend of the handle of the Great Dipper is thought to be at least forty times as massive as the sun. Algol is periodically eclipsed by a dark body revolving about it. From the length of the eclipse, combined with other data obtained spectroscopically, a diameter of 1,000,000 miles has been figured out for it.

No star sends us a measurable amount of stellar heat ; the entire body of stars gives one sixtieth as much light as the full moon, and decidedly mitigates the darkness

Stellar heat.

of the night. Seven billion stars like Sirius would be required to make night as bright as day now is.

DOUBLE STARS.

Double stars exist in considerable numbers, 10,000 being catalogued. Many more have been seen, but adjudged to be too faint to deserve attention, until their brighter brethren have been investigated. A double star appears as one to the naked eye, but is split up, by telescopic or spectroscopic aid, into two stars.

Optical doubles. An optical double is one the components of which are not really close together; one of the two components lies far beyond the other, but in nearly the same line of sight.

Physical doubles. In a physical double star, or binary, the two stars are neighbors subject to one another's attraction. Each of the two stars revolves about their common center of gravity. Such a system is unlike ours, where a number of comparatively small and cool bodies revolve about a large hot body. In a binary system there are two suns, often equal in size, which revolve like partners in a waltz. Each of them may be surrounded by a troop of planets for aught we know. If Jupiter were transported to the vicinity of Alpha Centauri, and became a planetary attendant upon it, the largest telescopes would seek for it in vain.

Does gravity bind binaries? It is not yet known that the force of gravitation, which keeps the planets in their orbits, controls the motion of binary stars, but there is so much evidence in favor of this supposition that it is accepted as a fact. Since the spectroscope shows that the stars are composed of elements found on the earth and the sun, as well as in other planets, comets, and meteors, there is no good reason for thinking that the same materials, when found in the stars, will not attract each other according to the same law which we observe in the solar system. When the orbits of double stars are computed upon the assumption that their motion is due to the force of gravity, and when their relative positions are predicted for years to come, the predictions are verified by the motions actually observed. A mass of evidence is continually accumulating to show that physical, chemical, and mechanical laws, discovered by experimentation upon terrestrial bodies, hold good throughout the visible universe.

The history of the discovery of the duplicity of Sirius strengthens the view that the universe is a wonderful unit, subject throughout its wide extent to laws which are the expression of the will of its Creator. During the first half of the nineteenth century thousands of accurate observations of the right ascension and declination of Sirius were made. The more earnestly accuracy was sought, the more impossible it was to make the observations agree with one another. It became evident that Sirius was not fixed on the face of the sky. *Sirius.*

More than half a century ago the illustrious German astronomer Bessel attacked the problem, and announced that Sirius was moving in a tiny curve, and that this curvilinear motion was probably a case of orbital revolution, in which an unknown companion took part. A few years afterward two other German astronomers made a yet more thorough discussion, and reached the conclusion that the companion made a complete revolution in fifty years. They also pointed out the direction in which the companion then lay from Sirius, and the direction in which it was moving. Eight years later their confidence was rewarded by the discovery of the disturbing body by Alvan G. Clark, who was not aware *A curvilinear motion.* *A companion.*

of the prediction made by the two Germans. The companion is not τοδοϋ as bright as the main star, but it is one half as heavy. It is therefore a much cooler object than Sirius, and may in the course of ages become a genuine planet, though an enormous one.

Spectroscopic doubles. Perhaps the most interesting class of double stars embraces those in which the two components are so close together that they can never be separately seen. Though the two may be equal in size and brightness, they look like one perfectly round body, no matter how high the magnifying power employed. Their existence becomes known through the spectroscope. If the bodies are just alike, each of them gives a particular

FIG. 135.—MOTION OF THE COMPONENTS OF A DOUBLE STAR.

spectrum ; if they are at rest the two spectra coincide ; but if they are in motion in a plane turned nearly edgewise to us, one body at a certain point in its orbit is moving away from us quite rapidly, while the other is approaching. This is the state of affairs when the bodies are at A and B, Fig. 135.

Shifting of the lines. The lines in the spectrum of one body are therefore shifted in one direction, and the corresponding lines in the other spectrum move in the other direction. At the instant when the bodies are at C and D respectively neither of them is being carried by its orbital revolution toward the earth or away from it. The spectral lines are therefore not shifted by the orbital revolution at that time.

When the stars are at C and D their spectra coincide; when they are at A and B the spectra are separated, and corresponding lines, which formerly coincided, now stand side by side. In a word, the dark lines sometimes appear single and sometimes double, the doubling recurring at regular intervals.

Spica, in Virgo, is a rapid spectroscopic binary, the revolution being completed in four days. If the components are equal they are but 6,000,000 miles apart, and each is a third heavier than the sun.

A system not infrequently contains three or more revolving suns. An interesting quadruple system is found in Epsilon Lyræ, one of the faint stars near Vega. It has already been described under the constellation Lyra. Theta Orionis, which is in the great nebula in Orion, is a sextuple star. There are many instances of multiple stars, where several are grouped together. Stars in a given group may be really close together, so as to form a revolving system, or they may be like optical doubles, in which one star is a great ways beyond the other. Zeta Cancri is composed of three visible stars, two of which are close together and constitute a binary system. The third star seems to revolve about the binary, but its motion is subject to irregularities, thought by some to be due to an invisible member of the system.

Multiple stars.

STELLAR SPECTRA.

When stars are examined with the spectroscope, great diversities between them become apparent. The spectra are so various that it is impossible to make a satisfactory classification of them. Yet by considering only certain broad characteristics a few types may be distinguished.

Type I. This type embraces the white or bluish stars, which are far more numerous than others. Sirius, Vega, and Altair belong to it, and the entire group is often called Sirian. The principal lines in the spectrum are

Sirians.

due to hydrogen; other lines are faint and few. Two thirds of these stars are in the Milky Way.

Solars.

Type II. Yellowish stars having spectra similar to that of our sun are placed under this head; such are Pollux, Capella, and Arcturus, which are called solar stars. The spectrum is rich in lines belonging to various metals. Solar stars are distributed equably over the heavens. The light of a Sirian star is more intense than that of a solar, but the latter gives on the average a greater quantity of light, because of its greater size.

Variables.

Type III. Orange and red stars, together with most of those which fluctuate in brightness, belong to this class, which includes Betelgeuse and Antares. Their spectrum contains many dark bands, one edge of which is sharply defined, while the other is diffuse; the sharp edge is on the side next to the violet end of the spectrum.

Deep red stars.

Type IV. The stars belonging to this type are few in number, faint, and generally of a deep red color. The spectrum is banded as in Type III., but the sharper edge of each band is on the side next to the red end of the spectrum.

Bright-line stars.

More than fifty stars have been discovered, whose spectra are different from any of the preceding, in that they contain bright lines, thought to be due to extensive gaseous envelopes enwrapping them. They are of especial interest because they seem to form a connecting link between nebulæ and other stars. Bright lines, thought to be due to masses of vapor hotter than the underlying photosphere, are at times seen in the spectrum of the sun. Most of the stars in Orion exhibit a special variety of spectrum, which is not often met outside of that constellation.

The Fixed Stars.

So many different varieties of spectra are known that Prof. E. C. Pickering* says : {The universe is a unit.}

In general it may be stated that with a few exceptions all stars may be arranged in a sequence, beginning with the planetary nebulæ, passing through the bright-line stars to the Orion stars, thence to the first type stars, and by insensible changes to the second and third type stars. The evidence that the same plan governs all parts of the visible universe is thus conclusive.

The opinion that different spectra belong to different stages of development has much in its favor, but more complete investigations must be made before any far-reaching theory can command the entire consent of spectroscopists. {Is development indicated?}

VARIABLE STARS.

Many stars are inconstant in brightness, and bear the designation of variables; the number of known variables is now (1896) nearly four hundred, but new ones are being found continually. Certain compact clusters contain a large number of variables. They are not included in the number specified above.

The most marvelous class of variables is the temporary stars which appear occasionally, often blazing up with a wonderful display of luminous energy, and then fading into insignificance, or entire invisibility. Perhaps the most famous of these is Tycho's star, which he perceived while out walking on a November evening in 1572. It was in the constellation of Cassiopeia, and was nearly as bright as Venus at her best. For several days it was visible in broad daylight, but began to lose its splendor in December; fifteen months later it was too faint to be seen. Tycho measured its place as well as it could be done without the aid of a telescope, {Temporary stars.}

---

* Director of the Harvard College Observatory.

which had not then been invented. There is now a faint star near the place assigned by him, but it is not certain that the two objects are the same.

Nova Aurigæ. The most remarkable recent temporary star is Nova Aurigæ (the new star in Auriga). It was first seen by an amateur Scottish astronomer on January 24, 1892, being then of the fifth magnitude. It had, however, previously impressed itself on a photographic plate exposed at Harvard on December 10, 1891. It was not on a photograph of the same region made at Heidelberg on December 8. It must therefore have burst out suddenly between these two dates. Its spectrum was at once investigated : two spectra were found ; one was a bright-line spectrum, the other an absorption or dark-line spectrum. The lines in the two spectra were not in their normal positions, but were shifted in such a way as to indicate that there were two bodies moving in different directions. During February and March the

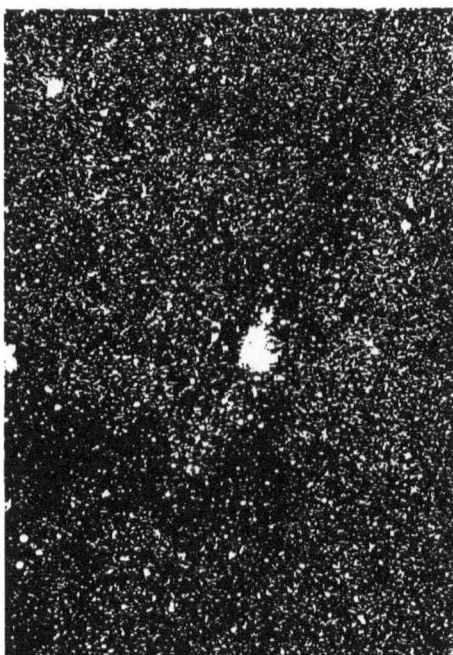

FIG. 136.—A RICH PORTION OF THE MILKY WAY.

A strange spectrum.

brightness of Nova fluctuated irregularly; after March 6 its magnitude diminished rapidly, and in six weeks it was barely visible in the Lick telescope. Four months afterward it was bright enough to be seen in a three-inch telescope, and looked like a small round nebula. The shifting positions of the spectral lines denoted large and variable velocities, and are very difficult to explain.

One hypothesis as to the cause of the outburst is that two large bodies moving swiftly barely missed colliding, and created great tidal disturbances, which in turn led to tremendous eruptions similar to solar prominences, but on a vastly greater scale. Another theory is that a dark body plunged into some cosmical cloud, like the vast nebulous masses, which photography reveals here and there. When it passed out of the cloud in the spring it rapidly cooled off; in the fall it encountered another such cloud, which brightened it up again. The observations are, however, too complicated to be explained fully by any hypothesis yet advanced. *Cause of the outburst.*

Very different from a temporary star is Algol, the Demon Star, so named by the ancients; it is in the constellation Perseus. Usually it is a star of the second magnitude, but at regular intervals of $2^{d.}$ $20^{hrs.}$ $48^{min.}$ $56^{sec.}$ it drops to the fourth magnitude; it remains faint for only twenty minutes, and brightens again until it reaches its usual luster. Its light is varying during $9^{hrs.}$ $45^{min.}$ of each period. The periodical darkening is a partial eclipse caused by a dark body revolving about a bright one: this is rendered practically certain by spectroscopic measurements, which show that Algol alternately retreats from us and approaches us, just as if it were one star of a revolving system. The dark companion is computed to be of nearly the same size as the sun; the main star has a diameter one fifth greater. *Algol.*

The distance between their surfaces is only 2,000,000 miles. Less than a dozen variables, which suffer eclipse like Algol, are known.

Mira.

Mira (the marvelous) is a strange variable located in Cetus; its changes have been observed for three hundred years. It occupies eleven months in running the gamut of its variations. During most of this time it is invisible to the naked eye, though an opera-glass shows it; but once in eleven months it rises in a few weeks to a maximum brightness, remains thus for about a week, and then sinks back slowly to its former faintness, the entire change occupying three months and a fraction. Sometimes its greatest brilliancy does not equal that of the faintest of the seven stars in the Great Dipper; at other times it rivals the brightest of them. At the time of a maximum its spectrum glows with a profusion of bright lines. The strange behavior of this star and others of its class may be explained by periodical eruptions like the solar prominences, though on a much larger scale. The periodicity of such eruptions is as mysterious as that of sun-spots.

Irregular variations.

There are variables which are unlike Algol or Mira, some of them being seemingly hopelessly irregular in their variations. The cause of their variability can only be conjectured. They may be afflicted with enormous spots, or subject to collisions with meteoric streams; great protuberances may also complicate matters, while rotation upon an axis may tend to give a certain regularity to the variations.

Clusters.

Aggregations in which the stars are to be counted by tens or hundreds of thousands are known as clusters. Several of the stars in the cluster of the Pleiades can be seen with the naked eye, and many more are brought out by an opera-glass. Præsepe in Cancer and the double cluster in Perseus look like bright spots on the sky, and are split into separate stars by a small telescope. All these are coarse clusters.

The finest compact cluster in the northern hemisphere is located in Hercules. One who knows just

The great cluster in Hercules.

FIG. 137.—THE GREAT GLOBULAR CLUSTER IN HERCULES.

where to look for it can see it as a hazy faint star. A large telescope is needed to resolve the entire cluster into separate stars. It is globular in form, and near its center the stars appear fairly to touch one another; at the edge the stars are more scattered, and branch out in pretty sprays. Such a cluster has been called an "island universe," as though it were a system apart

An "island universe."

from other stars, sunk in well-nigh infinite depths of space; according to this view the stars which appear so crowded are really separated by intervals comparable with the distance from the sun to Alpha Centauri or Sirius. If this were true a spectator on one of those distant orbs might look about him, and see a heavens like our own, spangled with novel constellations, and dotted here and there with clusters, one of which contained our own sun and the bright stars familiar to us.

<small>The theory rejected.</small>
But this theory is no longer held. In certain parts of the heavens clusters, nebulæ, and individual stars of various degrees of brightness are so associated that there is little probability that the clusters are isolated groups lying at inconceivable distances beyond the other objects.

In the great Hercules cluster each star must be subject to the gravitating influence of the others; but no motion has been detected yet. Photography may eventually lead to the detection of changes. The general opinion is that the cluster in Hercules, and others of similar appearance, are composed of much smaller stars than the sun.

<small>Is the universe spherical?</small>
If it were possible to survey the sidereal universe from without, as now we look at the Hercules cluster, would it too appear globular?

The first fact to be considered is that the vast majority of the stars lie in the Milky Way, which forms a girdle around the celestial sphere. Now if we were near the center of a spherical cluster, like that in Hercules, throughout which the stars were distributed with any approach to uniformity, they would appear to be about equally numerous in whatever direction we looked. There would be no point within the sphere from which the vast majority of the surrounding stars would have the appearance of a ring like the Galaxy. We therefore reject the hypothesis of sphericity and try again.

Suppose that an aquarium is a circle ten feet in diameter, in which the water is a foot deep. The body of water has the shape of a thin cheese. Let the aquarium be well stocked with minnows, and let a single fish somewhere near the center look about him. When he looks horizontally, no matter toward what point of the compass, he sees a goodly number of his companions. If he looks straight up or down he sees comparatively few. If he looks obliquely upward or downward he sees more fish than when he looked straight up, and fewer than when he looked horizontally. If he had an agile brain and pondered over the matter, would he not conclude that the reason why he saw the most fish when looking horizontally, was that the aquarium extended farthest in that direction? The more he studied the case the more confident would he be that the aquarium was cheese-shaped. *[Illustration of an aquarium.]*

Does not this illustration represent what an astronomer sees when he looks about? If he looks toward the Milky Way, which appears to surround him, he sees a large number of stars. It has been stated that the further he looks from the Milky Way the fewer stars he sees. Is it not reasonable then to suppose that the sidereal universe occupies a space shaped somewhat like a thin cheese or a silver dollar?

But more persistent inquiry will bring out some interesting facts. Those stars whose distances from us have been measured are mostly bright, and are scattered pretty evenly in all directions from us, showing no tendency to crowd together near the Milky Way; their spectra are chiefly like the sun's spectrum. *The sun therefore is a member of a cluster of stars similar to* *[The solar cluster.]*

itself in composition and probably globular in form.

The form of the Milky Way. The faint stars in and near the Milky Way are, almost without exception, at distances which defy our powers of measurement. Of faint stars of any particular order of brightness those near the Milky Way are in general further from us than those in other parts of the heavens. Shall we not say then that most of the stars in the Milky Way constitute a ring surrounding us? Stars whose spectra are like that of Sirius are very abundant in and near the Galaxy, and scattered sparsely in other regions; this fact has led Professor Pickering to say that the Milky Way may well be regarded as "a distinct cluster of stars, to which, from its composition or its age, the sun does not seem to belong."

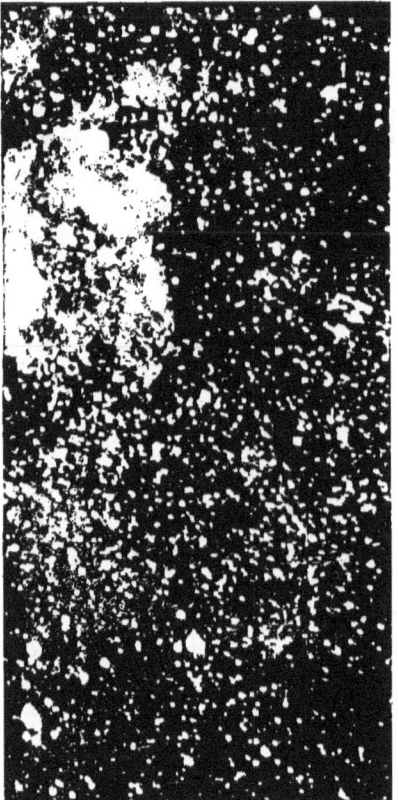

FIG. 138.—CLOUDY REGION IN THE MILKY WAY.

Saturn on a huge scale.

The mental picture of the stellar universe which springs from the preceding considerations rudely resembles the planet Saturn. Within is a ball of stars, of

The Fixed Stars.

which the sun is one. Surrounding the ball is an irregular ring composed of faint stars in and adjacent to the Milky Way. Such a theory as this cannot be considered final, but it commends itself as the best that can be devised in the light of present knowledge.

Our next inquiry is about the motion of this stupendous system; the only available light comes from a study of the movements of a great many stars scattered in all parts of the heavens. Many stars are moving slowly across the face of the sky, despite their designation of fixed stars. Star No. 1830 in Groombridge's catalogue moves a degree in five hundred years. Arcturus, which also has a large proper motion, has shifted its position by an equal amount during the Christian era. Such rapid motions are quite exceptional. If a star is moving toward us or from us, its velocity of approach or recession is obtained by spectroscopic observations; no velocity yet measured exceeds fifty miles a second. A star which is moving directly toward us, or away from us, has no "proper motion," because it does not alter its position on the face of the sky. *(Proper motions of stars.)*

Many groups of stars have a common proper motion. Only a few out of four hundred stars in the Pleiades, whose proper motions have been measured, refuse to drift along in the same direction as the others. It may almost be laid down as a principle that most of the stars in any group drift together, as though they were really connected. *(Some groups have a common motion.)*

The stars are going in all directions, so that it seems impossible to deduce any general results about their movements. But patient study of large numbers of proper motions has clearly brought out a prevailing drift. Stars in Hercules and Lyra are spreading apart very slowly; those on the opposite side of the celestial sphere are coming together. *(A prevailing drift.)*

A passenger on a ferry-boat plying between two cities at night sees lights along the wharves of each city. The lights in one set are spreading apart; in the other they are coming closer together. He knows at once that he is going toward the spreading lights. In like manner the astronomer concludes that the sun, carrying along its family of planets, is moving toward that region of the heavens which Hercules and Lyra grace. Whether the sun is moving in a straight line, or in the majestic sweep of some grand orbit, cannot yet be decided.

Is there a central sun? There is a persistent idea that there exists a central sun, about which all the starry hosts move obediently in vast cycles of time. But the motions of the stars are so complex that no one can hope to locate a point about which all bodies in the universe revolve.

Various systems. There are hosts of subsidiary systems, which are orderly in their ongoings. The solar system is ruled despotically by the sun. Binary systems move in proper fashion, bound by a common tie. The stars composing a group like the Pleiades seem to be impelled toward a common goal. Thus the entire sidereal universe is composed of groups which are practically independent of one another. There is, in the present state of astronomical knowledge, no inkling of a general plan in accordance with which all the stars move.

Is there evidence of design? But the design of the Creator may not involve any particular form of orderly movement which the mind of man has yet conceived. The fact that the molecules which compose a marble statue do not revolve about a common center, or move in curves whose sinuosities can be embraced in a formula, does not detract from its beauty, or argue the absence of design. The entrancing beauty shines forth, and speaks eloquently of the cunning hand of the sculptor.

CHAPTER XVIII.

THE NEBULÆ.

> "Regions of lucid matter taking forms,
> Brushes of fire, hazy gleams."
> — *Tennyson.*

NEBULÆ are cloud-like masses, of a great variety of form. Planetary nebulæ are small and round; they are usually somewhat brighter in the center than at the edge. If there is a very marked central condensation, the object may be called a nebulous star. Annular nebulæ are ring-shaped, brighter at the edge than near the center. Spiral nebulæ exhibit coils, like those of a watch-spring, or a corkscrew. The largest nebulæ are irregular in form and enormous in extent, being the largest visible objects in the universe; they dwarf everything else into insignificance. Photographs of Orion show that a large part of the constellation is involved in a great nebula. Many clusters contain nebulous matter within their boundaries; large nebulæ often appear to shelter stars within their ample folds.

Different classes of nebulæ.

About 8,500 are now known; new ones are being continually discovered. Photography offers a distinct advantage for the work of discovery, since the sensitive film captures objects too faint to impress the eye. They are not scattered uniformly over the sky; near the Milky Way few are to be found. Where stars are few nebulæ abound, being most numerous near the galactic poles, as previously stated.

Discovery and distribution.

No one has succeeded in measuring the distance of a

Distances.

nebula, though repeated attempts have been made upon planetary nebulæ. No nebula invites such an attack, unless it has some nuclear point which can be bisected

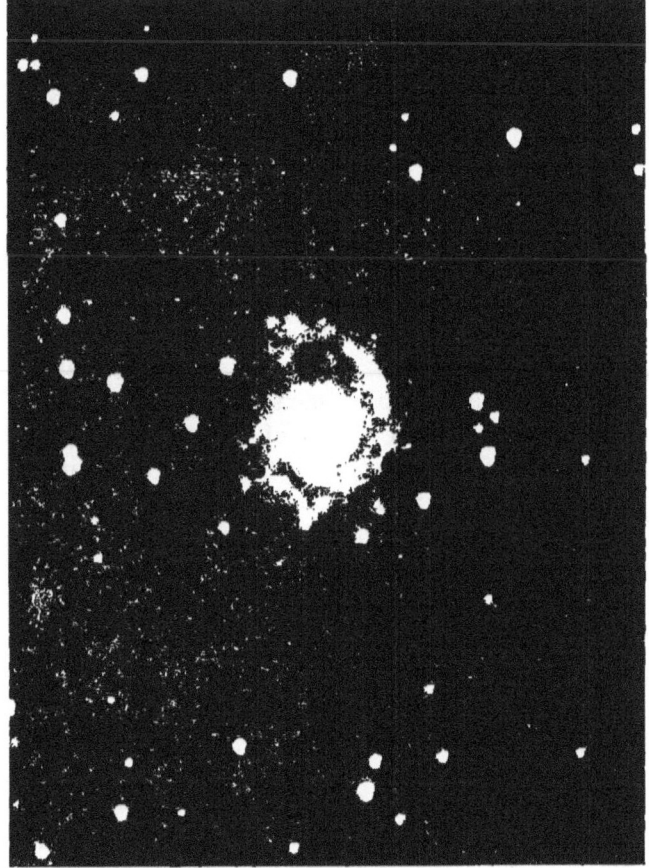

FIG. 139.—A SPIRAL NEBULA.

Association with stars.

with the spider-web of a micrometer. Yet they are in many cases so associated with stars that one cannot doubt that they are at the same distances.

In the Pleiades nebulous wisps connect certain stars; some of the brighter stars of the cluster are involved in nebulosity. The sextuple star Theta Orionis lies in a dark place in the great nebula in Orion. The appearance suggests that some of the adjacent nebulous matter has been used up in forming the stars. Four groups of lines in the spectrum of the stars coincide with corresponding groups in the spectrum of the nebula, and render it very probable that the stars actually lie in the nebula, instead of being merely in line with it. The nebula therefore is at the same distance as the stars. *Similar spectra.*

As spectroscopic observations have shown, their velocities are of the same magnitude as those of stars. *Motions.*

Drawings of a given nebula made at the same time by observers using different instruments vary so much in detail that a comparison of one set of drawings with another gives no secure evidence of change in the form of the nebula. The case of the trifid nebula in Sagittarius deserves mention in this connection. It contains a curious dark rift, in which Herschel and other observers saw a triple star, in the early part of the nineteenth century. This star, which has not moved appreciably with reference to other stars in the vicinity, now lies in the edge of the nebulous matter adjacent to the rift. The nebula must either have changed its form or drifted. While the outlines of the central portion of the great nebula in Orion remain unchanged, there are anomalous variations in the brightness of different portions of it. *Changes.*

Most of the nebulæ are too faint to give perceptible spectra. About half of the spectra thus far examined are composed of a few bright lines, which come from glowing gases. The presence of incandescent hydrogen is amply demonstrated; helium is fairly recognized, and also sodium. The remaining spectra are chiefly *Spectra.*

continuous bands of color such as would be given by heated liquid or solid bodies, or gases subjected to great pressure. A few nebulæ give both spectra. Nebulæ may contain solid or liquid bodies which are not sufficiently luminous to manifest themselves.

The great nebula in Andromeda is easily seen with the naked eye. A small telescope shows that it has a bright ball near the center, and is spindle-shaped. The magnificent photographs taken of late years reveal a very interesting structure. The whole rudely resembles Saturn, the central ball being surrounded by a ring; in the ring are dark curved lanes, as though the structure was spiral. Two smaller balls outside of the ring suggest planets yet uncondensed. There appeared in 1885 close to the nucleus of the nebula a new star which could be seen with an opera-glass; in a few months it had vanished. It was probably a

FIG. 140.—THE NEBULA OF ORION PHOTOGRAPHED. Exposure, fifteen minutes.

The Andromeda nebula.

FIG. 141.—THE NEBULA OF ORION PHOTOGRAPHED. Exposure, two hours.

fortuitous condensation or local brightening of the nebulous matter, its spectrum being like that of the nebula.

The great nebula in Orion is the most wonderful in the heavens. Its most brilliant portion is in the sword-handle of the giant. One easily sees there three stars in a row; the middle star is surrounded by a feeble glow

The nebula in Orion.

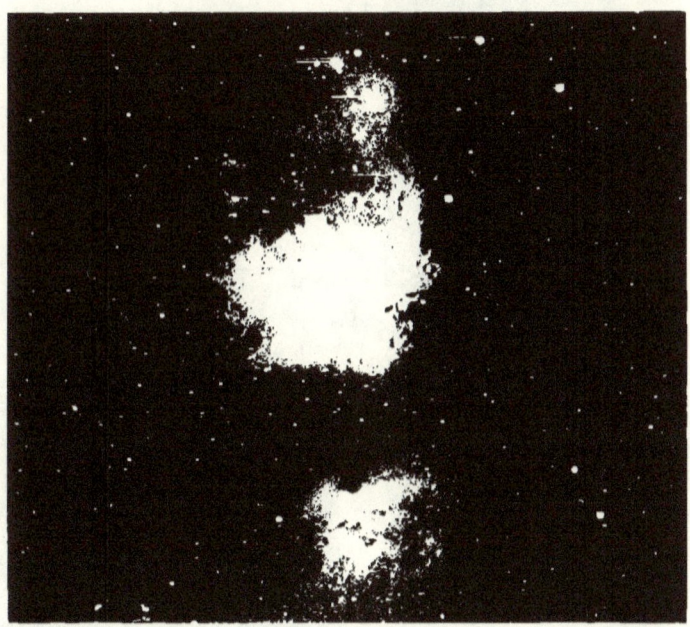

FIG. 142.—THE NEBULA OF ORION PHOTOGRAPHED.   Exposure, nine hours.

coming from the nebula. Galileo has left no record of it, much as he scoured the heavens. Cysatus, who was following a comet in 1618, first came across it, and compared the comet with it. As telescopes improved, the star which it envelops was split into four, called the Trapezium; later two more were added to the four. Dark spots were seen in the cloud, and enormous wing-like extensions of faint nebulosity, which gave the neb-

The Trapezium.

ula the appearance of a ghostly bat of prodigious size. The spectroscope then revealed the bright-line spectrum of glowing gas, though portions of the nebula have square corners and bright ribs and dark vacuities. Finally photography scored a signal triumph by extending the nebula in wraith-like arms which embrace a large part of Orion. Perhaps the exceptional richness of the constellation is due to the vastness of the nebular quarry from which the stars were hewn.

> " Where striving o'er the dim, ethereal plain,
> Orion brandishes his flaming sword,
> And shakes ajar the awful vestibule
> Of heaven's stupendous treasury of suns,
> Set for a jewel in the mighty hilt."

The Magellanic clouds. The Magellanic clouds, or nubeculæ, are invisible in the United States, because they are too near the south celestial pole. They resemble detached sections of the Milky Way, the larger one being of the size of the bowl of the Great Dipper, while the smaller is one fourth as large. These marvelous aggregations may well be likened to celestial show-cases, in which are displayed specimens of sidereal wonders. While nebulæ and clusters fight shy of one another in other parts of the heavens, they are here mingled indiscriminately. Globular clusters are found in all stages of condensation, and irregular clusters of various degrees of coarseness. Irregular nebulæ of curious forms, and neat little elliptical ones, are thickly scattered over a background rich in stars. In places the stars are minute and packed as though they were the closely woven texture of a celestial fabric.

The raw material of worlds. A peculiar interest inheres in the study of nebulæ, since they are thought to be the chaotic world-stuff from which stars, clusters, suns, planets, and satellites have been evolved. Milton adumbrates this idea in the second book of "Paradise Lost," where he describes Satan pausing a moment at the open mouth of hell, ere he set out across the abyss which lay before him, seeking for the abode of man.

> "Into this wild abyss,
> The Womb of Nature, and perhaps her grave,
> Of neither sea, nor shore, nor air, nor fire,
> But all these in their pregnant causes mixed.
> Confusedly, and which thus must ever fight,
> Unless the Almighty Maker them ordain,
> His dark materials to create new worlds:
> Into this wild abyss the wary fiend
> Stood on the brink of hell, and looked awhile,
> Pondering his voyage: for no narrow frith
> He had to cross."

Men may properly be abashed before the problem of the development of the universe, but they have not hesitated to attack it, working out a theory concerning the origin of the solar system, and following the same line of thought with reference to the countless bodies which make up the sidereal heavens. The famous hypothesis, which has been slowly elaborated during a century and a half, is familiarly known as the "nebular hypothesis." Suggested by Kant and Swedenborg it was treated from a mathematical standpoint by Laplace at the close of the eighteenth century. Since that time it has undergone modification in details, but the outline of the original fabric of thought remains.

The nebular hypothesis.

According to this theory the materials which are now to be found in the sun and planets were originally diffused through a nebula of vast extent. The nebula may have been a mass of heated gas, but was probably a cloud of cold dust. The mutual attractions of its particles caused it to assume a globular form, to acquire

The beginning of the solar system.

a rotatory motion, and to become hotter. The smaller it became, the more rapidly it whirled; it was flattened at the poles and bulged at the equator. The "centrifugal force" finally became so great that the central attraction could no longer restrain matter in the equatorial regions, and a ring escaped at the equator. Or if there were some place on the equator where the matter was denser than in adjoining regions, a lump was formed at this dense spot, and the lump was left behind, instead of a ring.

<small>Rings or more compact masses are left behind.</small>

The original body rotated still more swiftly; another ring or another ball was liberated. If some portion of an abandoned ring was markedly more dense than the rest of it, it gradually attracted to itself the adjacent matter, and finally formed another rotating body (a planet), which in turn threw off rings or balls of matter to form satellites. If a ring were pretty homogeneous it might condense into a multitude of bodies like the asteroids, or the rings of Saturn, which are by some considered an ear-mark of the creative process.

<small>Formation of planets.</small>

A liberated ball would form a planet more quickly than a ring would. The planets and satellites gradually liquefied and solidified, falling in temperature at the same time. Minute bodies like the satellites of Mars lost their heat quickly, and are probably now solid throughout. On larger bodies a crust was formed, and the central fires have not yet died out; such is the case of the earth. Still larger bodies, like Jupiter and Saturn, have probably not cooled off sufficiently to permit the formation of a solid crust. The sun, which holds in fiery embrace most of the matter in the original nebula, will begin to cool off whenever his huge mass begins to liquefy.

<small>Further history of the planets.</small>

Such is the nebular hypothesis, briefly stated. Some

years ago it was supposed that the retrograde motions of the satellites of Uranus and Neptune, and the rapid motion of the inner moon of Mars, which completes a revolution in less than one third of a Martian day, were objections to the theory. But these anomalies have now received satisfactory explanations. *Objections.*

Let us now travel in imagination throughout the

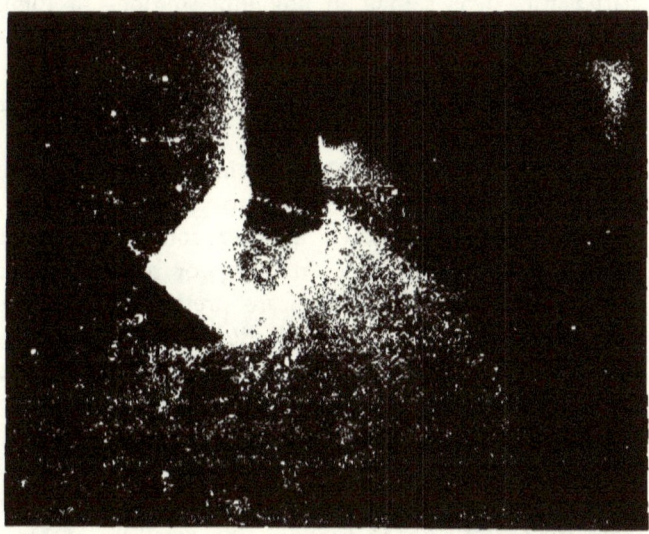

FIG. 143.—A DRAWING OF THE CENTRAL PART OF THE GREAT NEBULA IN ORION.

universe, investigating the nebulæ, the stars, the earth, the moon, the planetary system, and finally the sun, that they may give their mute testimony to the truth or falsity of the nebular hypothesis. *A broad investigation.*

Scattered over the sky we find vast inchoate masses of faintly gleaming matter, some of the most stupendous of which are revealed by photography alone, being too faint for the most powerful visual apparatus. Surely here is the raw material which the theory demands. *The raw material.*

The next step.

The nebula in Orion.

Planetary nebulæ.

The Pleiades.

Other associations of nebulæ and stars.

The next step in the process is illustrated by the great nebula in Andromeda, in the center of which is a bright globe. The surrounding matter is arranged in rings or whorls, as if there were a motion of rotation, disengaging rings of tenuous matter. Has any of the disengaged material assumed a spherical form? Look again at this wonderful nebula and see the two outlying globes.

Study the latest photograph of the nebula in Orion, and let the gigantic spiral tell its own story. See the stars in the Trapezium, and the dark space in which they lie, as if some of the nebulous matter had been used up in forming them. Examine their spectra and behold the bright lines, which tally with lines in the spectrum of the nebula. Does not a heated gas produce a spectrum of bright lines?

Pass in review hundreds of planetary nebulæ. Are they not circular? Have not some of them faint condensations in their centers? Have not some brighter condensations? Do not a considerable number exhibit a spiral structure? Can we not arrange known nebulæ in orderly sequence from those composed of the dimmest world-stuff up to those which have justly received the appellation of nebulous stars? Is the testimony of the nebulæ inconclusive? We turn to the stars.

Let us study various photographs of the Pleiades. Why does a nebulous bridge run from this faint star to its neighbor if there be no relation between nebulæ and stars? Why does this other nebulous ray connect a row of small stars? Why are so many of the brighter stars apparently involved in nebulosity? Why do rays run out from this large nebula to these faint stars?

Why are there so many stars all over the heavens which appear to be enveloped with nebulous matter? How are certain very complicated stellar spectra to be explained? Are not the stars giving them surrounded by enormous gaseous envelopes?

Has not our attention been already called to the fact that almost all stars can be arranged in a sequence from planetary nebulæ onward to the most highly finished orbs, according to the characteristics of their spectra? While this is true, let us be candid and admit that such a sequence must be considered only as a possible hint of progressive development. *Is there a sequence?*

Is the testimony of the nebulæ and stars insufficient? We turn to the earth.

Is the earth a cold, dark, solid body, far removed in nature from the heated objects which we have considered thus far? Take a thermometer down deep holes in the earth's crust, and see the column of mercury slowly rise. Listen to the rumbling of yonder volcano; see the steamy cloud rising from it, and the scorching outpourings which have rolled down its sides; ask the geologist whether the granite of our mountains has ever passed through primeval fires. Give heed to his statement that statuary marble is limestone transformed by heat. Is there not a preponderance of evidence in favor of the view that mountain chains are wrinkles of the earth's crust formed while it was contracting? Is there no hint in the fact that if the earth were heated to incandescence its spectrum would resemble the sun's? *The earth.*

Is the testimony of the nebulæ, the stars, and the earth inconclusive? We turn to the moon.

He who examines the moon with a telescope and studies its formations will hardly deny that indications of an igneous origin are written in large characters over its scarred visage. On this point let us listen to Nasmyth and Carpenter, two English students of the moon: *The moon.*

We trust then that we, on our part, have shown that the

study of the moon may be a benefit not merely to the astronomer, but to the geologist, for we behold in it a mighty medal of creation, doubtless formed of the same material and struck with the same die that molded our earth, but while the dust of countless ages and the action of powerful disintegrating and denuding elements have eroded and obliterated the earthly impressions, the superscriptions on the lunar surface have remained with their pristine clearness unsullied, every vestige sharp and bright as when it left the Almighty Maker's hand.

A medal of creation.

Is the testimony of the nebulæ, the stars, the earth, and the moon insufficient? We turn to the planetary system, and group some observed harmonies under four heads.

I. Jupiter, Saturn, Uranus, and Neptune are large bodies of small density. According to the nebular theory were they not formed from large rings of small density? Mars, the earth, Venus, and Mercury, on the other hand, are small bodies of great density.

II. All the planets revolve eastward about the sun, their orbits being nearly circular, and lying nearly in the same plane.

III. All the known rotations of the planets are eastward, the planes of their equators being nearly coincident with those of their orbits.

IV. The satellites of the planets revolve in planes which do not deviate much from the equators of their primaries; they also revolve in the direction in which their primaries rotate. The positions of the planes of the equators of Uranus and Neptune are, however, unknown.

Is the testimony of the nebulæ, the stars, the earth, the moon, and the planetary systems insufficient? We turn to the sun.

The sun.

It has been stated that the sun's outpour of radiant energy is accounted for by the supposition that it is slowly contracting in bulk. If it is contracting, was it not larger one thousand years ago than to-day? Was it not still larger one hundred thousand years ago? Can we not go back in thought through the long ages of which geologists tell us, and see the sun larger yet and more diffuse? If we may be bold to peer into appalling abysses of past time, do we not at last see in dim outline the mists of a gigantic nebula, from which the solar system has been formed by such a process as we have sketched?

Is not the chain of evidence so complete as to compel our assent? If this were a matter of ordinary business, if shares of stock in the nebular hypothesis were for sale, would you not consider them a good investment? *What shall we say?*

If you were to consult an astronomer, before making this intellectual investment, what would he say? He would reply that if you wished to invest in an hypothesis, he could heartily recommend the nebular hypothesis; he himself had taken stock in it. But he would beg you to remember that there is a vast difference between an hypothesis and an ascertained fact, and that this particular hypothesis could never attain the certainty of a demonstration. He would remind you that a man who has a limitless duration of time to draw upon, and an infinite extent of space to put the creations of his imagination in, ought to be able to invent a far-reaching theory which would seemingly agree with almost any orderly series of facts. Though it does not now seem at all probable, yet it is possible that in the centuries to come new facts may be discovered and new laws formulated, to which the nebular hypothesis will be compelled to yield, as the Ptolemaic theory yielded after fourteen centuries to the Copernican, and as Newton's corpuscular theory of light gave way to the wave theory. *An astronomer's opinion.* *Possible overthrow of the theory.*

334   A Study of the Sky.

The subtlety of nature.   Some day the wreck of the nebular hypothesis may furnish a fresh illustration of the doctrine of Bacon that the subtlety of nature transcends in many ways the subtlety of the intellect and senses of man, and may call men's attention anew to the real depth of their ignorance concerning the fundamental causes of natural phenomena. Across the chasm of centuries still rings the old poetic outburst, "Lo, these are parts of His ways; but how little a portion is heard of him? but the thunder of his power who can understand?"

We have been threading the mazes of the past: what shall we say of the future? In the

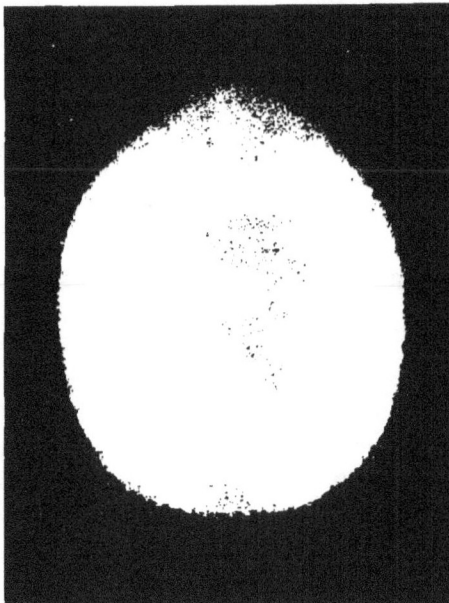
FIG. 144.—THE RING NEBULA IN LYRA.

A glance ahead.   chapter on the sun we have already considered the future of the solar system, and we now turn to the sidereal universe.

The stars seem to be radiating away their stores of energy, just as the sun is. The best light that we have *The stars die out.* reveals Arcturus the magnificent or Sirius the glowing as a dull cold corse, when ages have rolled away. If these stellar princes are at last to sink into eternal night, shall we not prophesy the same fate for the lesser orbs?

To be sure, their places may be filled by new stars condensed from nebulæ now seen and from others which are not yet bright enough to show themselves. But the death knell of these new worlds must be sounded at last, unless there be some intervention of which we have no hint. *New ones appear and die in turn.*

If such be the fate of the sidereal universe, why should we repine? If our reasoning be correct the human race will perish long before the sidereal universe loses the splendid energies whose manifestations bring us so much delight. We have no evidence that there are inhabitants of other worlds, who would be overwhelmed in the universal rout. The peopling of planets surrounding other suns with intelligences is but a vagary of the fancy. *Why repine?*

If the Creator spoke the universe into existence, may he not speak it out of existence, when once it has fulfilled his purposes? But let us call a halt, ere we wander further in paths of groundless and fruitless speculation. We may rest in the assurance that He who has controlled the worlds for ages past still holds them in the hollow of His hand, and orders their destinies aright. Radiant suns are not needed to shed light and heat upon the City Beautiful, whose walls are jasper and whose gates are pearl. "For the glory of God doth lighten it and the Lamb is the light thereof." *The Creator is supreme.*

INDEX.

A chromatic telescope, 131.
Adam, 17, 20.
Adams, J. C., 269.
Æsculapius, 107.
Age of the sun, 204.
Albireo, 98.
Alcor, 45, 60.
Alcyone, 73.
Aldebaran, 53, 72.
Algol, 81, 305, 313.
"Almagest," 24, 26.
Alpha Centauri, 305.
Alphabet, Greek, 55.
Alphonso, 26.
Altair, 53, 105.
Andromeda, 37, 39, 48, 69, 324, 330.
Andromedes, 290, 292.
Angular measurement, 41.
Antares, 53, 101, 102.
Apennines, 214, 216.
Aphelion, 237.
Aquarius, 66.
Aquila, 53, 105.
Arabian astronomy, 25.
Arcturus, 36, 53, 87.
Aries, 70.
Arion, 104.
Aristotle, 23.
Aryans, 20.
Asteroids, 39, 246.
Astronomers, 111.
Auriga, 76.
Australian savages, 52.
Babylonian astronomy, 22.
Bacon, 128.
Barnard, E. E., 120, 250, 259, 264.
Bayer, 53.
Bede, 50.
Betelgeuse, 53, 74, 75.
Biela's comet, 281, 284, 293.
Binary stars, 306.
Bloomington, 299.

Bode's law, 247.
Boötes, 53, 87.
Brashear, J. A., 137.
Bread, 180.
Brenham township, 299.
Brightness of stars, 57.
Brooks, W. R., 286, 287.
Burnham, S. W., 126.
Campbell, W. W., 245.
Canals of Mars, 240.
Cancer, 83, 94.
Canis Major, 83.
Canis Minor, 85.
Capella, 36, 37, 76, 77, 84, 305.
Capricornus, 109.
Capture of comets, 273.
Cassiopeia, 48, 62.
Castor, 79.
Catalogue of stars, 54, 55.
Celestial meridian, 152.
Celestial sphere, 41, 42, 47.
Cepheus, 48, 49, 108, 109.
Ceres, 248, 250.
Cetus, 49, 69, 71.
Challis, Professor, 270.
Chamberlin Observatory, 145.
Chamberlin telescope, 141.
Chandler, S. C., 125.
Chinese astronomy, 21, 93.
Chromosphere, 189.
Chronograph, 157, 171.
Chronometer, 169.
Clark, A. G., 84, 307.
Clocks, 146, 172.
Clusters, 314.
Coal, 179.
Coma Berenices, 89.
Comet-groups, 274.
Comet hunters, 114, 271.
Comets, 39, 271.
Conjunction, 231, 237.
Constellations, 48.

Index.

Copernicus, 26, 32, 212.
Corona, 193, 230.
Corona Borealis, 92.
Coronium, 195.
Corvus, 91.
Craters, 212.
Cygnus, 98.
Declination, 55.
Declination axis, 139.
Deimos, 238.
Delphinus, 104.
Deneb, 98.
Diameter of a planet, 160.
Diffraction grating, 165.
Dipper, the Great, 36, 60, 61.
Dipper, the Little, 44, 61.
Distance of the sun, 181.
Dollond, John, 131.
Dome, 148.
Double stars, 123, 160, 306.
Draco, 99.
Druids, 52.
Duration of life on the earth, 204.
Earth shine, 209.
Eclipses, 224.
Ecliptic, 51.
Egyptians, 21.
Ellipse, 273.
Elongation, 232.
Encke's comet, 283.
Envelopes, 276.
Epicycles, 25.
Equator, celestial, 55.
Equinox, 55, 69.
Faculæ, 189.
Flamsteed, 54.
Fomalhaut, 67.
Galaxy, see Milky Way.
Galileo, 30, 128, 259.
Galle, 270.
Gauss, 248.
Gemini, 79.
Gould, B. A., 116.
Graduations, 150, 156.
Gravitation, 33, 306.
Great Plague, 29.
Grecian philosophers, 22.
Greek alphabet, 55.
Guinand, 131.
Habitability of Mars, 245.
Hall, Asaph, 238.

Hall, Chester Moor, 131.
Heat of the sun, 198, 201.
Helium, 192, 323.
Hercules, 53, 96, 315, 319.
Herodotus, 21.
Herschel, Caroline, 64, 266.
Herschel, William, 35, 64, 265.
Hesiod, 51.
Hindus, 52, 229.
Hipparchus, 23, 25, 86.
Holden, E. S., 114.
Holmes's comet, 282.
Huyghens, 260.
Hyades, 51, 72, 74.
Hydra, 92.
Hyperbola, 273.
Inferior planets, 231.
Inquisition, 31.
Iroquois Indians, 49.
Josephus, 20.
Judas Iscariot, 210.
Juno, 248, 250.
Jupiter, 31, 39, 128, 202, 237, 250, 253, 273, 328, 332.
Kant, 327.
Keeler, James E., 121, 255, 263.
Kepler, 29.
Krakatoa, 217.
Lacus Solis, 243.
Lagrange, 35.
Lalande, 54.
Laplace, 34, 286, 327.
Laws, Kepler's, 30, 33.
Laws, Newton's, 33, 34, 273.
Leo, 86, 291.
Leonids, 291, 294.
Lepus, 85.
Level, 151.
Leverrier, 269.
Lexell's comet, 286.
Libra, 103.
Lick Observatory, 155.
Lick telescope, 16, 259.
Lippershey, 128.
Lyra, 54, 95, 319.
Madrid, 300.
Magellanic clouds, 326.
Magnetic storms, 199.
Magnitudes of stars, 57.
Mark Twain, 204.
Mars, 27, 29, 39, 236, 250, 329.

Maxwell, Clerk, 263.
Mercury, 39, 231.
Meridian circle, 145, 149, 150, 152, 154.
Meteoric showers, 284, 290, 294.
Meteorites, 293, 294.
Meteors, 39, 288.
Mexicans, 52.
Micrometer, 124, 158, 272.
Milk-dipper, 108.
Milky Way, 17, 18, 31, 38, 99, 301, 316, 321.
Mira, 72, 314.
Mizar, 44, 45, 46, 60, 61, 62, 305.
Moon, 36, 205.
Motion of the heavens, 36.
Mountains of the moon, 214.
Mounting of a telescope, 138, 139.
Multiple stars, 309.
Nebulæ, 39, 271, 321.
Nebular theory, 327.
Neptune, 39, 268, 329, 332.
Newcomb, S., 115.
Newton, Isaac, 32, 119, 125, 129, 130.
Nova Aurigæ, 78, 312.
Object-glass, 138, 153.
Observatories, 143.
Okouari, 49.
Olbers, 248.
Ophiuchus, 106.
Opposition, 237.
Orion, 39, 53, 74, 102, 321, 323, 325.
Pallas, 248, 250.
Parabola, 273.
Paré, 280.
Pegasus, 49, 64.
Perihelion, 237.
Periodicity of sun-spots, 186.
Perseids, 290, 291.
Perseus, 49, 81.
Persians, 52.
Personal equation, 170.
Peruvians, 52.
Phases of inferior planets, 232.
Phobos, 238.
Photography, 165, 329.
Photosphere, 187.
Piazzi, 247, 248.
Pickering, E. C., 60, 117.
Pickering, W. H., 119.
Pisces, 68.
Planetary system, 39, 332.

Pleiades, 37, 51, 72, 319, 323, 330.
Pointers, 41.
Polar axis, 139.
Pole, celestial, 43, 62.
Pole-star, 41, 61, 62.
Pollux, 79.
Procyon, 85.
Prominences, 190, 230.
Proper motion, 319.
Ptolemaic system, 24.
Ptolemy, 24, 59.
Pythagoras, 22, 23.
Radiant, 289.
Red spot on Jupiter, 255.
Reflector, 130.
Refraction, 218.
Refractor, 131.
Regulus, 86.
Reticle, 151.
Rigel, 75.
Right ascension, 55.
"Rigveda," 20.
Rosse, 130.
Sagitta, 100.
Sagittarius, 109, 323.
Satellites, 40.
Saturn, 39, 259, 328, 332.
Schæberle, J. M., 197.
Schiaparelli, 233, 240, 241.
Schwabe, 186.
Scientific method, 20.
Scorpio, 101.
Serpens, 106.
Serpentarius, see Ophiuchus.
Sextant, 223.
Shadow of the earth, 15.
Shooting stars, 288.
Showers, meteoric, 284, 290, 294.
Sirius, 36, 37, 53, 74, 84, 304, 307.
Site of an observatory, 143.
Society Islanders, 51.
Solstice, 79.
Spectroscope, 162.
Spectrum analysis, 163.
Sphere, celestial, 41, 42, 47.
Spica, 90, 91, 309.
Spider-webs, 161.
Standard time, 168, 174.
Star-light, 305.
Starry skies, 15.
Stars, 38, 301.

Structure of the universe, 318.
Sun, 179.
Sun-spots, 182.
Superior planets, 237.
Swift, Lewis, 230, 287.
Swift's comet, 278.
Taurus, 54, 72.
Telescope, 128, 141.
Temporary stars, 311.
Tides, 205, 223.
Time, 117, 167, 223.
Transit, 231.
Trapezium, 76, 325, 330.
Tycho, 28, 29, 32, 63, 311.
Types of stellar spectra, 309.
Uranienburg, 29.
Uranus, 39, 247, 265, 268, 329, 332.
Ursa Major, 59.

Ursa Minor, 61.
Variable stars, 310, 311.
Vega, 36, 37, 62, 95, 305.
Venus, 31, 37, 38, 39, 128, 231, 234, 253.
Vernal equinox, 55, 69.
Vesta, 248, 250.
Vesuvius, 215.
Virgo, 90, 104.
Volcanoes, 215.
Watches, 176.
Watson, J. C., 230.
Weather, 201, 225.
Weigel, Professor, 50.
World's Fair, 211, 296.
Yerkes Observatory, 144.
Young, Charles A., 112, 191, 200.
Zodiac, 50, 51.
Zodiacal light, 294.

www.ingramcontent.com/pod-product-compliance
Lightning Source LLC
Chambersburg PA
CBHW030001240426
43672CB00007B/776